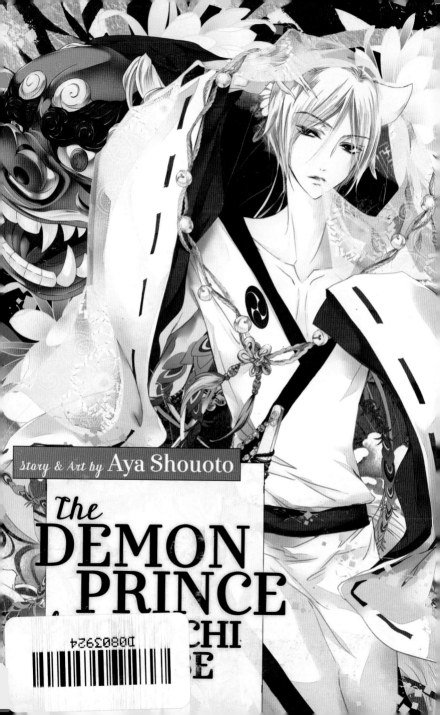

Story & Art by Aya Shouoto

The DEMON PRINCE

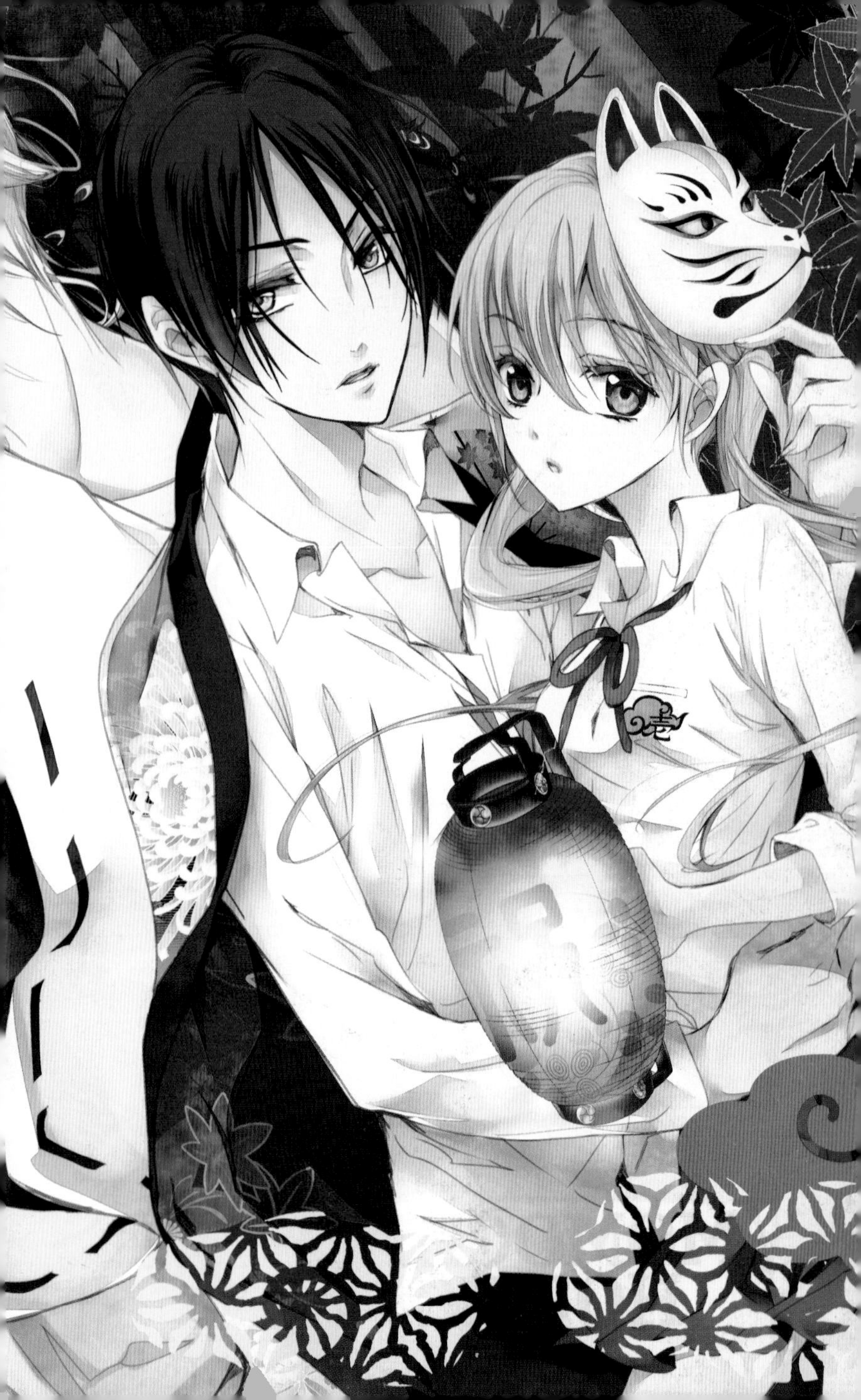

The Fourth Friend: Part 2

CHAPTER 8

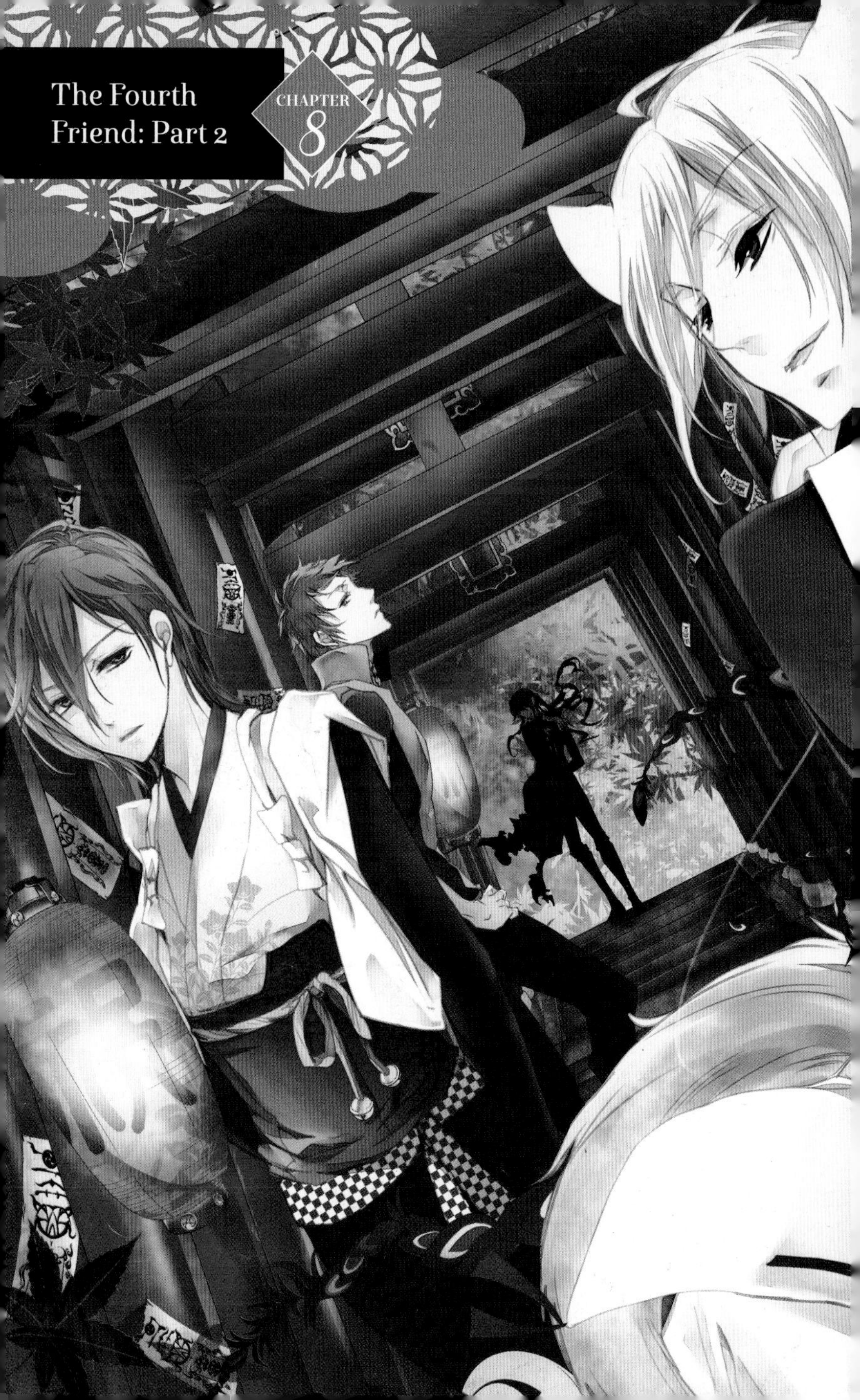

The DEMON PRINCE of MOMOCHI HOUSE ③

Contents

The Mysterious Residents of Momochi House

Aoi Nanamori

When he was 7 years old, he wandered into Momochi House and was chosen as the Omamori-sama. He transforms into a nue to perform his duties, but it seems this role was meant for Himari.

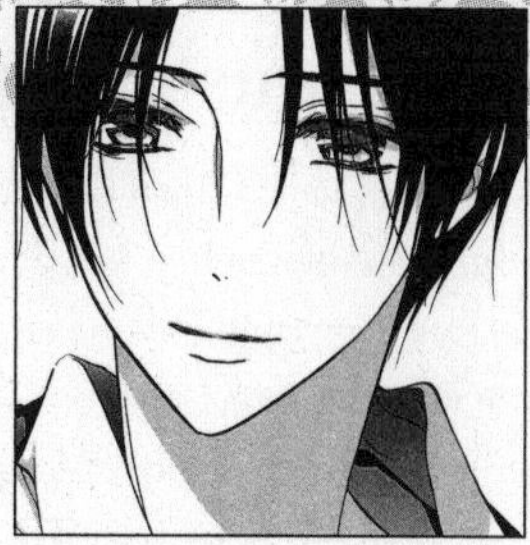

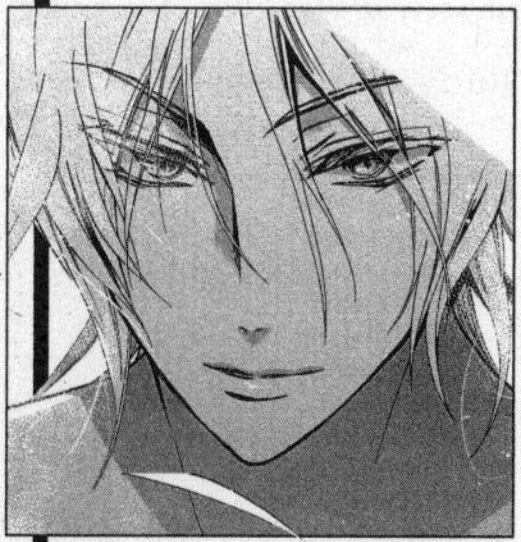

Omamori-sama (Nue)

An ayakashi, or demon, with the ears of a cat, the wings of a bird, and the tail of a fox. As the Omamori-sama, the nue protects Momochi House and eliminates demons who make their way in from the spiritual realm.

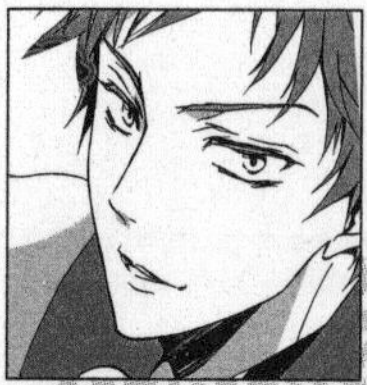

Ise

One of Omamori-sama's shikigami. He's an orangutan.

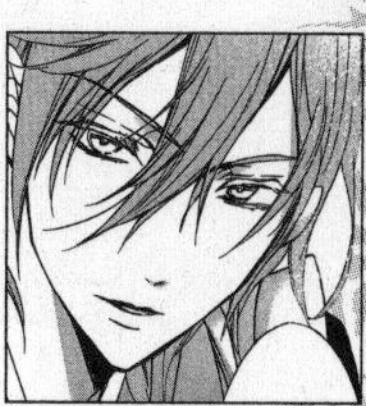

Yukari

One of Omamori-sama's shikigami. He's a water serpent.

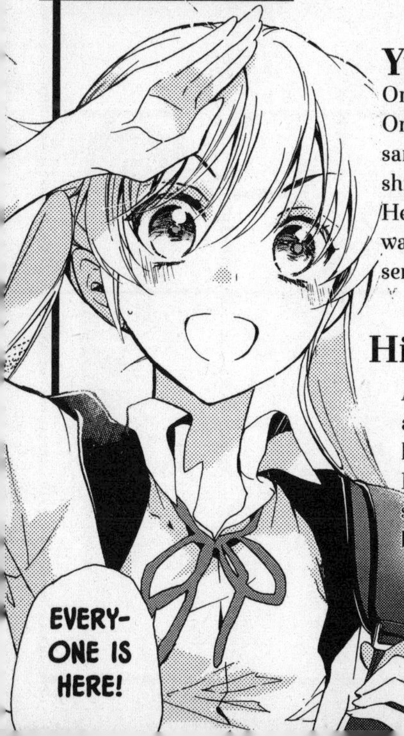
EVERY-
ONE IS
HERE!

Himari Momochi

A 16-year-old orphan who, according to a certain will, has inherited Momochi House. As rightful owner, she has the ability to expel beings from the house.

Lesser Yokai

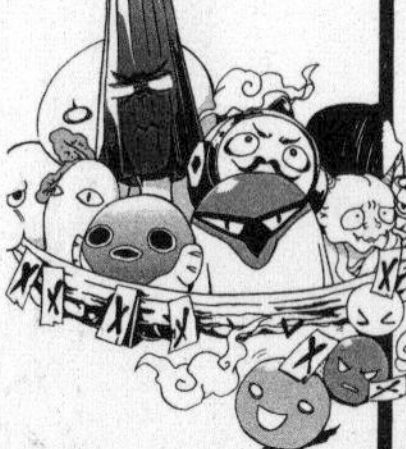

Momochi House: Story Thus Far

Himari has become accustomed to living in Momochi House and starts attending school. On her first day, she makes four friends who invite themselves over, curious to see the rumored haunted house. After meeting them, Aoi declares that one of her friends is already dead. This spirit was able to enter Momochi House because Himari—the landlady—allowed it. Her friend is absorbing Momochi House's energy and quickly transforming into a demon. Until Himari figures out who the dead person is, her other friends are in danger. But now another friend, Iizuka, has had her soul removed...

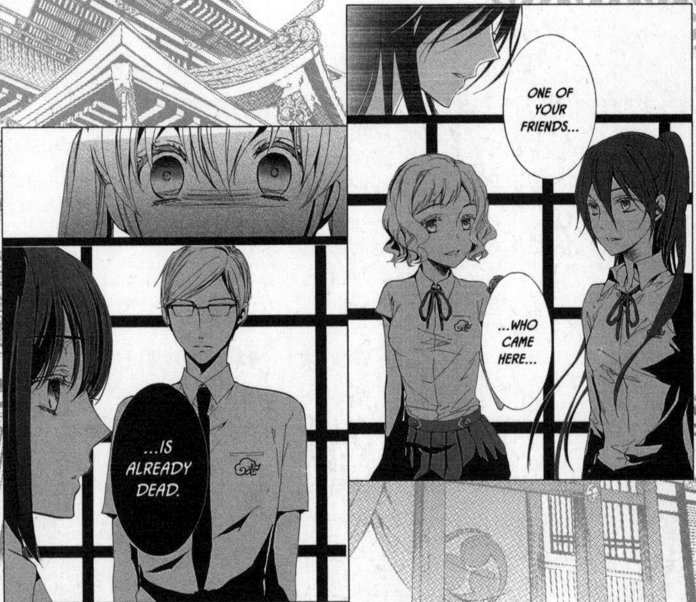
ONE OF YOUR FRIENDS...
...WHO CAME HERE...
...IS ALREADY DEAD.

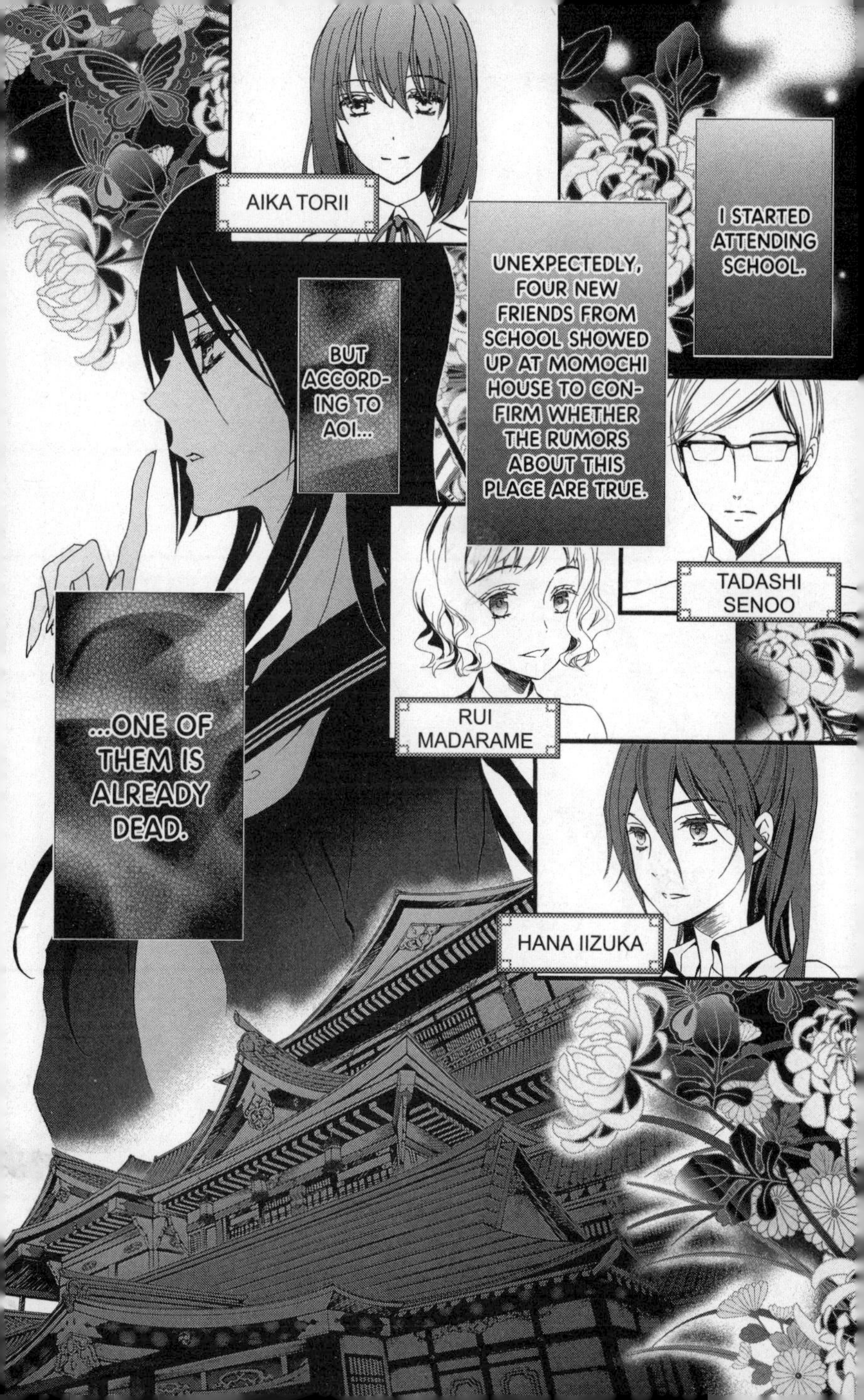
I STARTED ATTENDING SCHOOL.
UNEXPECTEDLY, FOUR NEW FRIENDS FROM SCHOOL SHOWED UP AT MOMOCHI HOUSE TO CONFIRM WHETHER THE RUMORS ABOUT THIS PLACE ARE TRUE.
AIKA TORII
TADASHI SENOO
BUT ACCORDING TO AOI...
RUI MADARAME
HANA IIZUKA
...ONE OF THEM IS ALREADY DEAD.

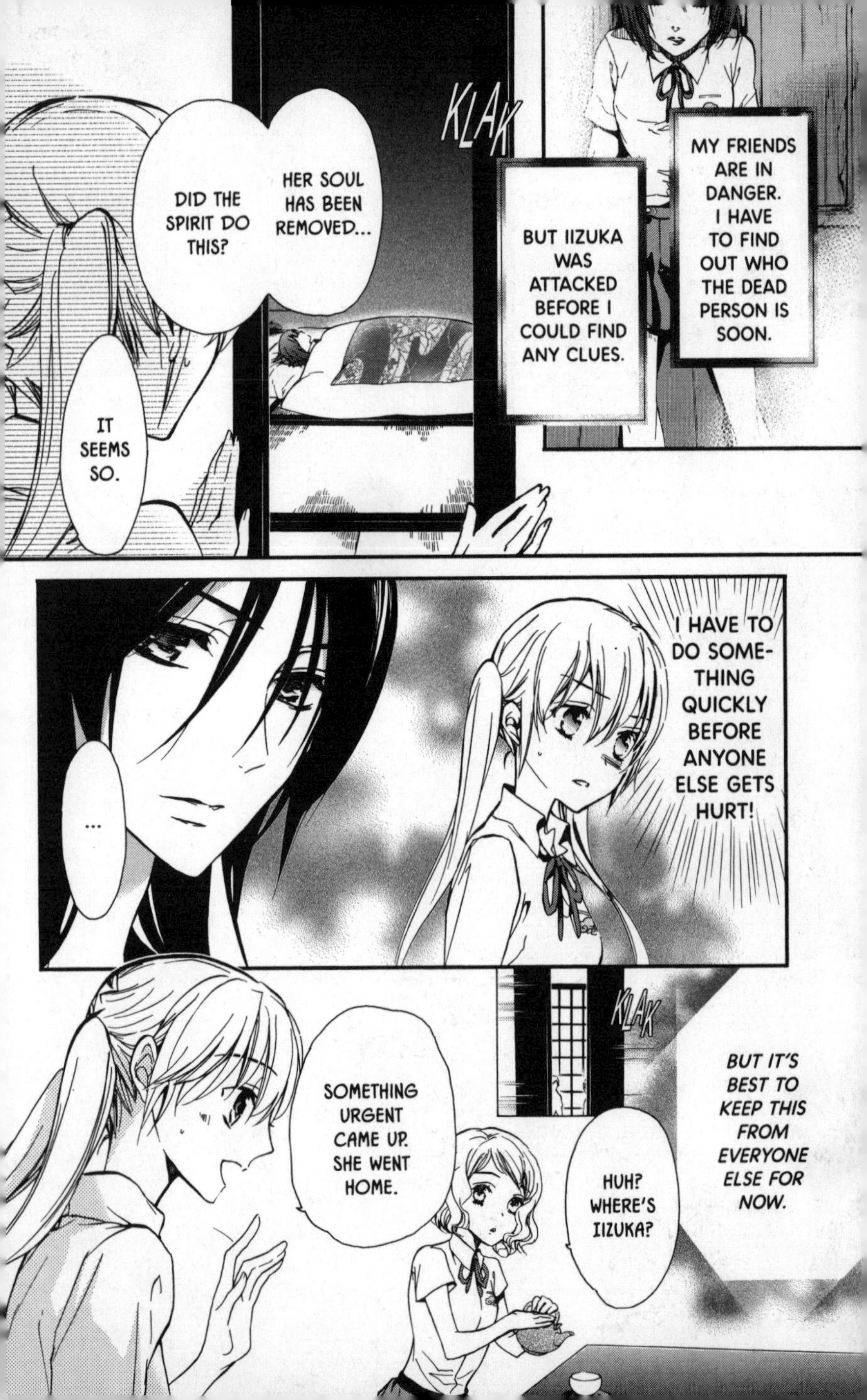
MY FRIENDS ARE IN DANGER. I HAVE TO FIND OUT WHO THE DEAD PERSON IS SOON.
BUT IIZUKA WAS ATTACKED BEFORE I COULD FIND ANY CLUES.
KLAK
HER SOUL HAS BEEN REMOVED...
DID THE SPIRIT DO THIS?
IT SEEMS SO.
I HAVE TO DO SOME-THING QUICKLY BEFORE ANYONE ELSE GETS HURT!
...
BUT IT'S BEST TO KEEP THIS FROM EVERYONE ELSE FOR NOW.
KLAK
HUH? WHERE'S IIZUKA?
SOMETHING URGENT CAME UP. SHE WENT HOME.

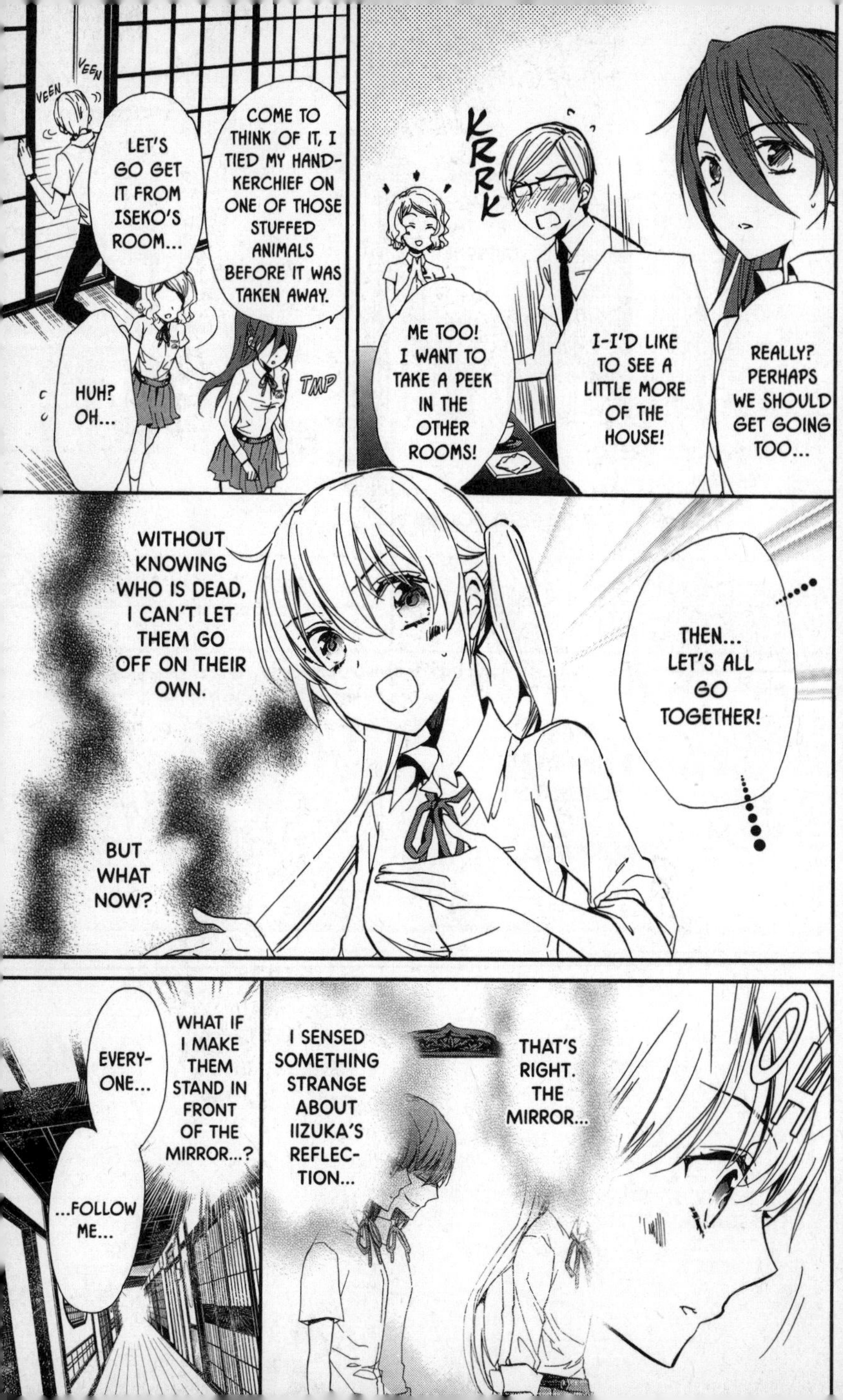
REALLY? PERHAPS WE SHOULD GET GOING TOO...
KRRK
I-I'D LIKE TO SEE A LITTLE MORE OF THE HOUSE!
ME TOO! I WANT TO TAKE A PEEK IN THE OTHER ROOMS!
COME TO THINK OF IT, I TIED MY HAND-KERCHIEF ON ONE OF THOSE STUFFED ANIMALS BEFORE IT WAS TAKEN AWAY.
VEEN
VEEN
LET'S GO GET IT FROM ISEKO'S ROOM...
TMP
HUH? OH...
THEN... LET'S ALL GO TOGETHER!
WITHOUT KNOWING WHO IS DEAD, I CAN'T LET THEM GO OFF ON THEIR OWN.
BUT WHAT NOW?
THAT'S RIGHT. THE MIRROR...
I SENSED SOMETHING STRANGE ABOUT IIZUKA'S REFLEC-TION...
WHAT IF I MAKE THEM STAND IN FRONT OF THE MIRROR...?
EVERY-ONE...
...FOLLOW ME...

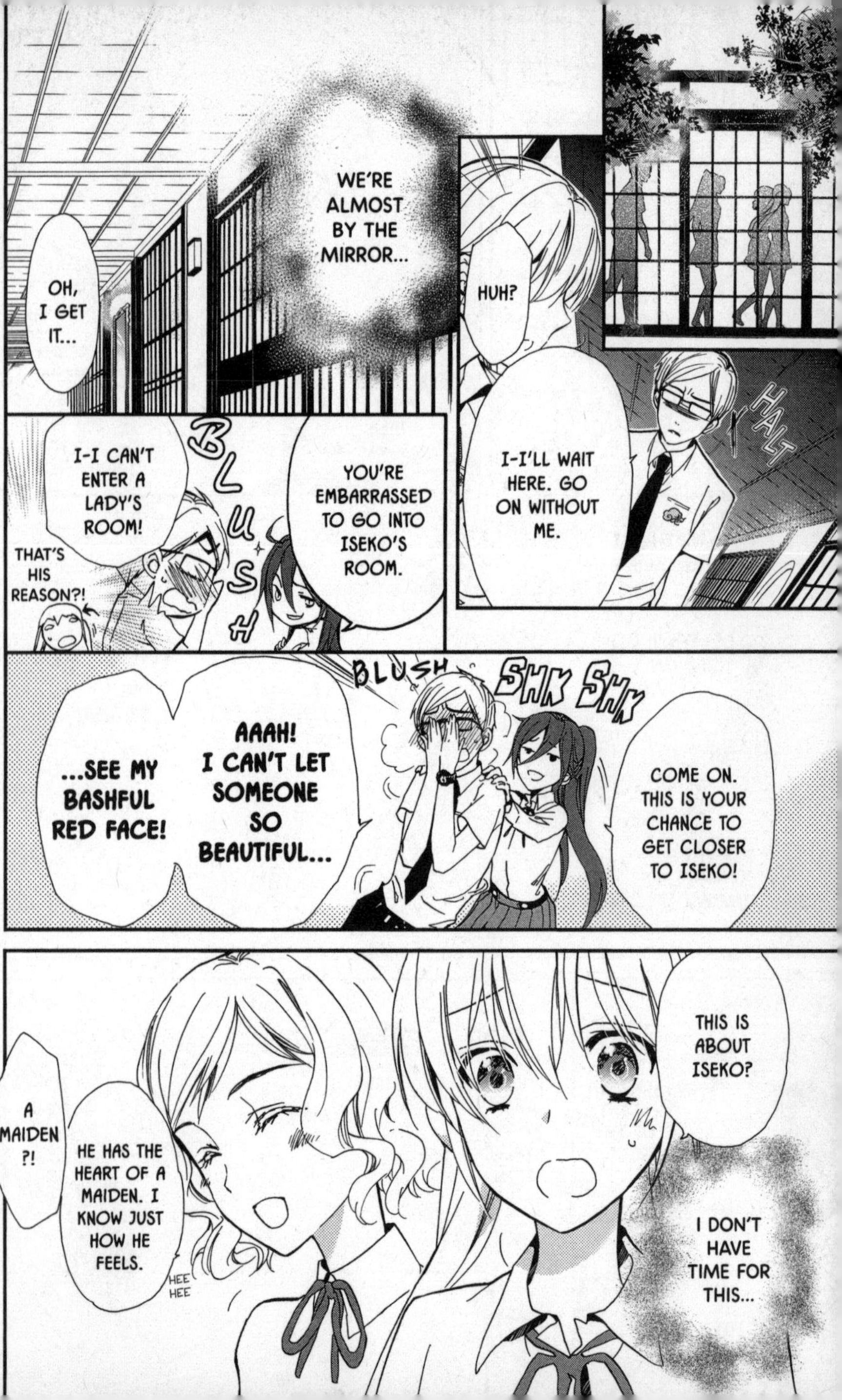
WE'RE ALMOST BY THE MIRROR...
HUH?
HALT
I-I'LL WAIT HERE. GO ON WITHOUT ME.
OH, I GET IT...
YOU'RE EMBARRASSED TO GO INTO ISEKO'S ROOM.
BLUSH
I-I CAN'T ENTER A LADY'S ROOM!
THAT'S HIS REASON?!
COME ON. THIS IS YOUR CHANCE TO GET CLOSER TO ISEKO!
SHK SHK
BLUSH
AAAH! I CAN'T LET SOMEONE SO BEAUTIFUL...
...SEE MY BASHFUL RED FACE!
THIS IS ABOUT ISEKO?
I DON'T HAVE TIME FOR THIS...
HE HAS THE HEART OF A MAIDEN. I KNOW JUST HOW HE FEELS.
HEE HEE
A MAIDEN?!

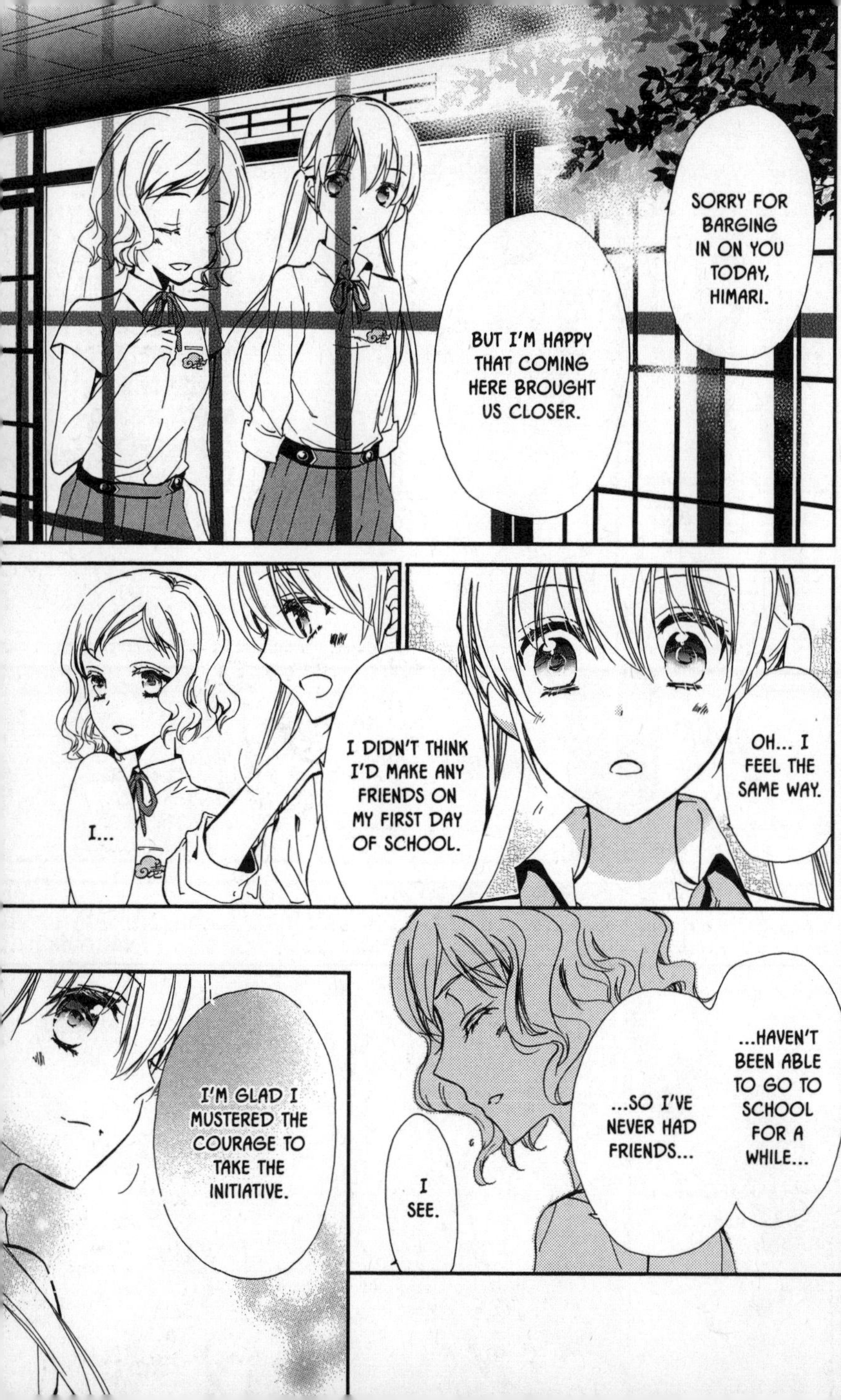
SORRY FOR BARGING IN ON YOU TODAY, HIMARI.
BUT I'M HAPPY THAT COMING HERE BROUGHT US CLOSER.
OH... I FEEL THE SAME WAY.
I DIDN'T THINK I'D MAKE ANY FRIENDS ON MY FIRST DAY OF SCHOOL.
I...
...HAVEN'T BEEN ABLE TO GO TO SCHOOL FOR A WHILE...
...SO I'VE NEVER HAD FRIENDS...
I SEE.
I'M GLAD I MUSTERED THE COURAGE TO TAKE THE INITIATIVE.

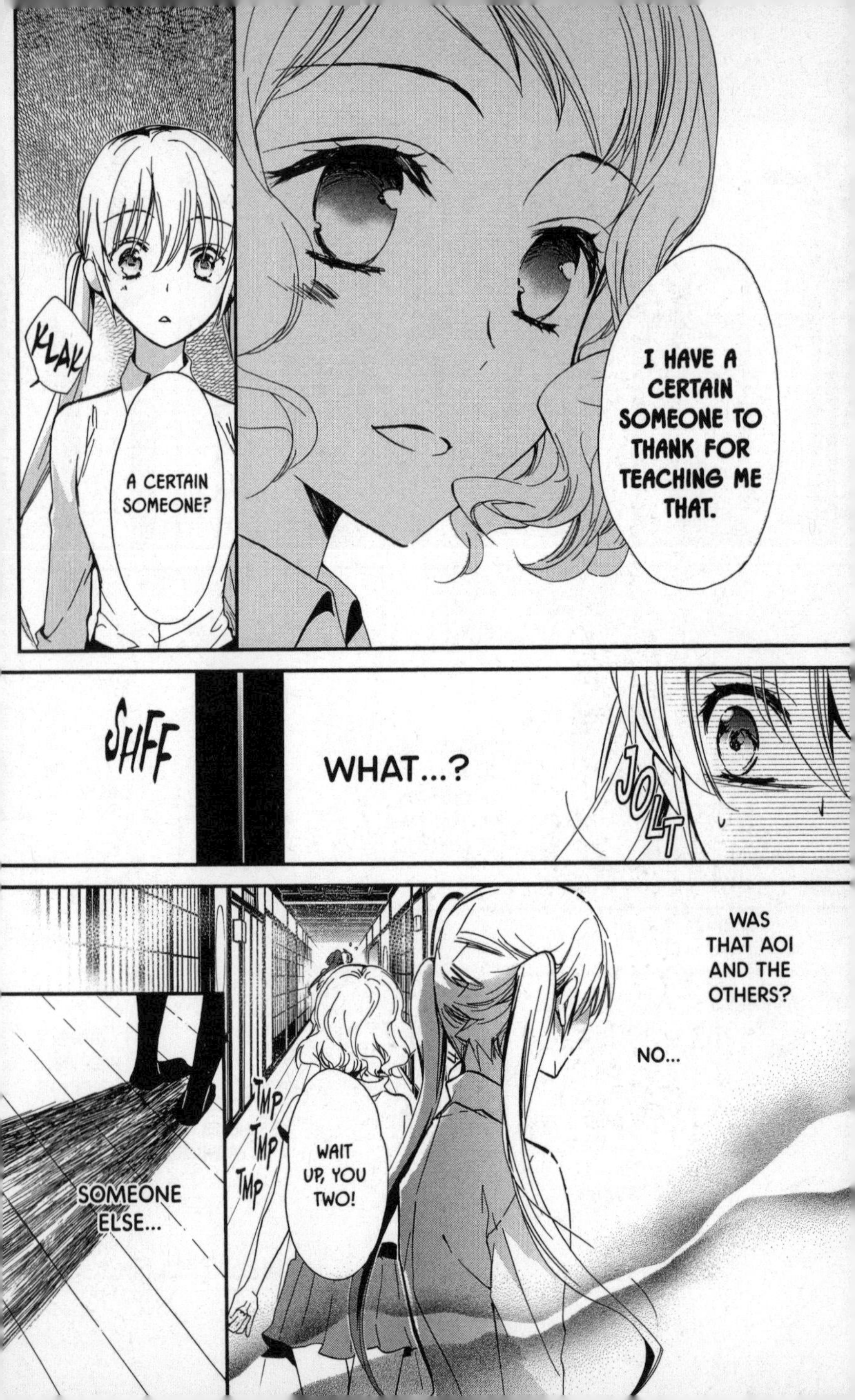
I HAVE A CERTAIN SOMEONE TO THANK FOR TEACHING ME THAT.
KLAK
A CERTAIN SOMEONE?
JOLT
WHAT...?
SHFF
WAS THAT AOI AND THE OTHERS?
NO...
WAIT UP, YOU TWO!
TMP TMP TMP
SOMEONE ELSE...

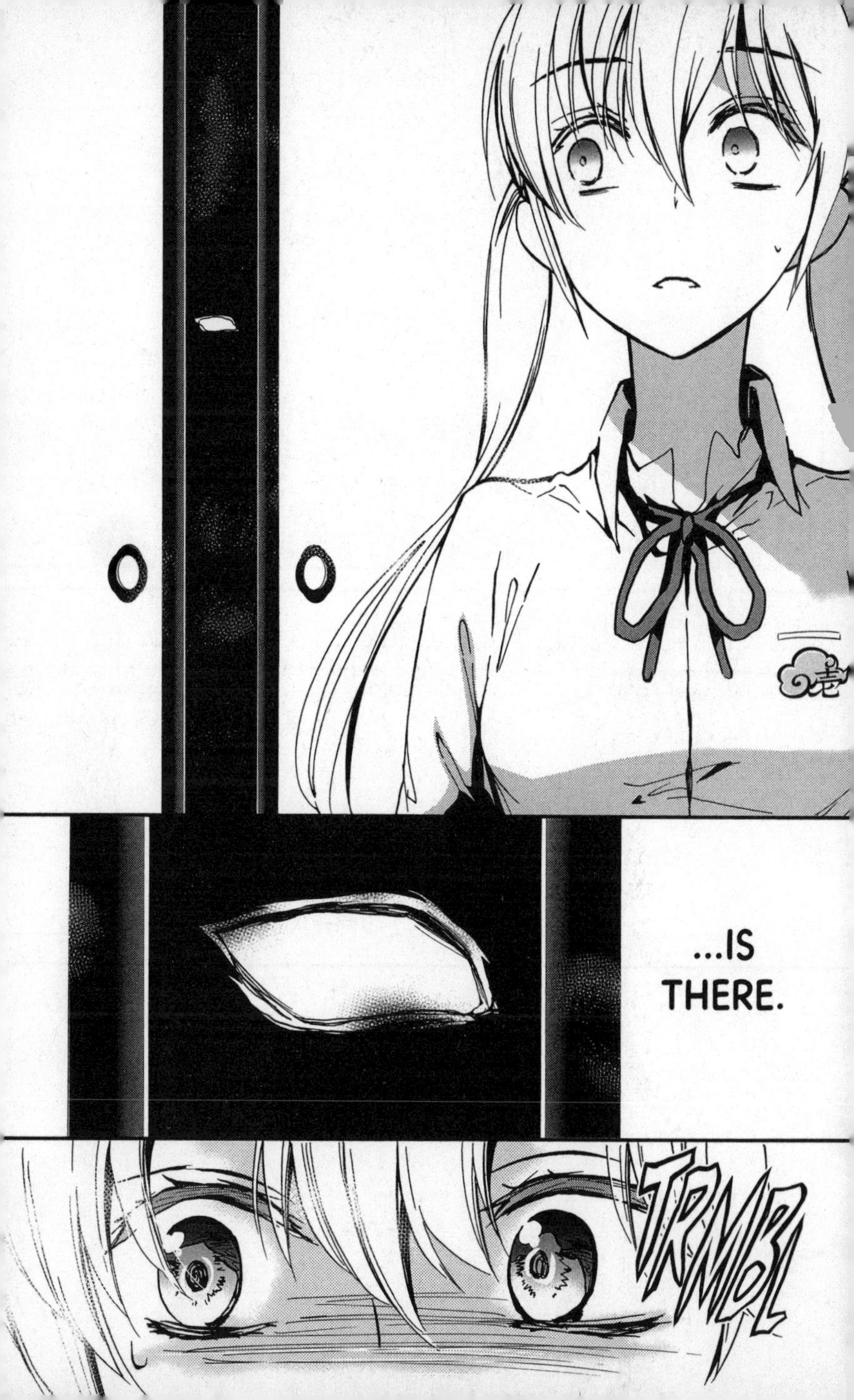
...IS THERE.
TRMBL

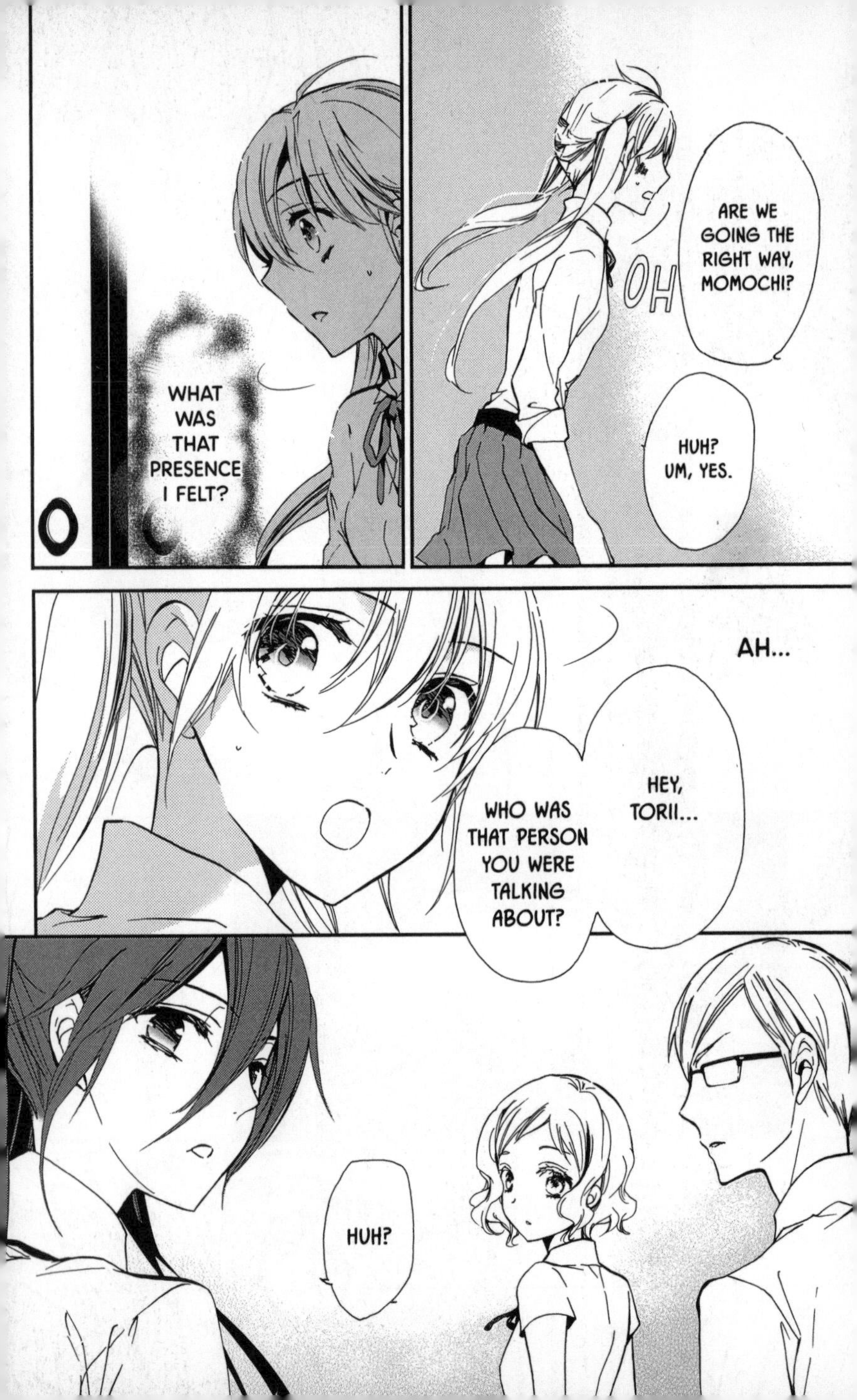
ARE WE GOING THE RIGHT WAY, MOMOCHI?
OH
HUH? UM, YES.
WHAT WAS THAT PRESENCE I FELT?
AH...
HEY, TORII...
WHO WAS THAT PERSON YOU WERE TALKING ABOUT?
HUH?

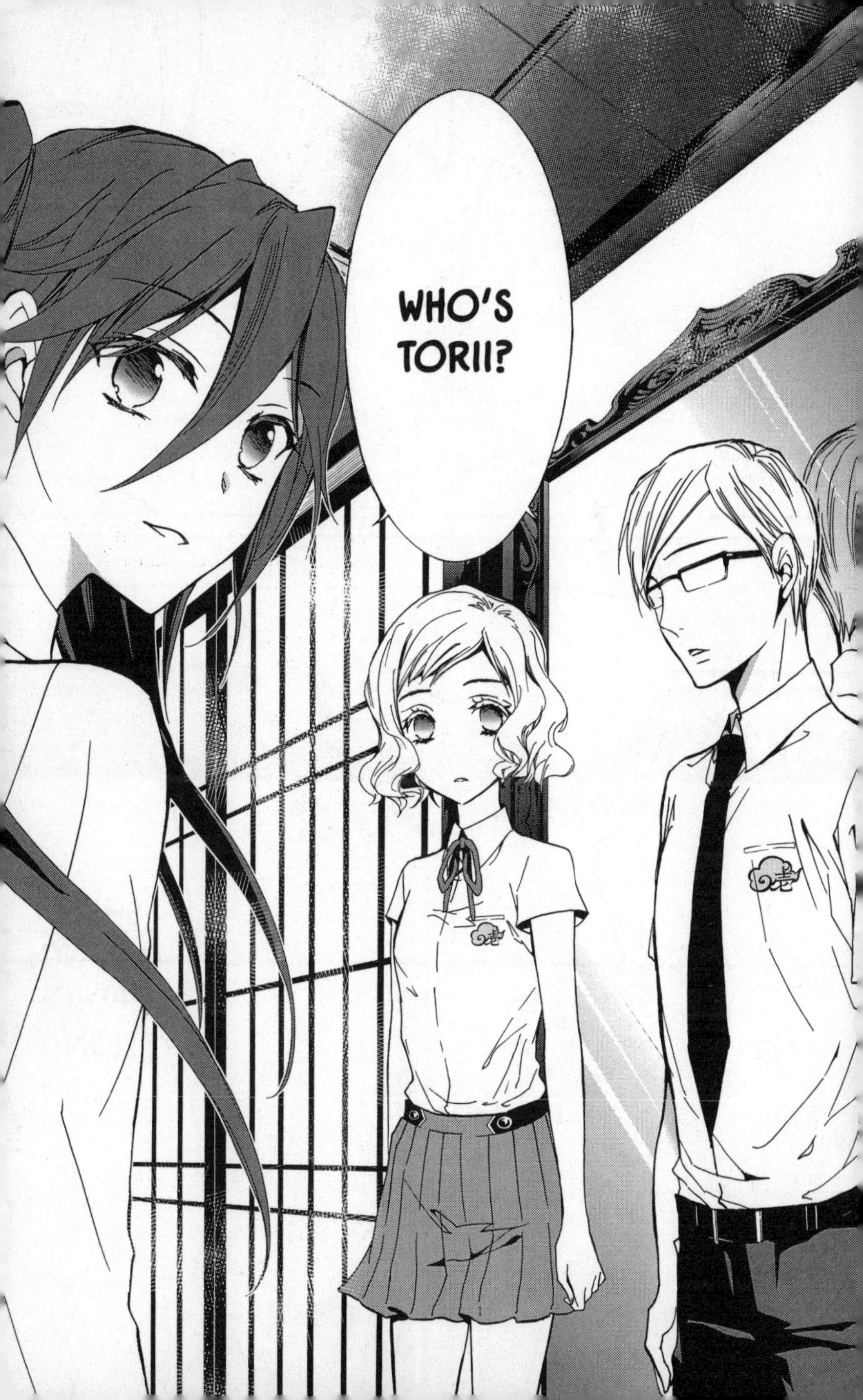
WHO'S TORII?

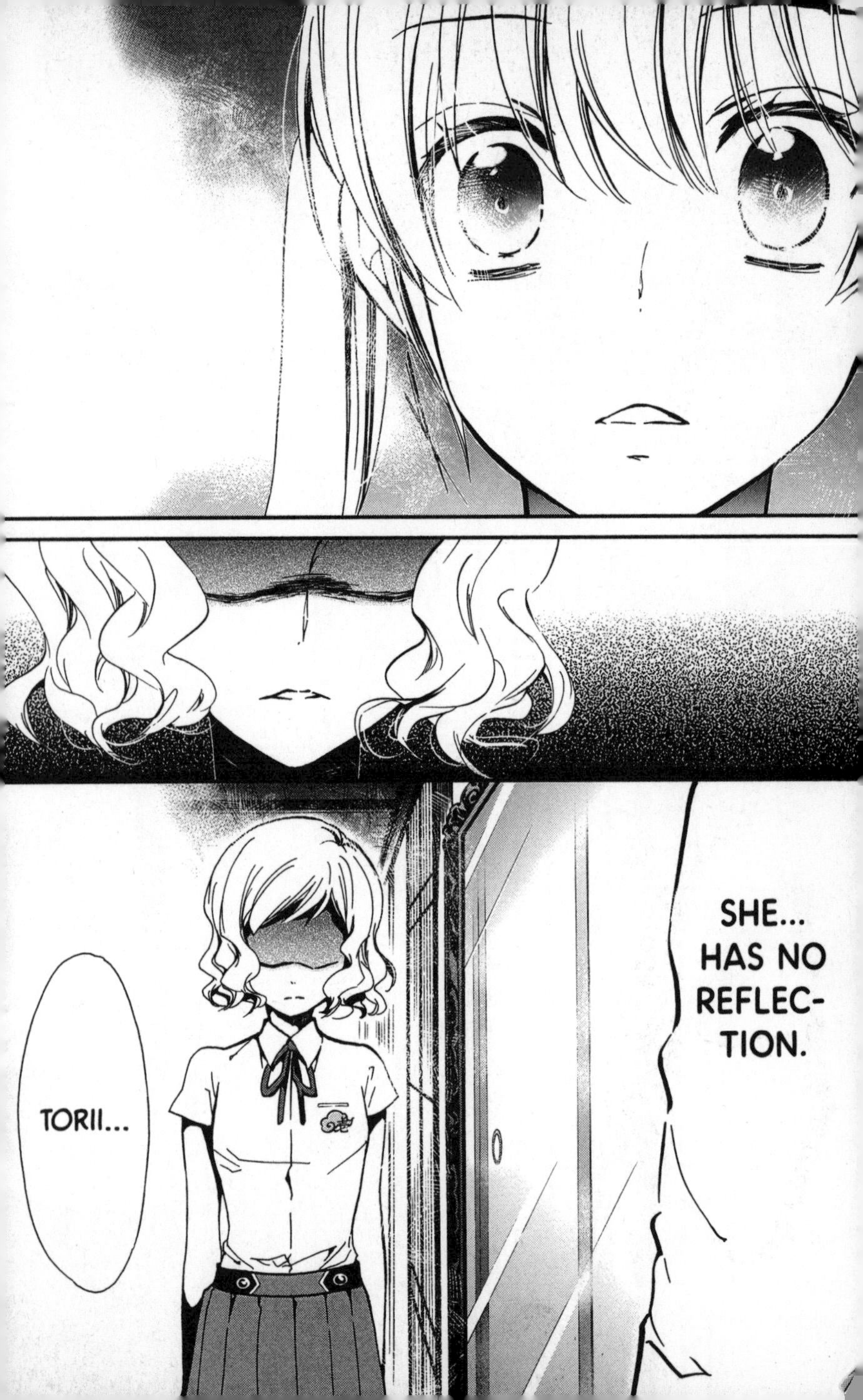
SHE... HAS NO REFLEC-TION.
TORII...

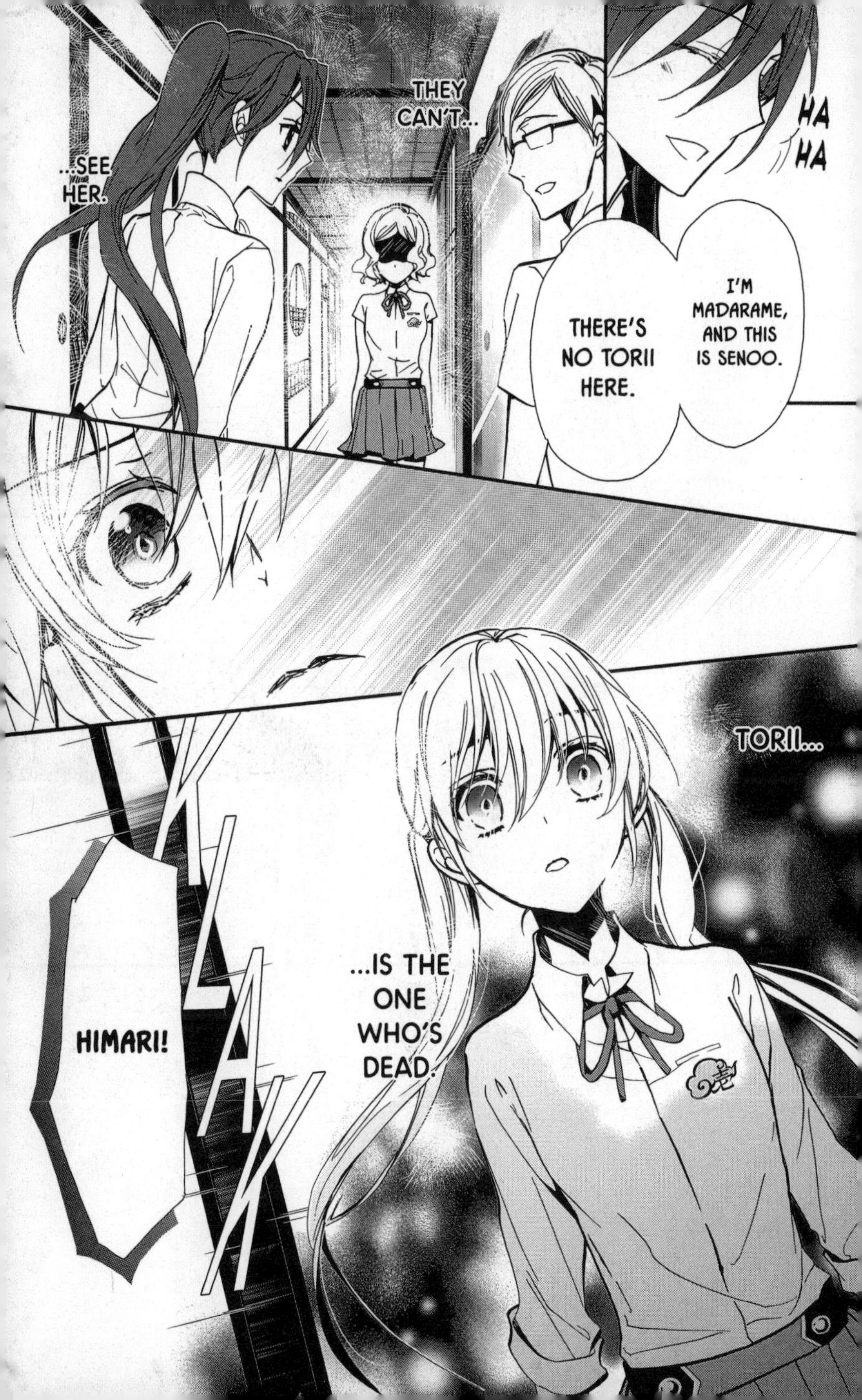
HA HA
I'M MADARAME, AND THIS IS SENOO.
THERE'S NO TORII HERE.
THEY CAN'T...
...SEE HER.
TORII...
...IS THE ONE WHO'S DEAD.
HIMARI!
KLAK

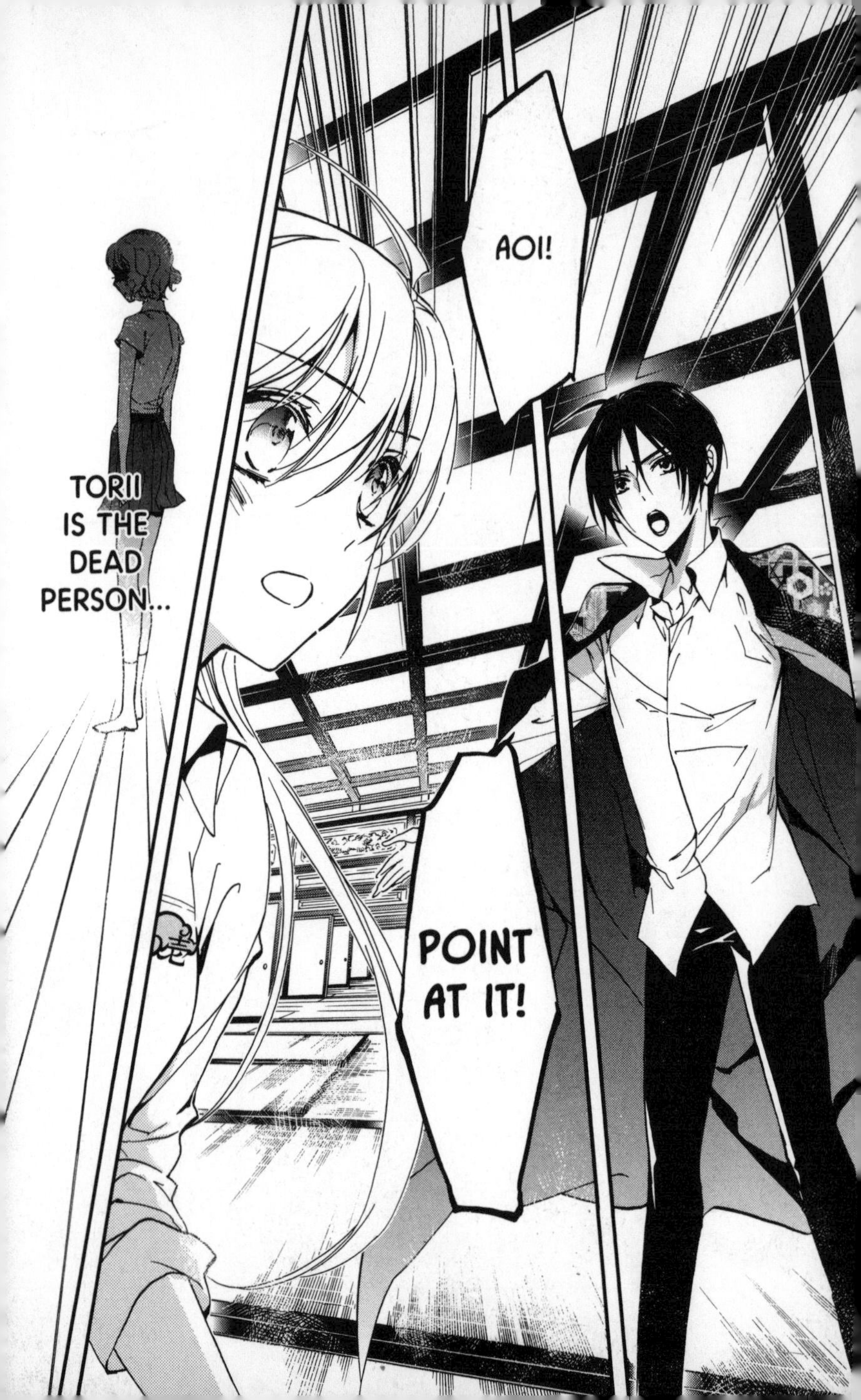
AOI!
POINT AT IT!
TORII IS THE DEAD PERSON...

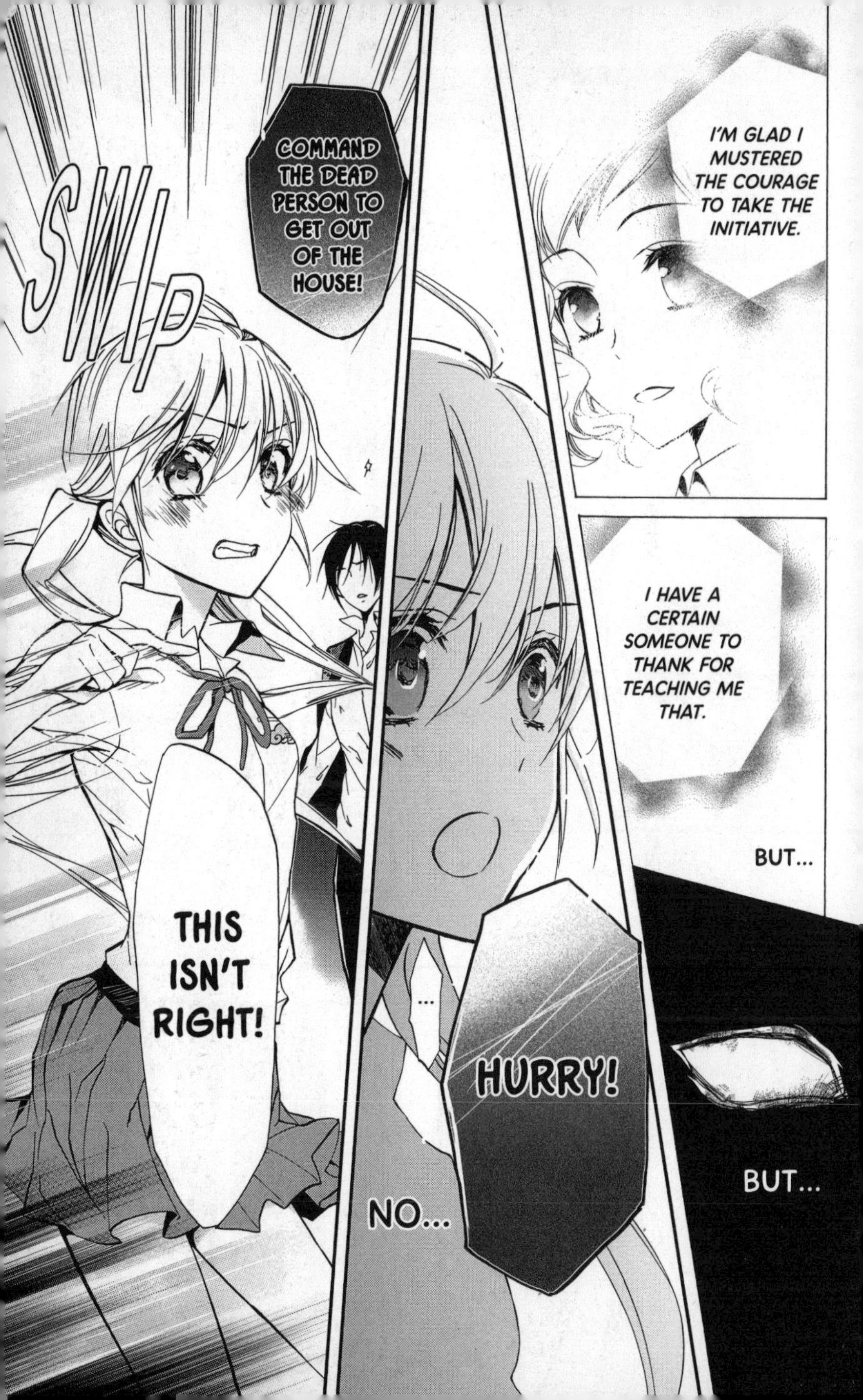
I'M GLAD I MUSTERED THE COURAGE TO TAKE THE INITIATIVE.
I HAVE A CERTAIN SOMEONE TO THANK FOR TEACHING ME THAT.
BUT...
BUT...
HURRY!
...
NO...
COMMAND THE DEAD PERSON TO GET OUT OF THE HOUSE!
SWIP
THIS ISN'T RIGHT!

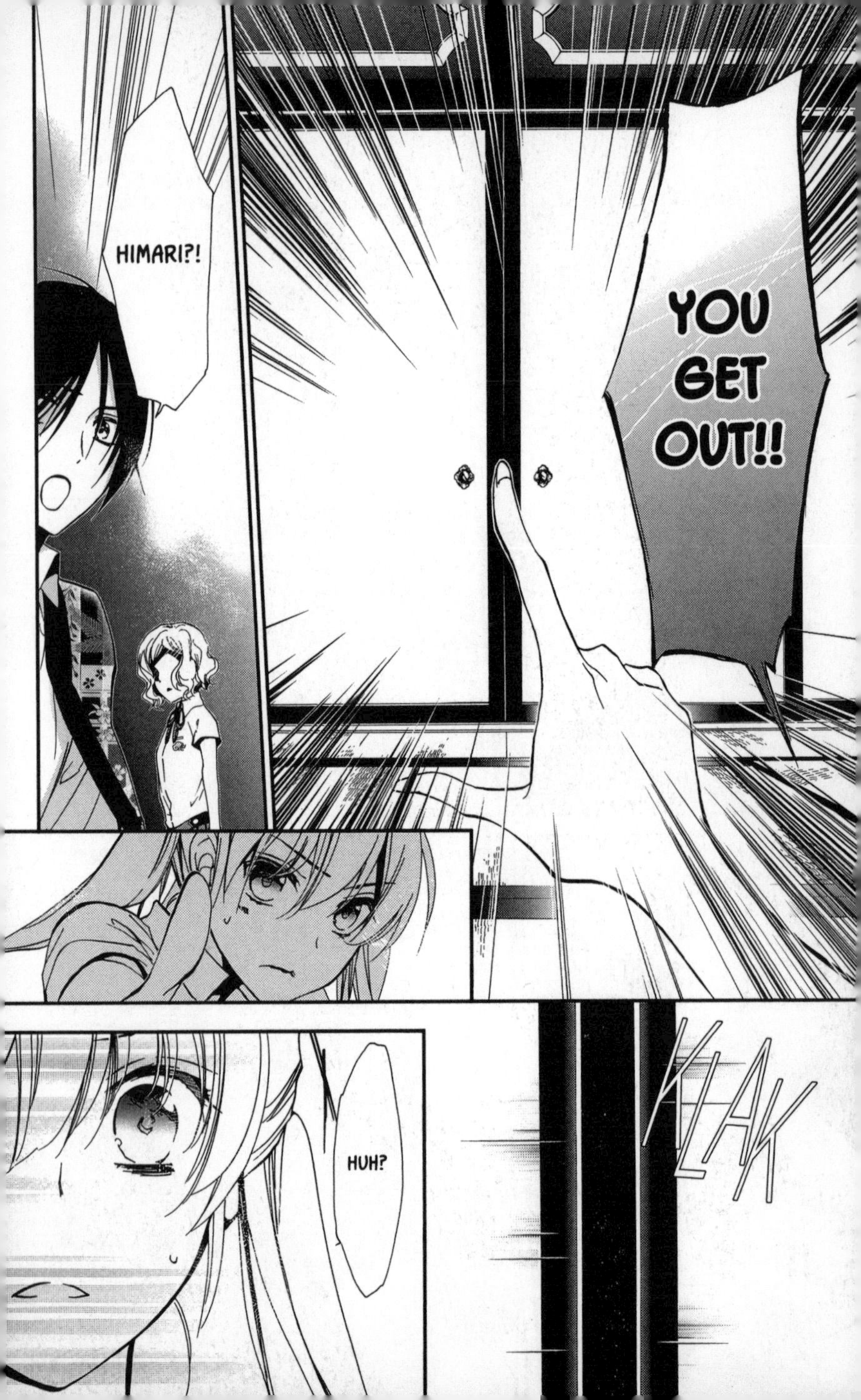
YOU GET OUT!!
HIMARI?!
KLAK
HUH?

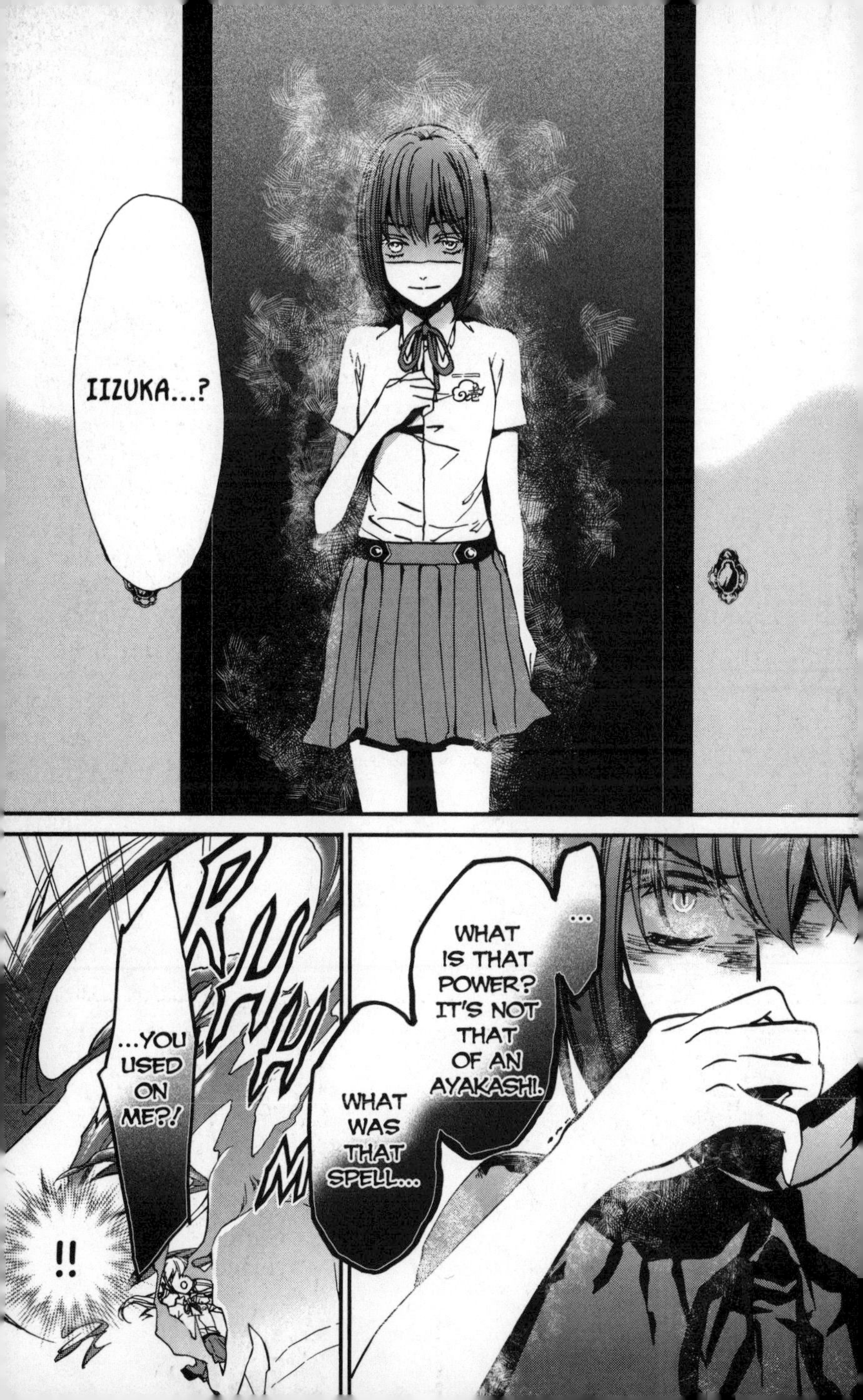
IIZUKA...?
...
WHAT IS THAT POWER? IT'S NOT THAT OF AN AYAKASHI.
WHAT WAS THAT SPELL...
...YOU USED ON ME?!
!!

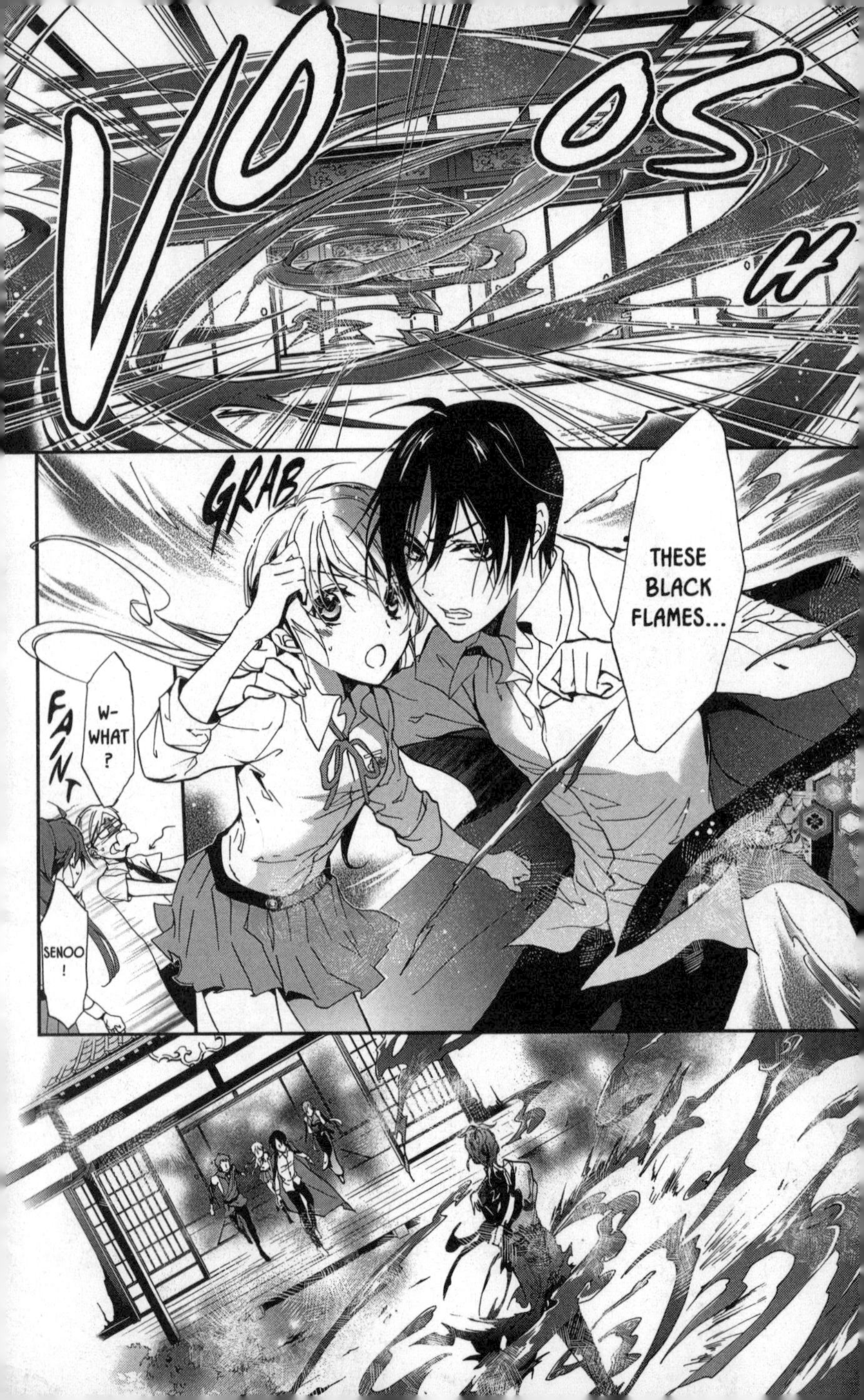
VOOSH
GRAB
THESE BLACK FLAMES...
W-WHAT?
FAINT
SENOO!

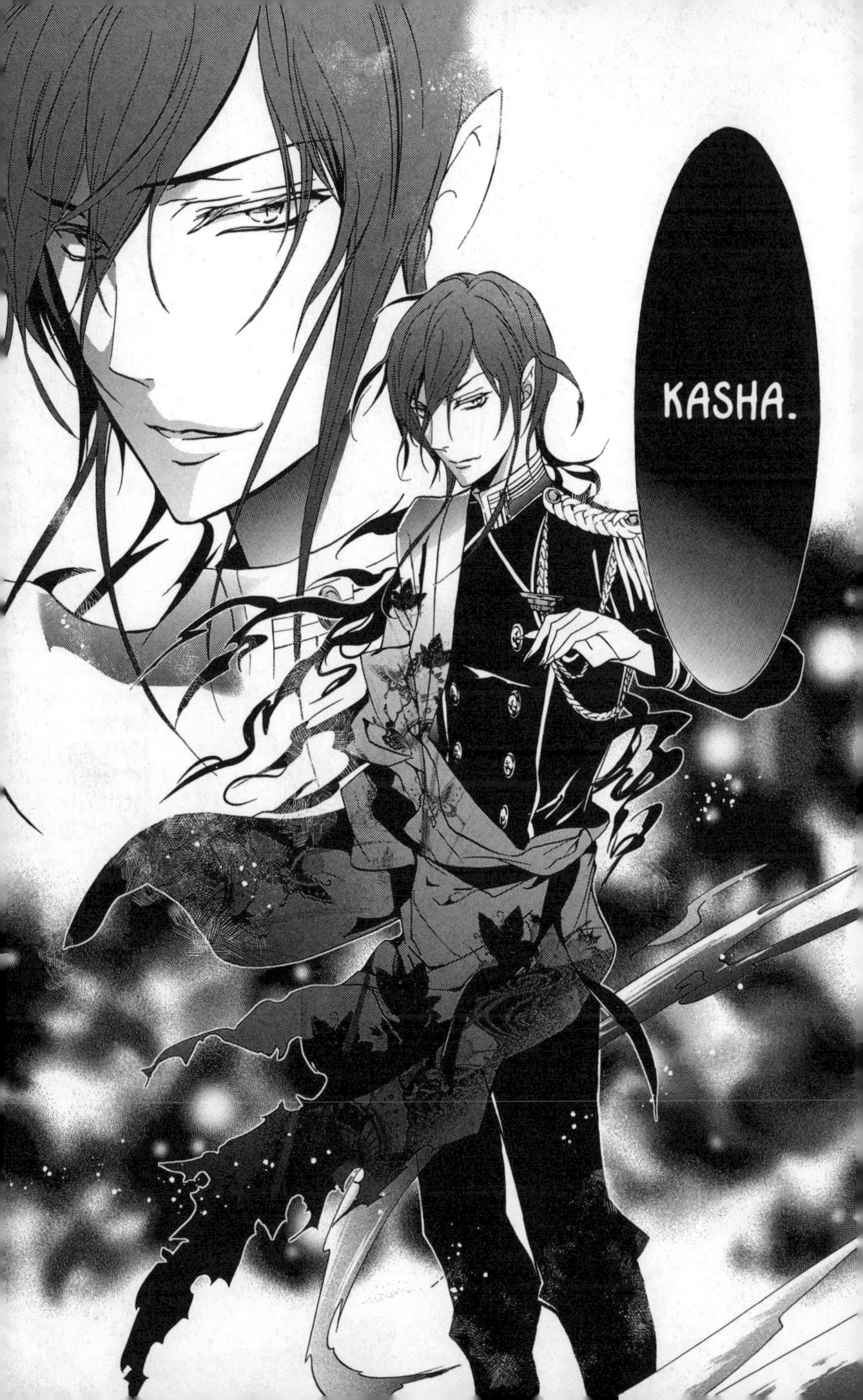
KASHA.

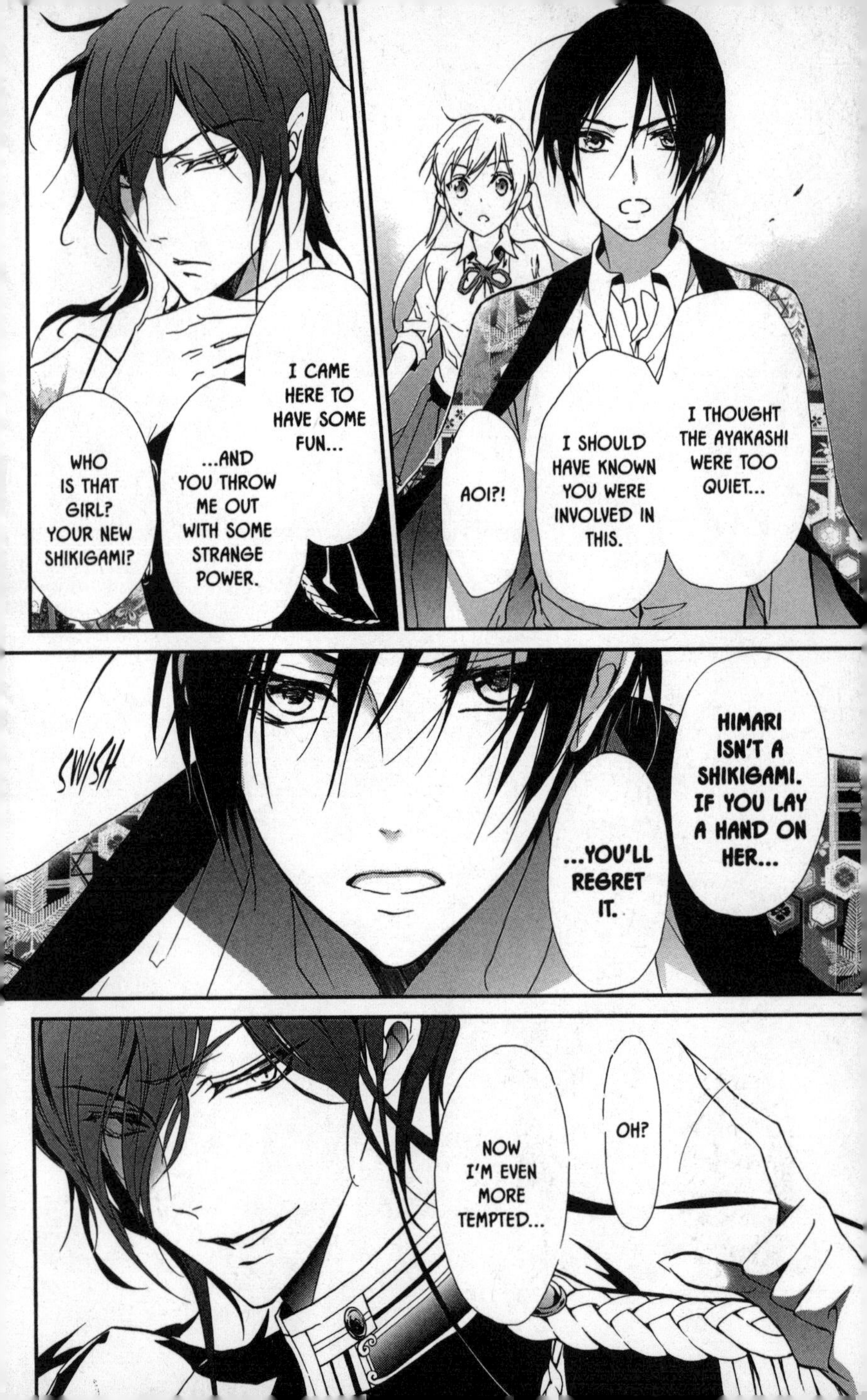
I THOUGHT THE AYAKASHI WERE TOO QUIET...
I SHOULD HAVE KNOWN YOU WERE INVOLVED IN THIS.
AOI?!
I CAME HERE TO HAVE SOME FUN...
...AND YOU THROW ME OUT WITH SOME STRANGE POWER.
WHO IS THAT GIRL? YOUR NEW SHIKIGAMI?
HIMARI ISN'T A SHIKIGAMI. IF YOU LAY A HAND ON HER...
...YOU'LL REGRET IT.
SWISH
OH?
NOW I'M EVEN MORE TEMPTED...

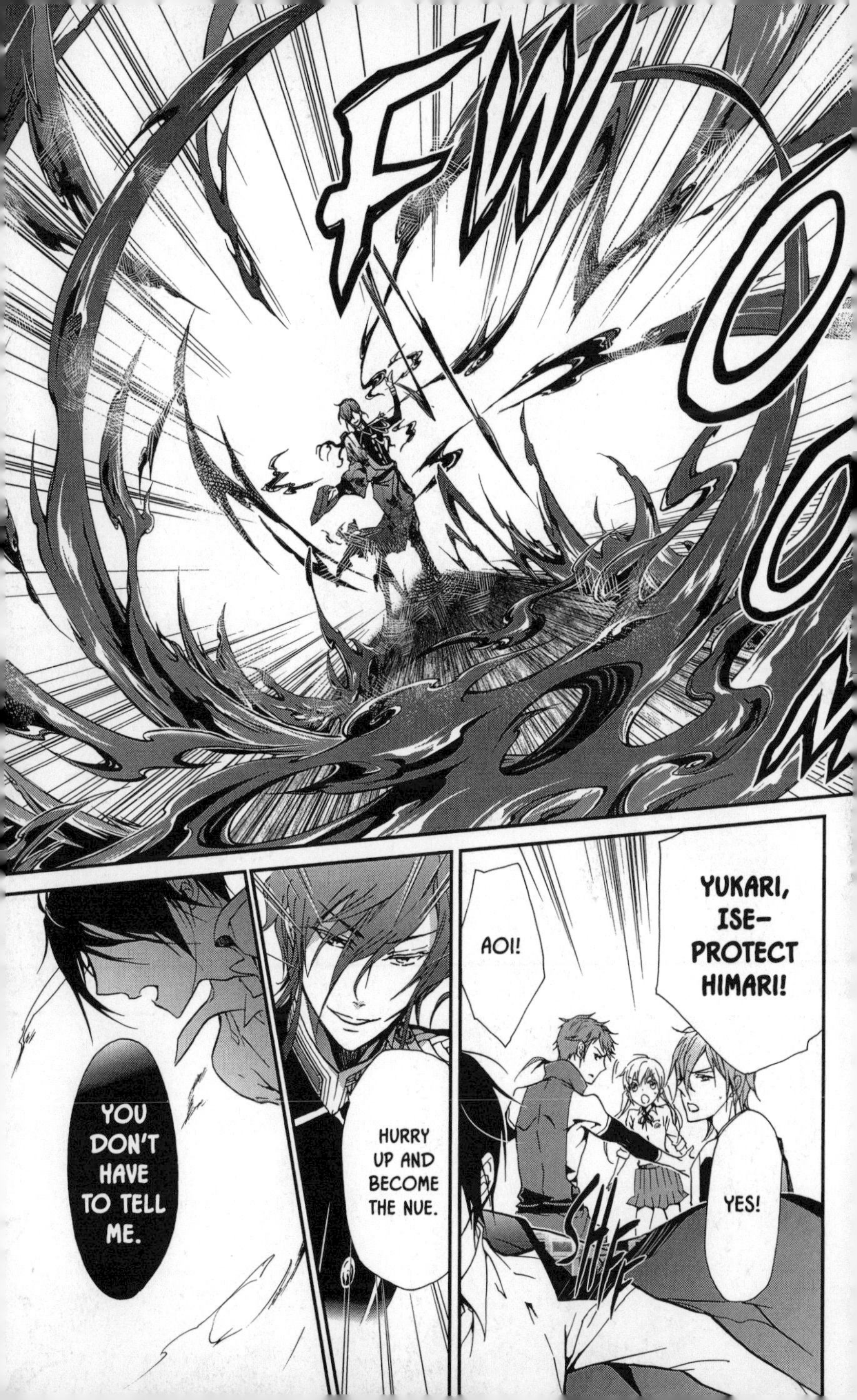
FWOOOM
YUKARI, ISE— PROTECT HIMARI!
AOI!
YES!
HURRY UP AND BECOME THE NUE.
YOU DON'T HAVE TO TELL ME.

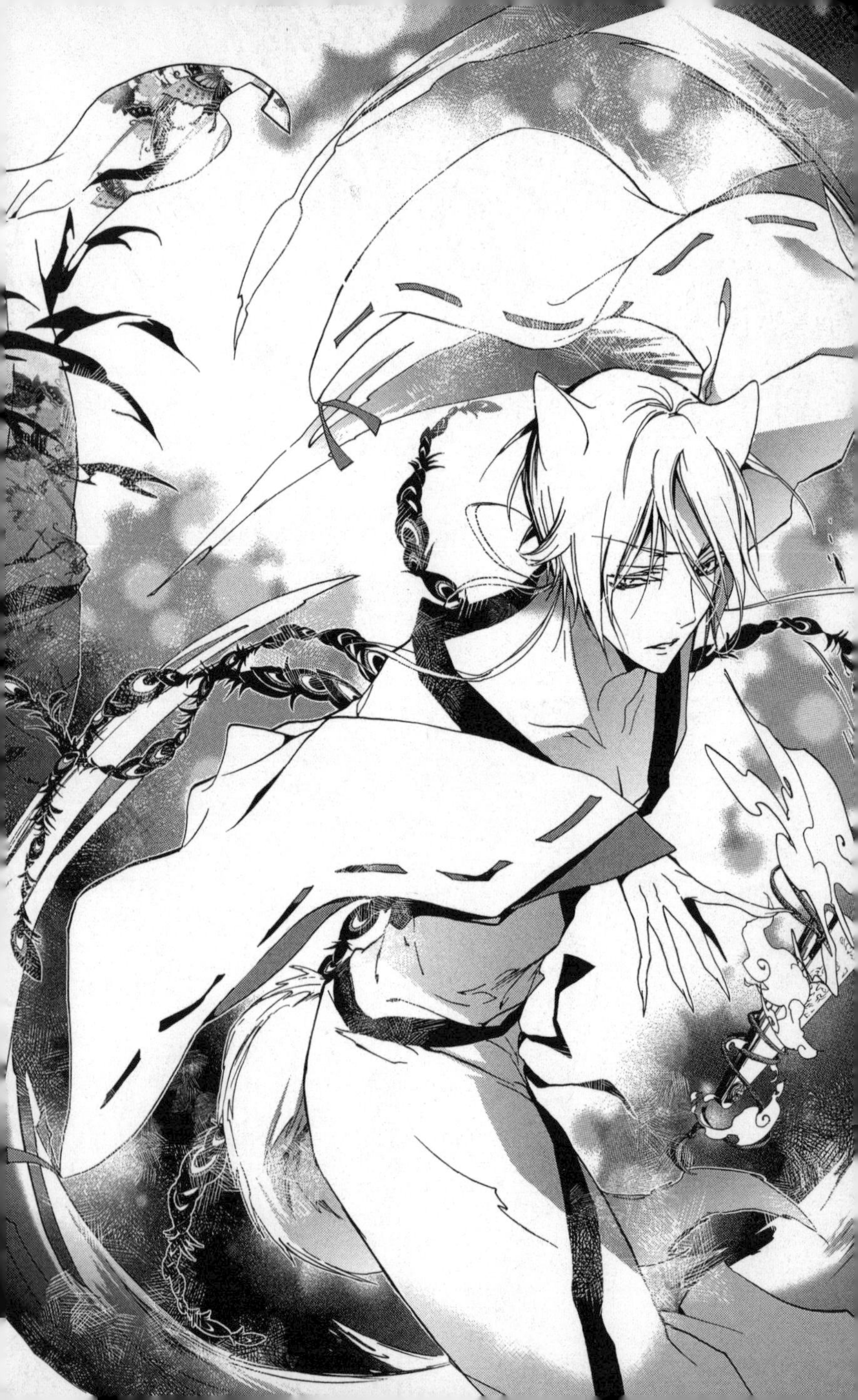

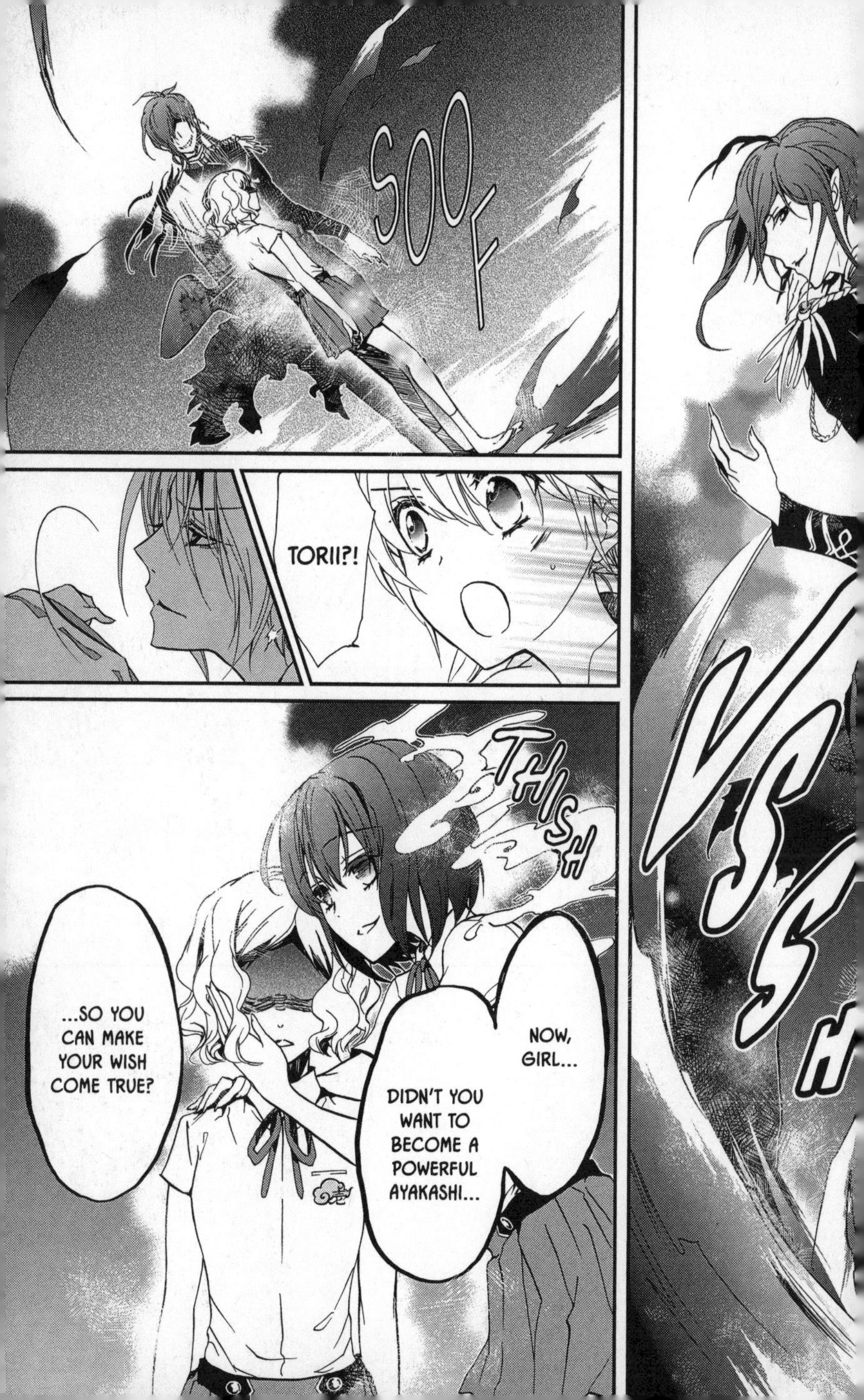
VSSH
SOOF
TORII?!
THISH
NOW, GIRL...
DIDN'T YOU WANT TO BECOME A POWERFUL AYAKASHI...
...SO YOU CAN MAKE YOUR WISH COME TRUE?

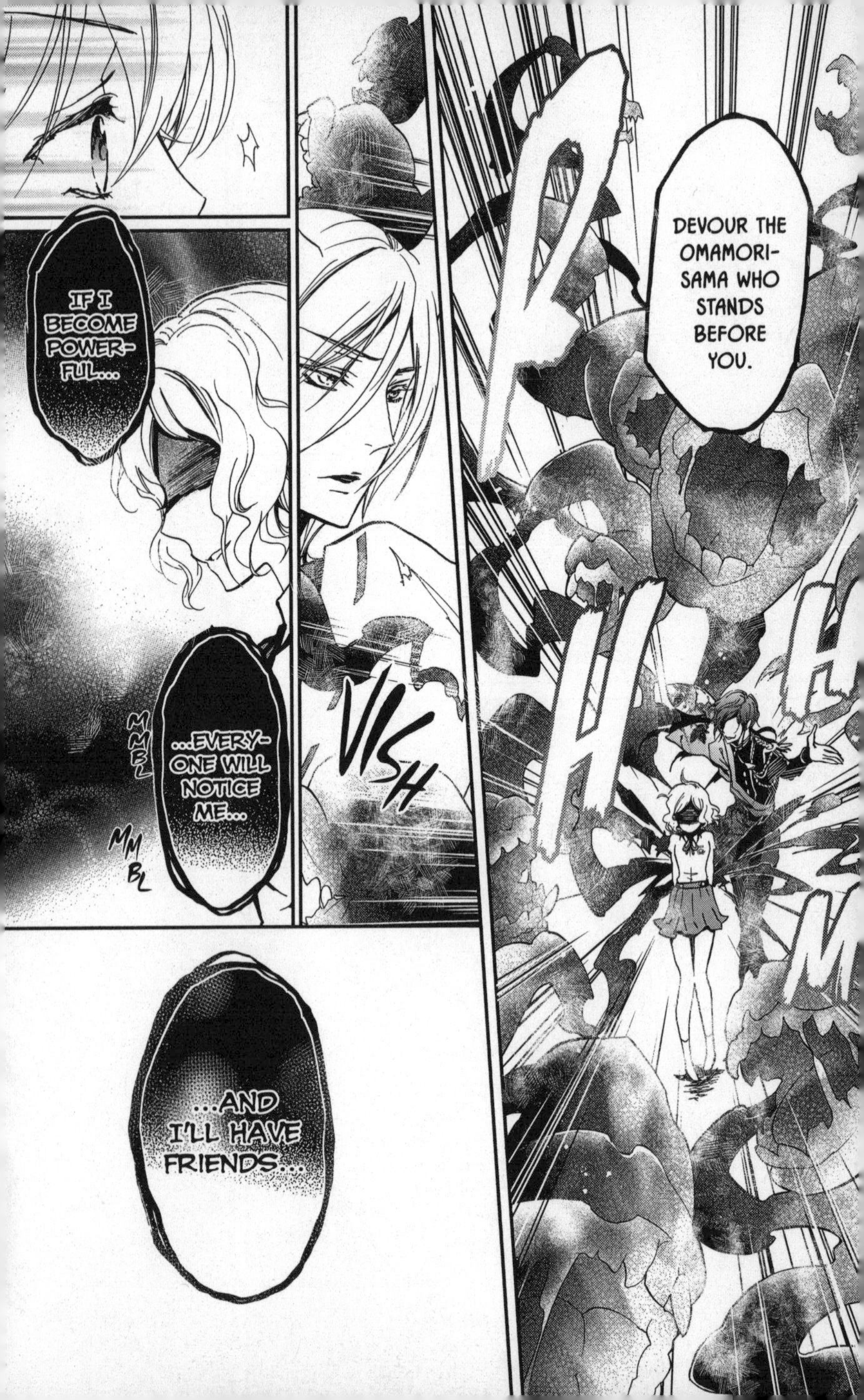
DEVOUR THE OMAMORI-SAMA WHO STANDS BEFORE YOU.
VISH
IF I BECOME POWER-FUL...
...EVERY-ONE WILL NOTICE ME...
MMBL
MMBL
...AND I'LL HAVE FRIENDS...

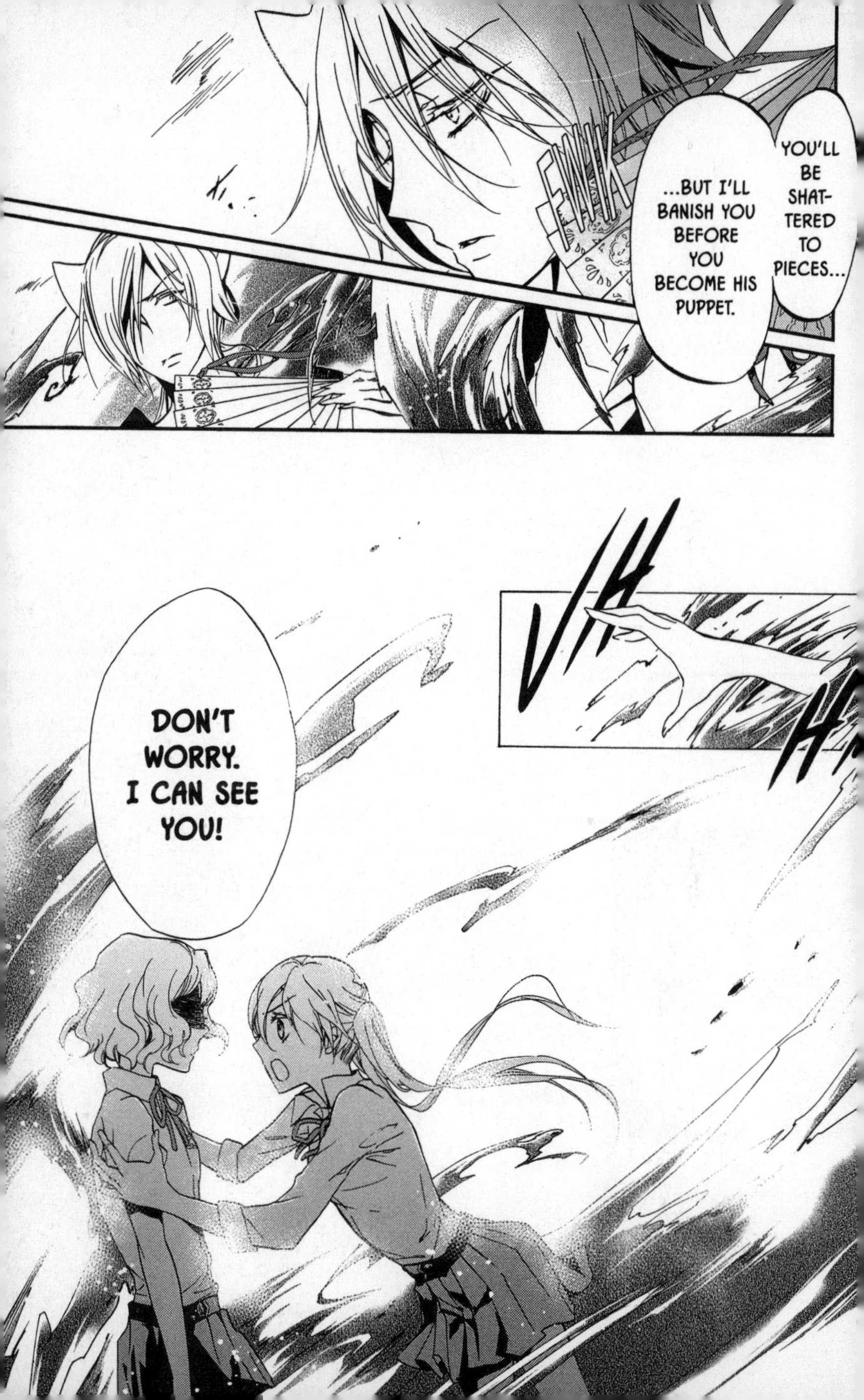
YOU'LL BE SHATTERED TO PIECES...
...BUT I'LL BANISH YOU BEFORE YOU BECOME HIS PUPPET.
DON'T WORRY. I CAN SEE YOU!

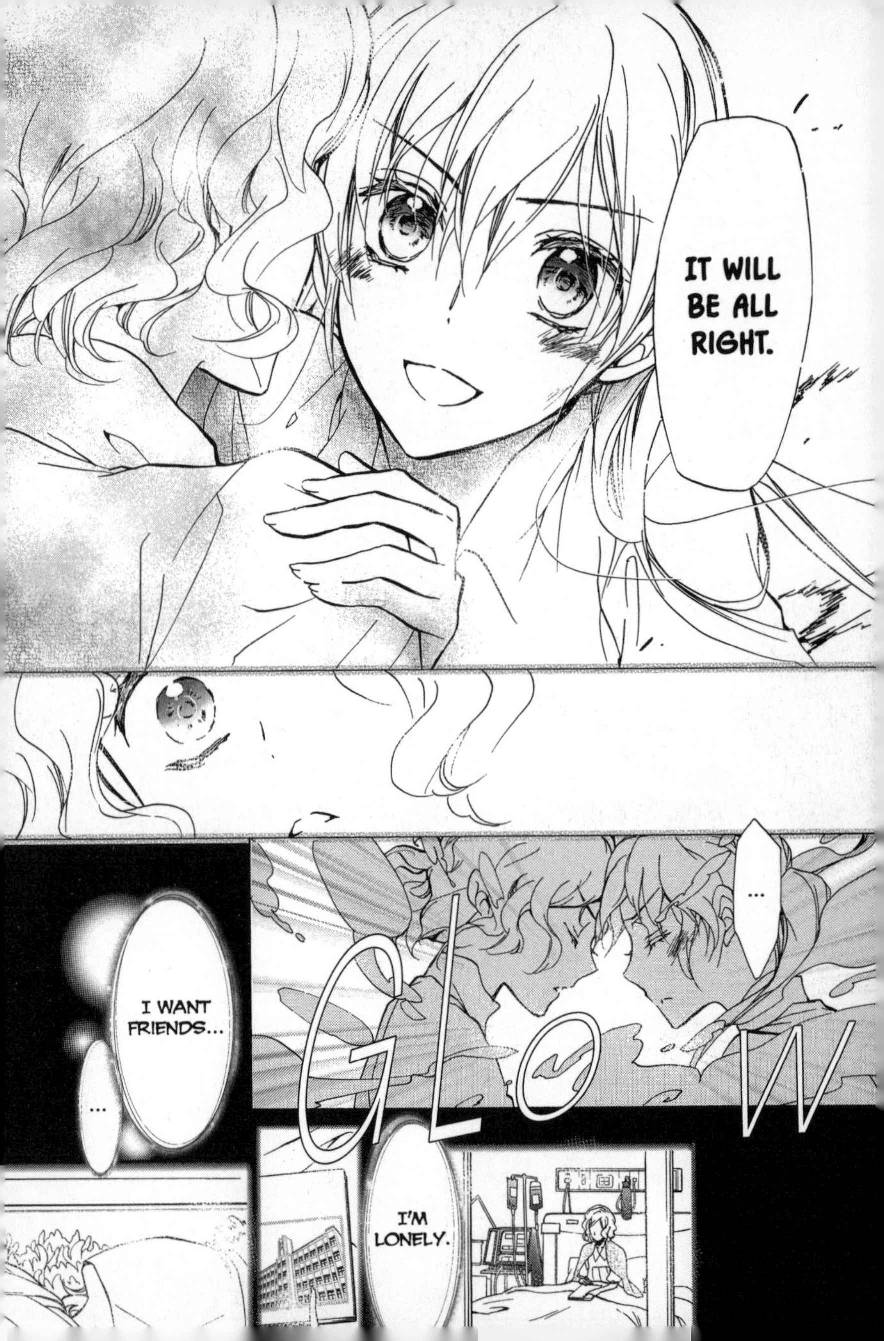
IT WILL BE ALL RIGHT.
...
GLOW
I WANT FRIENDS...
...
I'M LONELY.

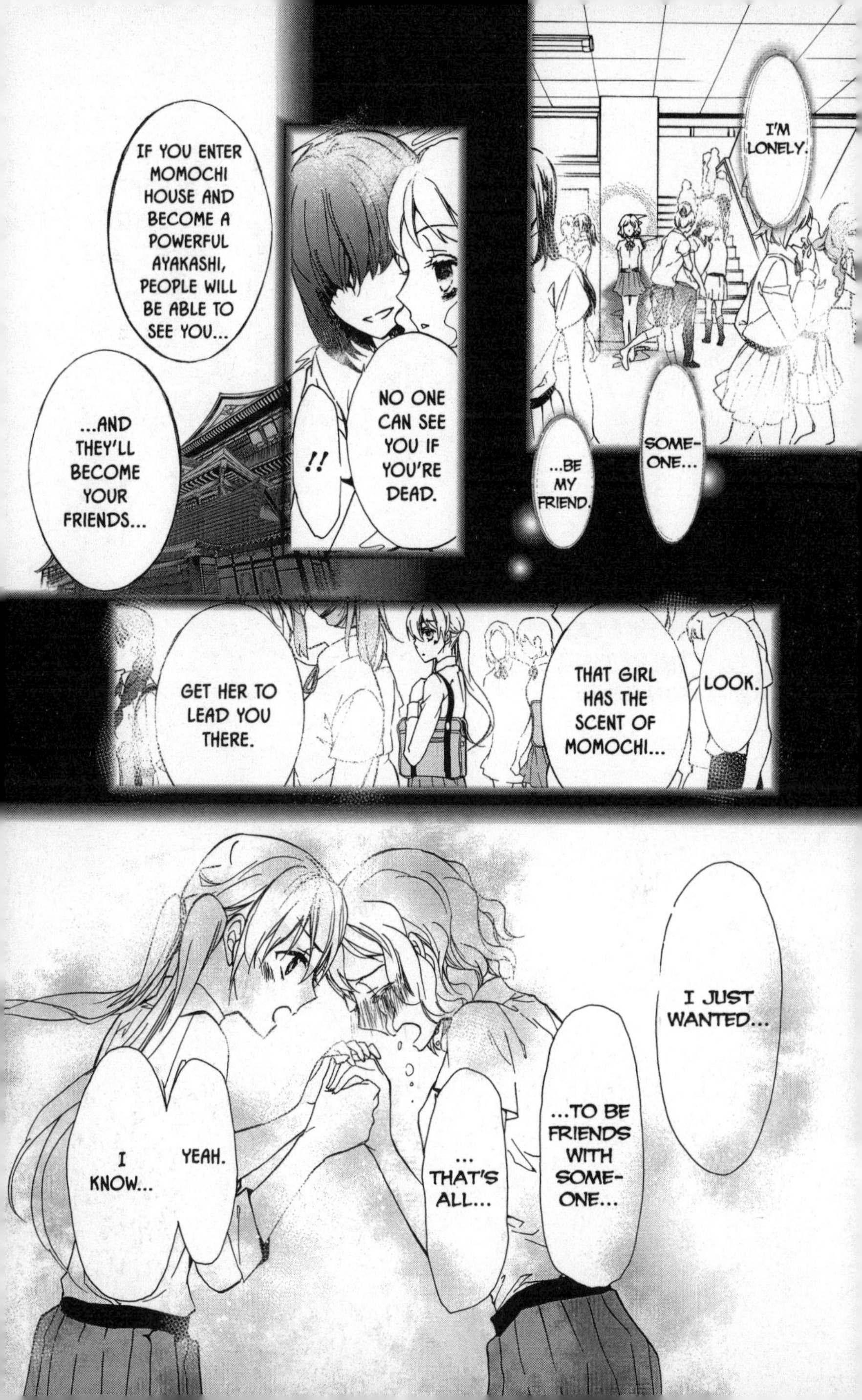
I'M LONELY.
SOME-ONE...
...BE MY FRIEND.
NO ONE CAN SEE YOU IF YOU'RE DEAD.
!!
IF YOU ENTER MOMOCHI HOUSE AND BECOME A POWERFUL AYAKASHI, PEOPLE WILL BE ABLE TO SEE YOU...
...AND THEY'LL BECOME YOUR FRIENDS...
LOOK.
THAT GIRL HAS THE SCENT OF MOMOCHI...
GET HER TO LEAD YOU THERE.
I JUST WANTED...
...TO BE FRIENDS WITH SOME-ONE...
...THAT'S ALL...
YEAH.
I KNOW...

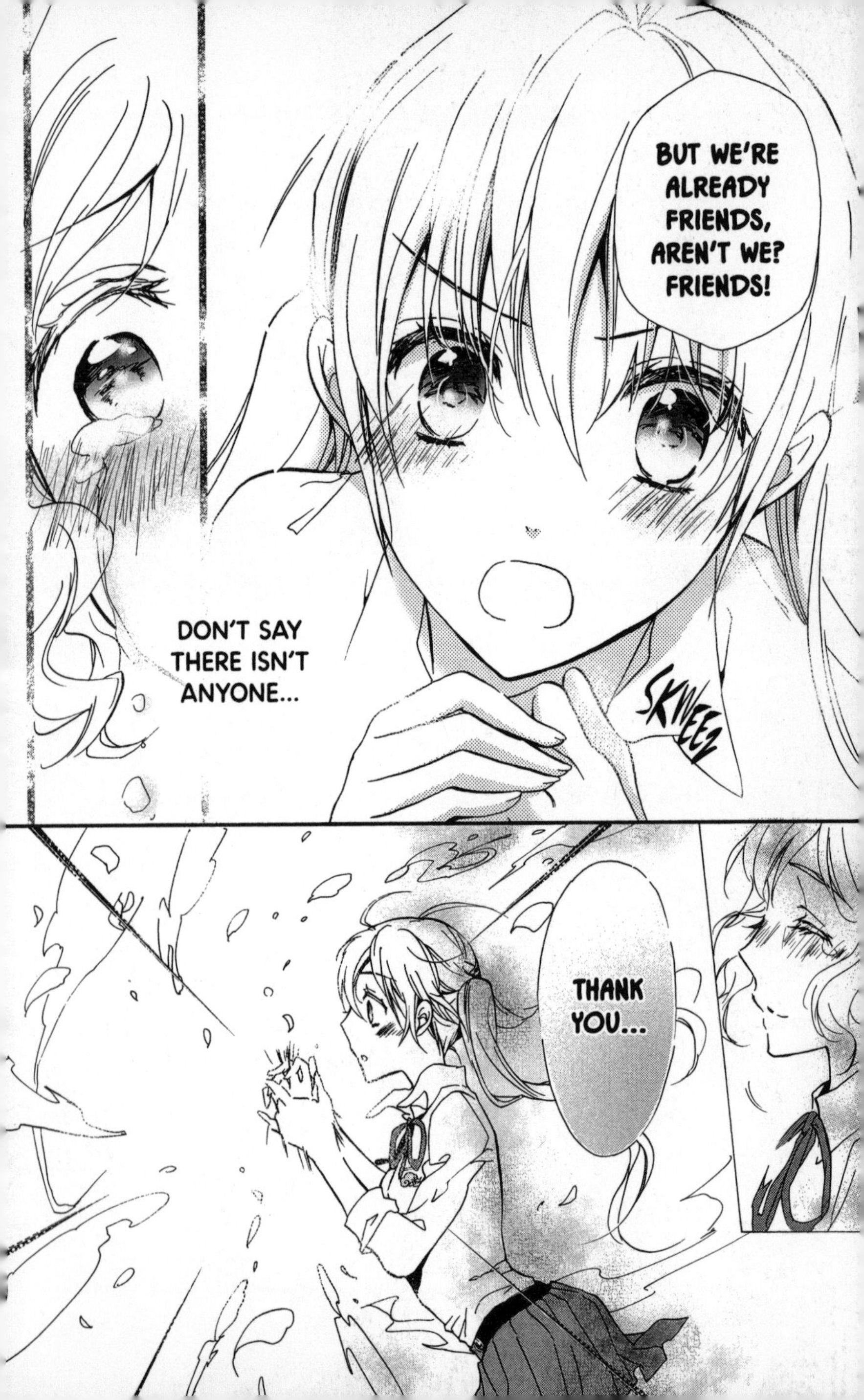
BUT WE'RE ALREADY FRIENDS, AREN'T WE? FRIENDS!
DON'T SAY THERE ISN'T ANYONE...
SKWEEZ
THANK YOU...

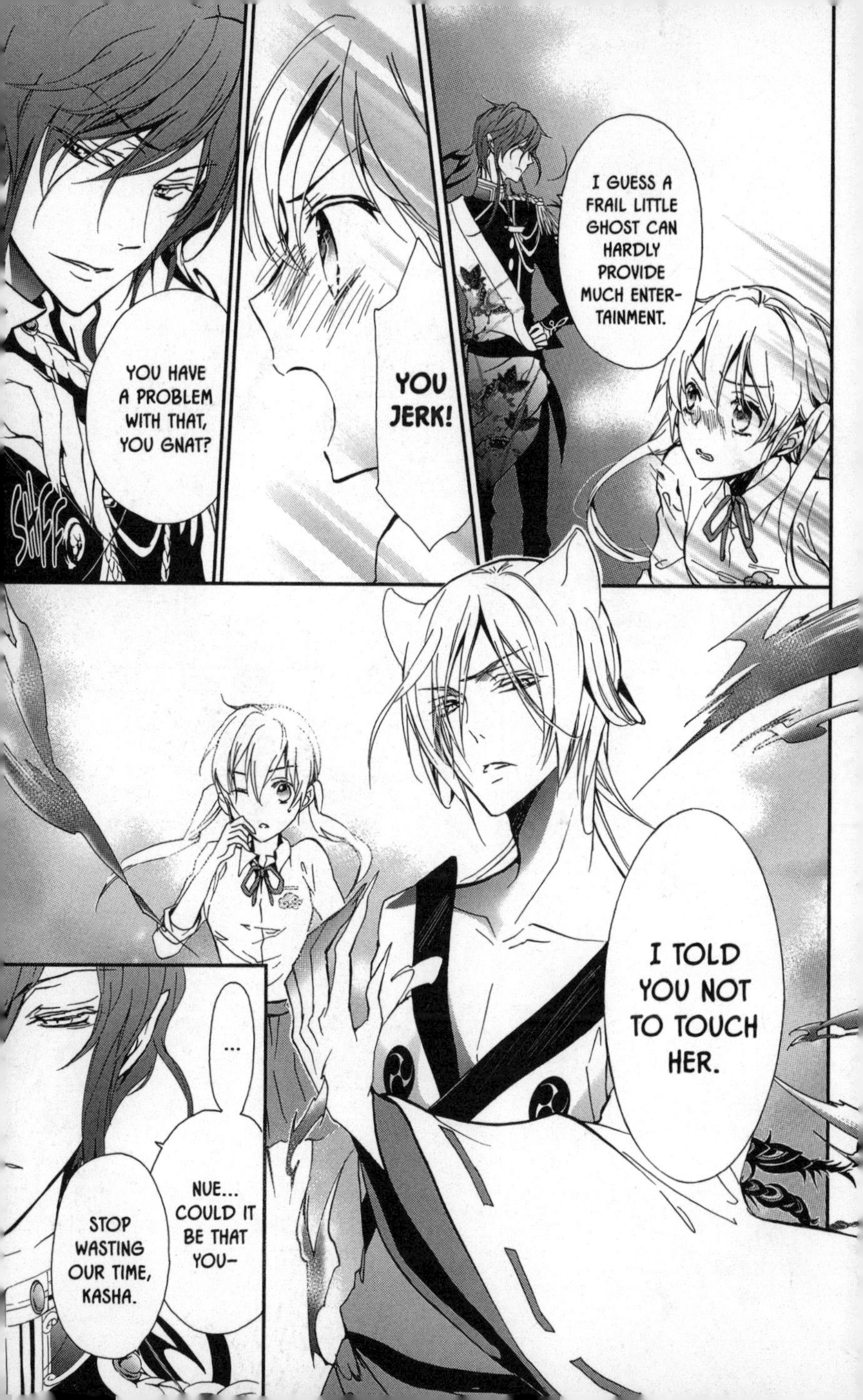
I GUESS A FRAIL LITTLE GHOST CAN HARDLY PROVIDE MUCH ENTER-TAINMENT.
YOU JERK!
YOU HAVE A PROBLEM WITH THAT, YOU GNAT?
I TOLD YOU NOT TO TOUCH HER.
...
NUE... COULD IT BE THAT YOU–
STOP WASTING OUR TIME, KASHA.

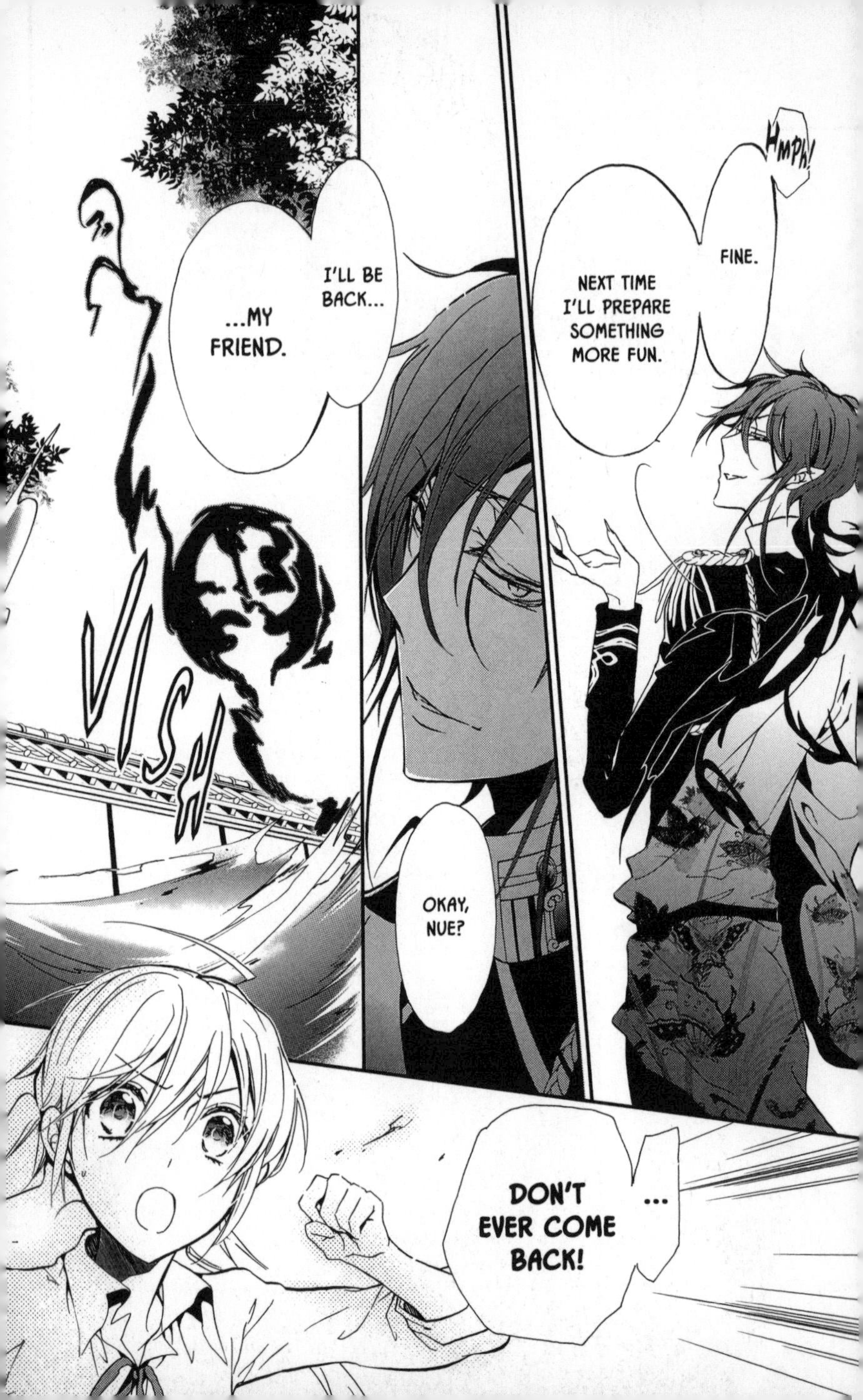
HMPH!
FINE.
NEXT TIME I'LL PREPARE SOMETHING MORE FUN.
OKAY, NUE?
I'LL BE BACK...
...MY FRIEND.
VISH
...
DON'T EVER COME BACK!

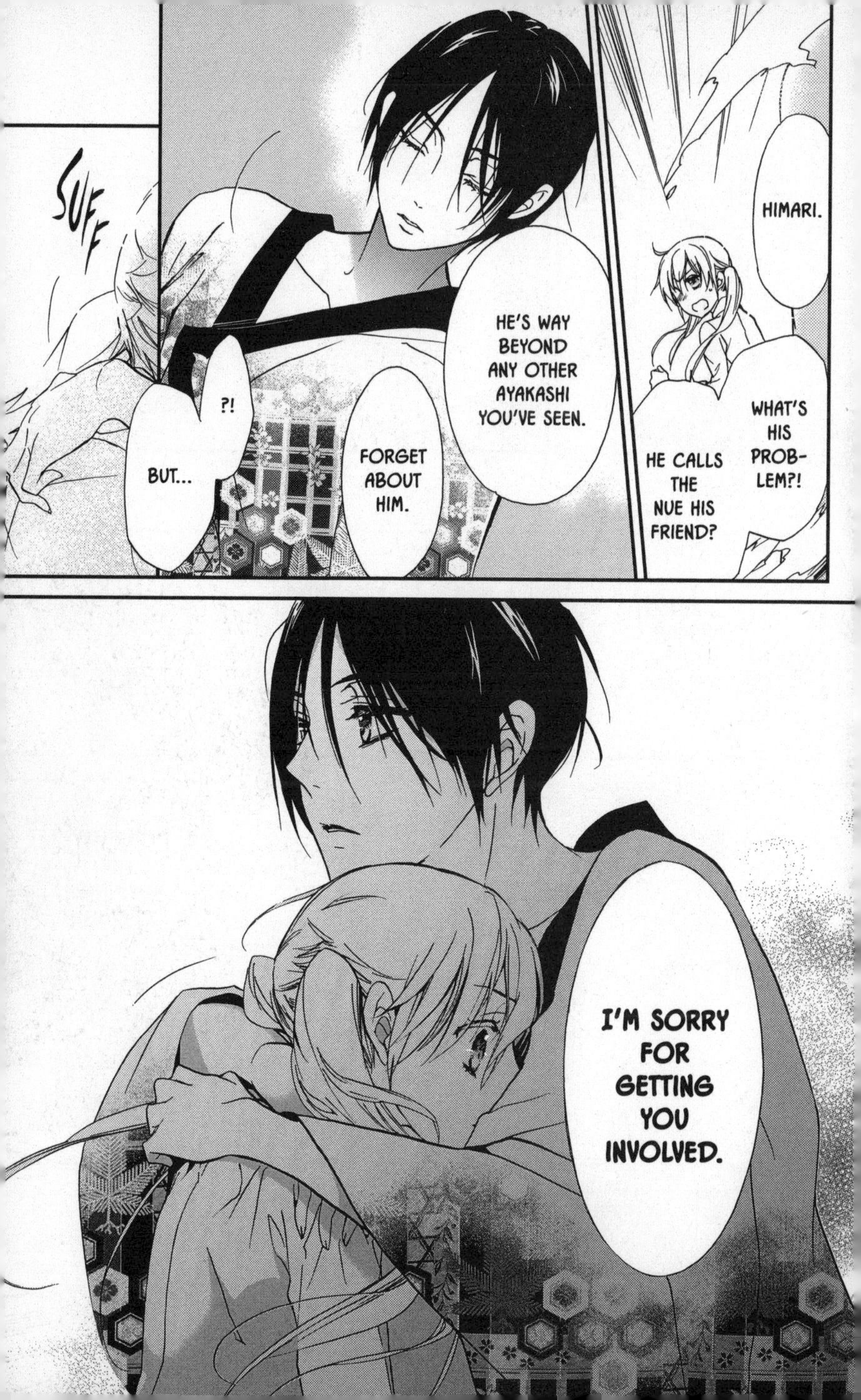
HIMARI.
WHAT'S HIS PROB-LEM?!
HE CALLS THE NUE HIS FRIEND?
HE'S WAY BEYOND ANY OTHER AYAKASHI YOU'VE SEEN.
FORGET ABOUT HIM.
SUFF
?!
BUT...
I'M SORRY FOR GETTING YOU INVOLVED.

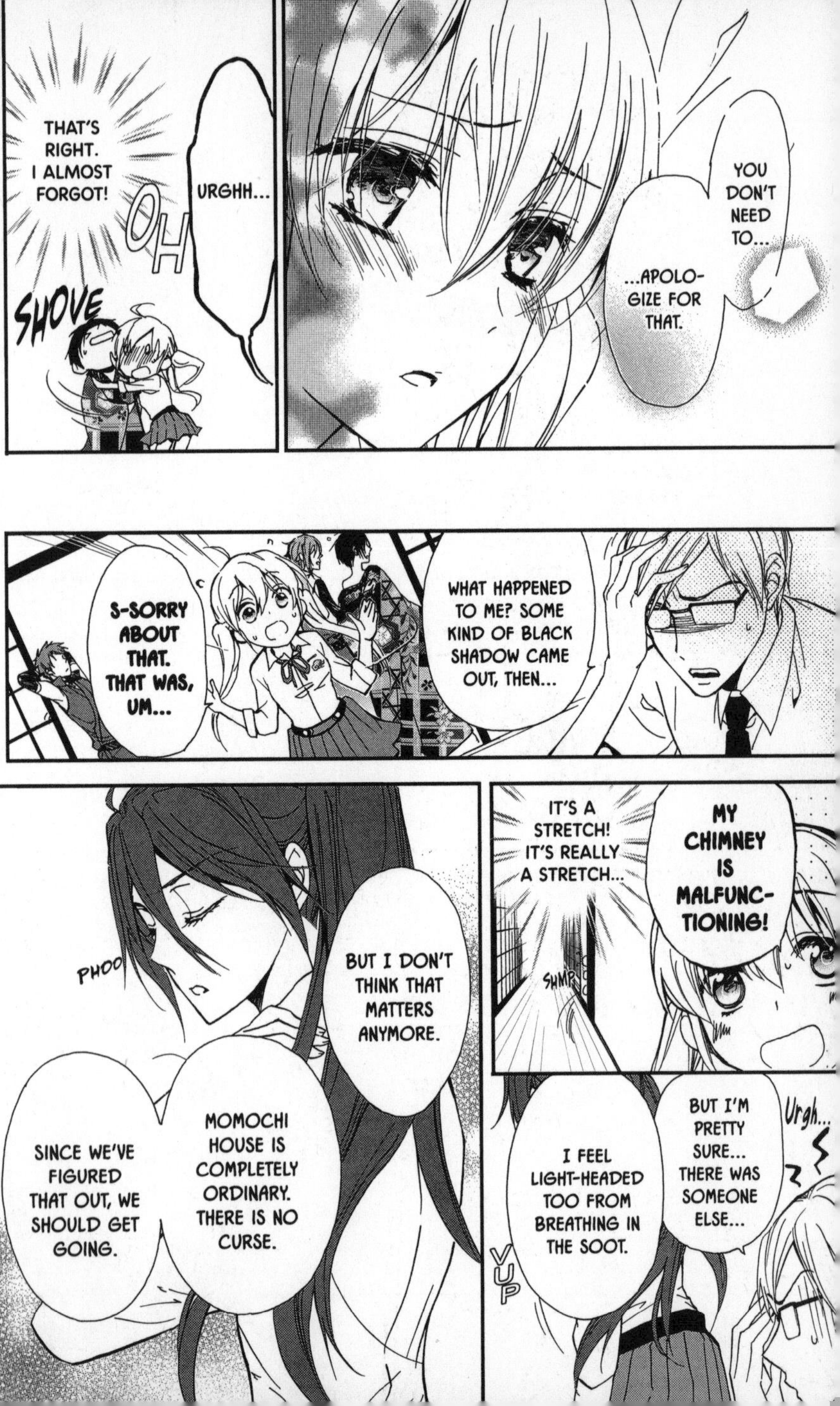
YOU DON'T NEED TO...
...APOLOGIZE FOR THAT.
URGHH...
OH
SHOVE
THAT'S RIGHT. I ALMOST FORGOT!
WHAT HAPPENED TO ME? SOME KIND OF BLACK SHADOW CAME OUT, THEN...
S-SORRY ABOUT THAT. THAT WAS, UM...
MY CHIMNEY IS MALFUNCTIONING!
IT'S A STRETCH! IT'S REALLY A STRETCH...
SHMP
Urgh...
BUT I'M PRETTY SURE... THERE WAS SOMEONE ELSE...
I FEEL LIGHT-HEADED TOO FROM BREATHING IN THE SOOT.
VUP
PHOO
BUT I DON'T THINK THAT MATTERS ANYMORE.
MOMOCHI HOUSE IS COMPLETELY ORDINARY. THERE IS NO CURSE.
SINCE WE'VE FIGURED THAT OUT, WE SHOULD GET GOING.

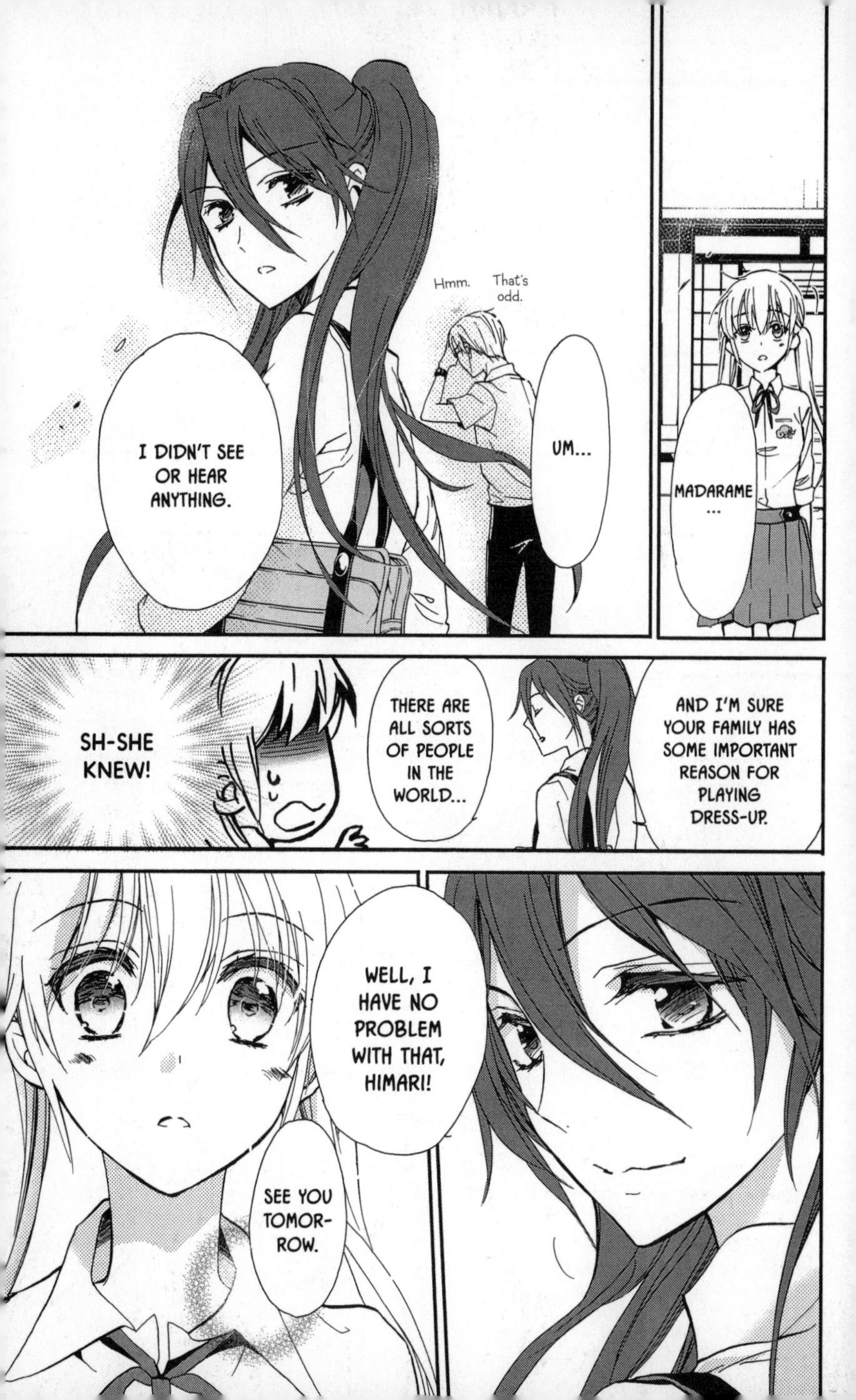
MADARAME ...
Hmm. That's odd.
UM...
I DIDN'T SEE OR HEAR ANYTHING.
AND I'M SURE YOUR FAMILY HAS SOME IMPORTANT REASON FOR PLAYING DRESS-UP.
THERE ARE ALL SORTS OF PEOPLE IN THE WORLD...
SH-SHE KNEW!
WELL, I HAVE NO PROBLEM WITH THAT, HIMARI!
SEE YOU TOMOR-ROW.

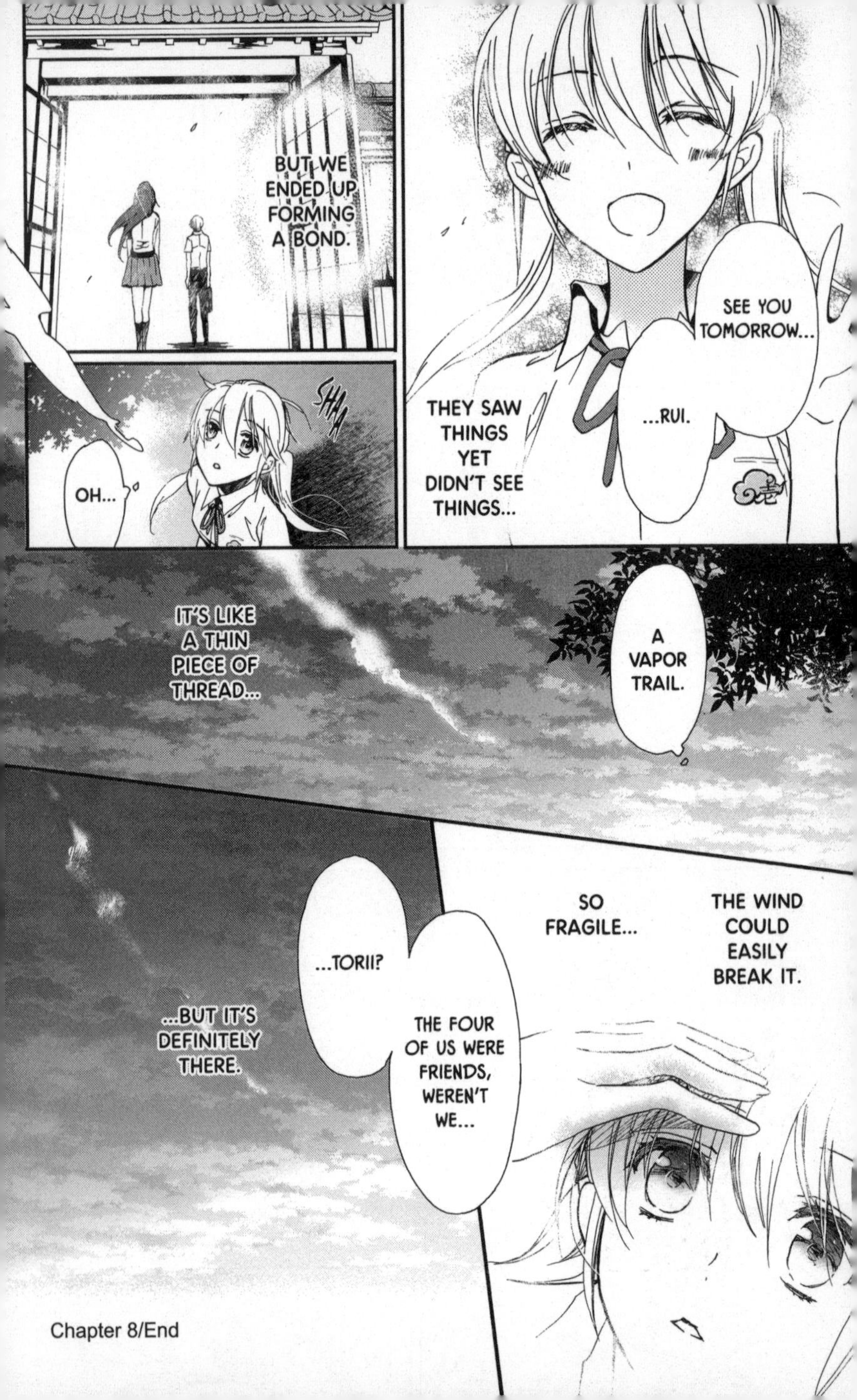
SEE YOU TOMORROW...
...RUI.
THEY SAW THINGS YET DIDN'T SEE THINGS...
BUT WE ENDED UP FORMING A BOND.
SHAA
OH...
A VAPOR TRAIL.
IT'S LIKE A THIN PIECE OF THREAD...
THE WIND COULD EASILY BREAK IT.
SO FRAGILE...
...TORII?
THE FOUR OF US WERE FRIENDS, WEREN'T WE...
...BUT IT'S DEFINITELY THERE.

Chapter 8/End

The
DEMON
PRINCE
of MOMOCHI
HOUSE

The
DEMON
PRINCE
of MOMOCHI
HOUSE

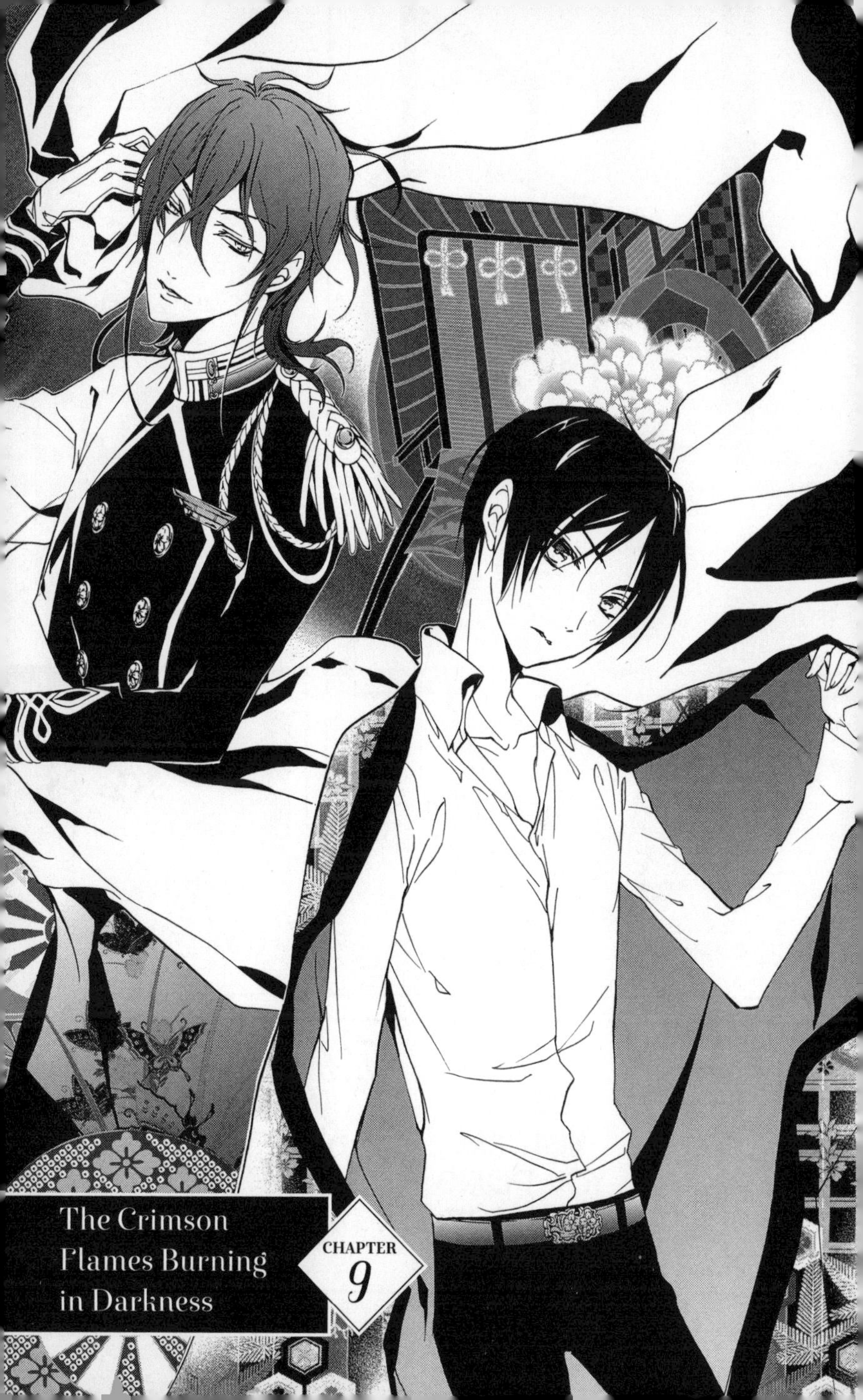
The Crimson Flames Burning in Darkness
CHAPTER 9

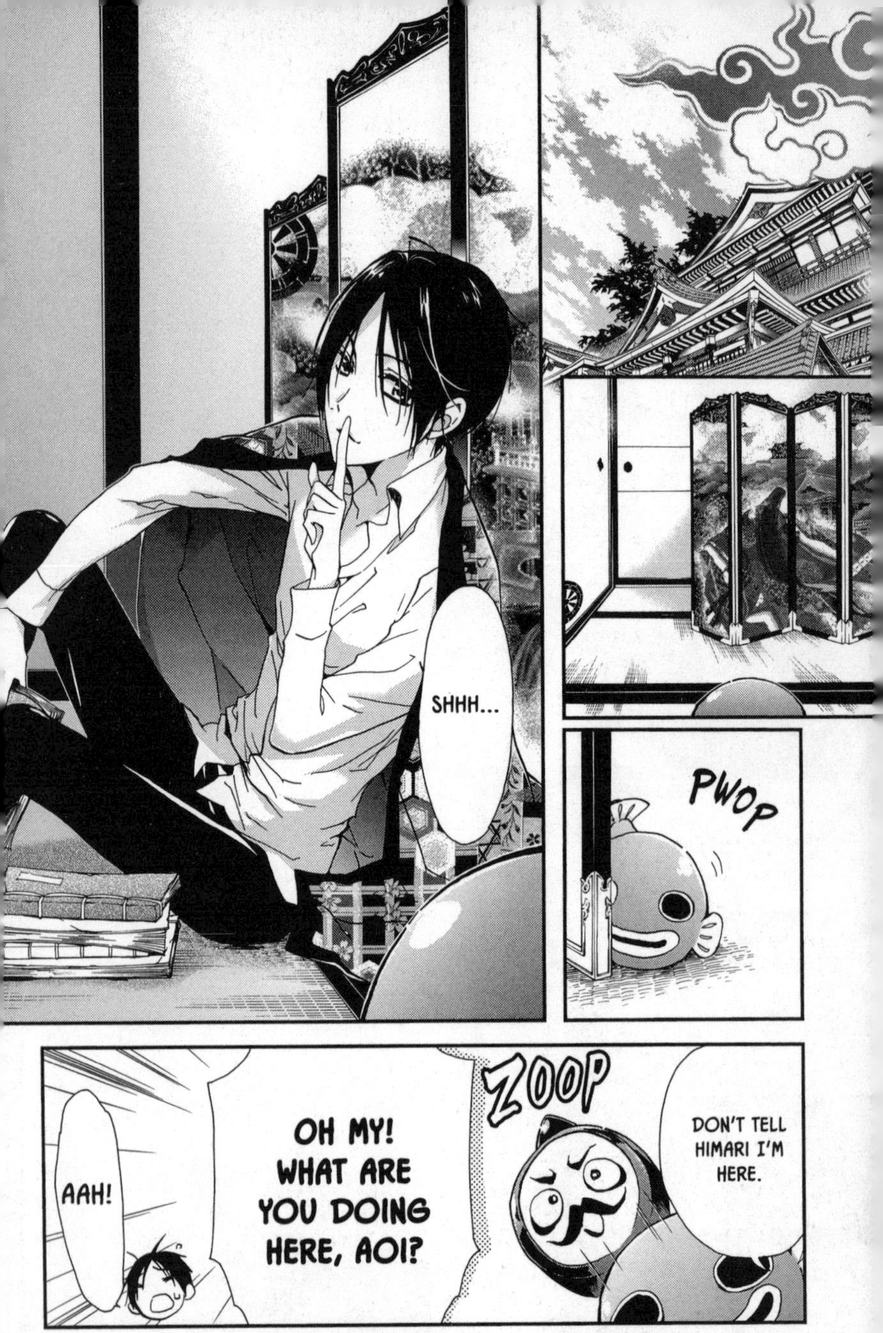
PWOP
SHHH...
DON'T TELL HIMARI I'M HERE.
ZOOP
OH MY! WHAT ARE YOU DOING HERE, AOI?
AAH!

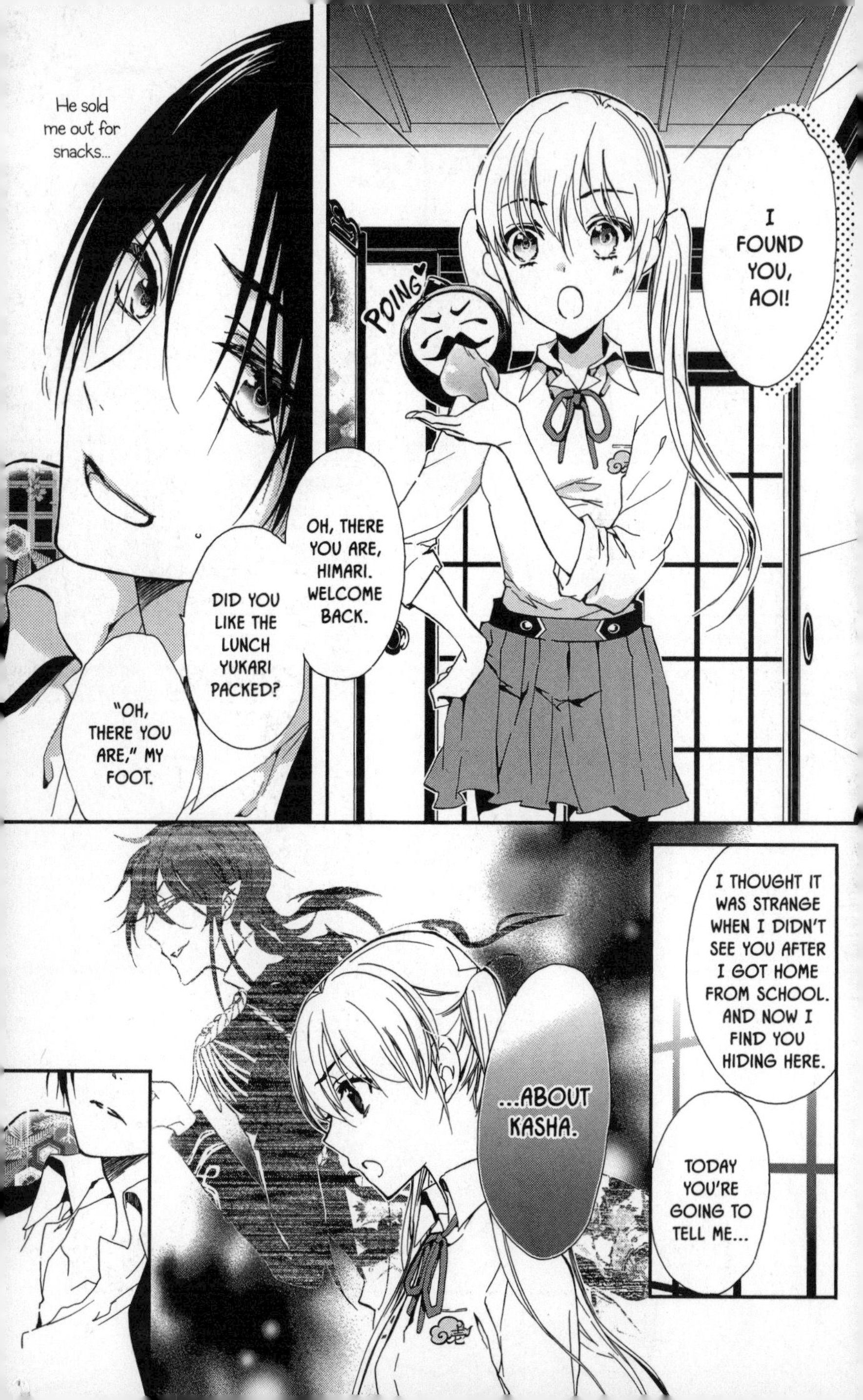
I FOUND YOU, AOI!
POING
OH, THERE YOU ARE, HIMARI. WELCOME BACK.
DID YOU LIKE THE LUNCH YUKARI PACKED?
He sold me out for snacks...
"OH, THERE YOU ARE," MY FOOT.
I THOUGHT IT WAS STRANGE WHEN I DIDN'T SEE YOU AFTER I GOT HOME FROM SCHOOL. AND NOW I FIND YOU HIDING HERE.
TODAY YOU'RE GOING TO TELL ME...
...ABOUT KASHA.

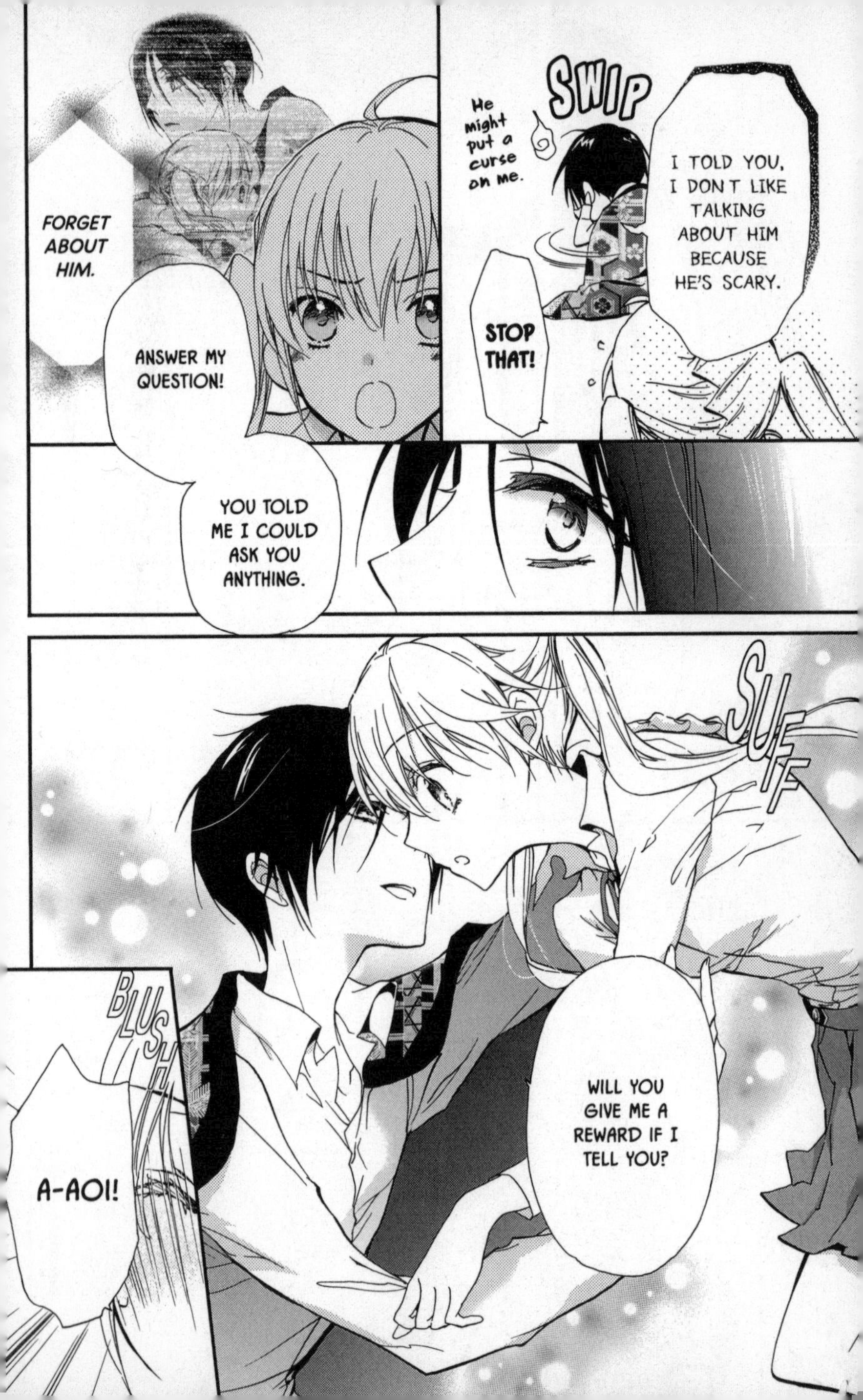
SWIP
I TOLD YOU, I DON'T LIKE TALKING ABOUT HIM BECAUSE HE'S SCARY.
He might put a curse on me.
STOP THAT!
FORGET ABOUT HIM.
ANSWER MY QUESTION!
YOU TOLD ME I COULD ASK YOU ANYTHING.
SUFF
WILL YOU GIVE ME A REWARD IF I TELL YOU?
BLUSH
A-AOI!

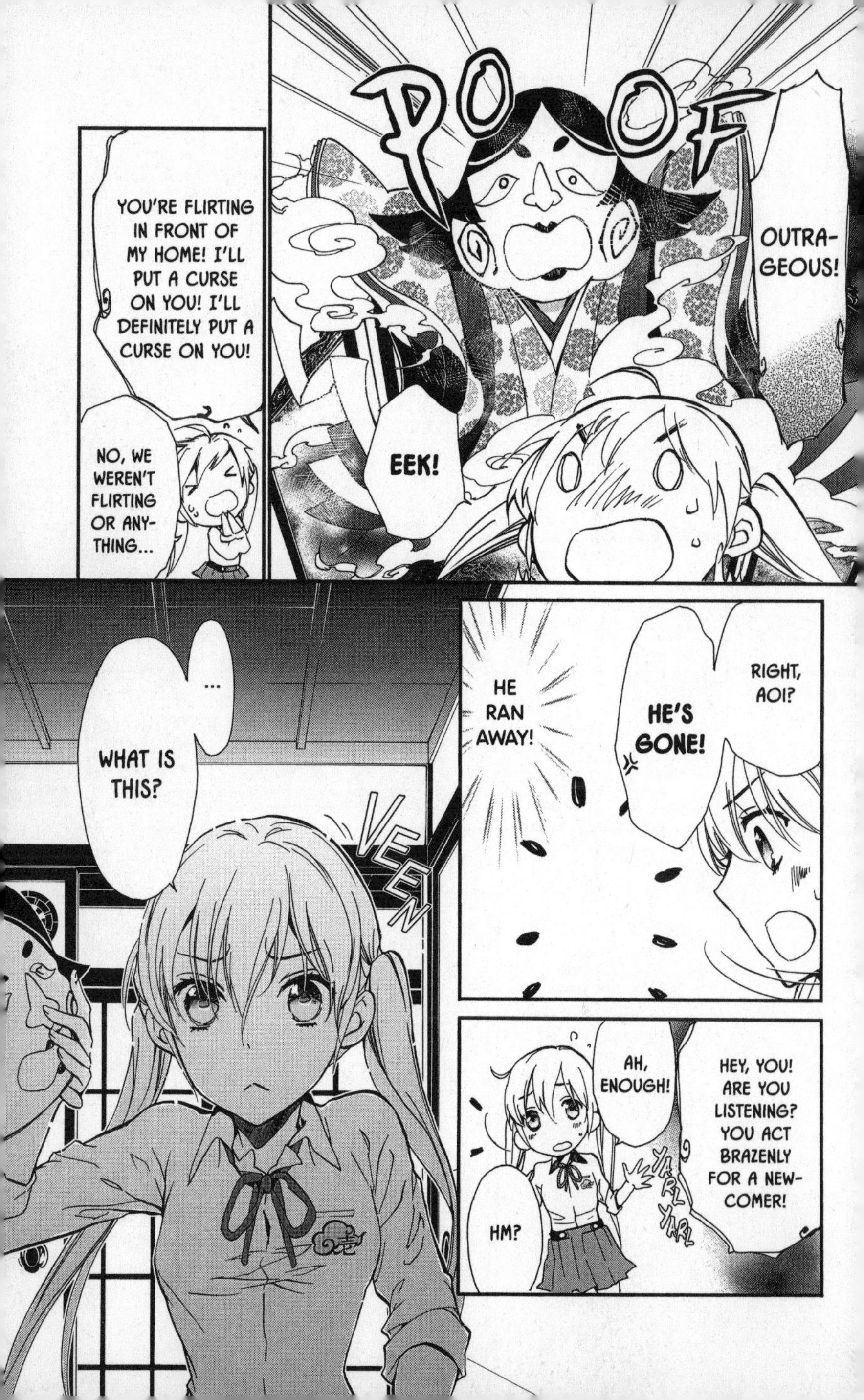
POOF
OUTRA-GEOUS!
EEK!
YOU'RE FLIRTING IN FRONT OF MY HOME! I'LL PUT A CURSE ON YOU! I'LL DEFINITELY PUT A CURSE ON YOU!
NO, WE WEREN'T FLIRTING OR ANY-THING...
RIGHT, AOI?
HE'S GONE!
HE RAN AWAY!
HEY, YOU! ARE YOU LISTENING? YOU ACT BRAZENLY FOR A NEW-COMER!
AH, ENOUGH!
YARL YARL
HM?
...
WHAT IS THIS?
VEEN

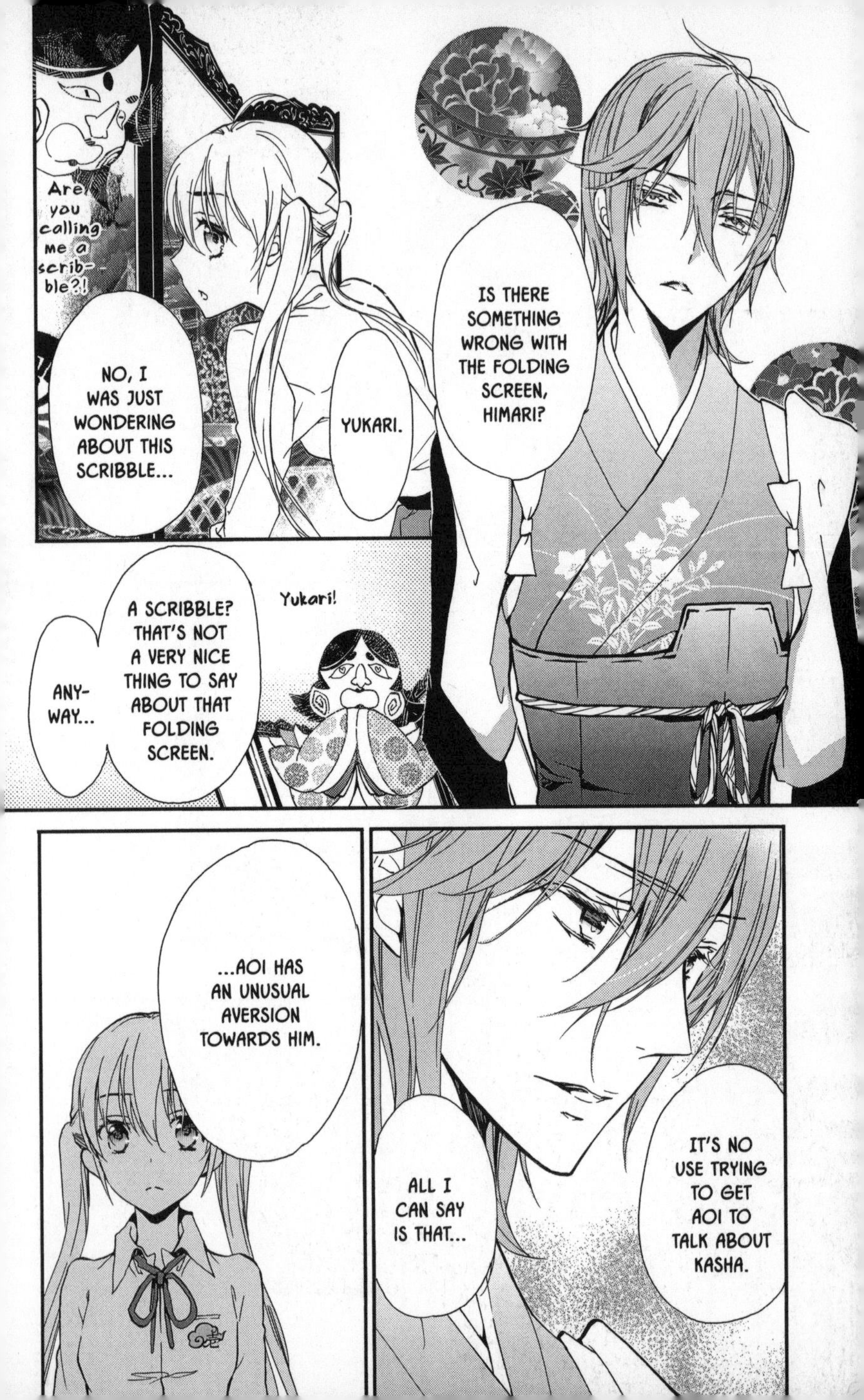
IS THERE SOMETHING WRONG WITH THE FOLDING SCREEN, HIMARI?
YUKARI.
NO, I WAS JUST WONDERING ABOUT THIS SCRIBBLE...
Are you calling me a scrib-ble?!
Yukari!
A SCRIBBLE? THAT'S NOT A VERY NICE THING TO SAY ABOUT THAT FOLDING SCREEN.
ANY-WAY...
IT'S NO USE TRYING TO GET AOI TO TALK ABOUT KASHA.
ALL I CAN SAY IS THAT...
...AOI HAS AN UNUSUAL AVERSION TOWARDS HIM.

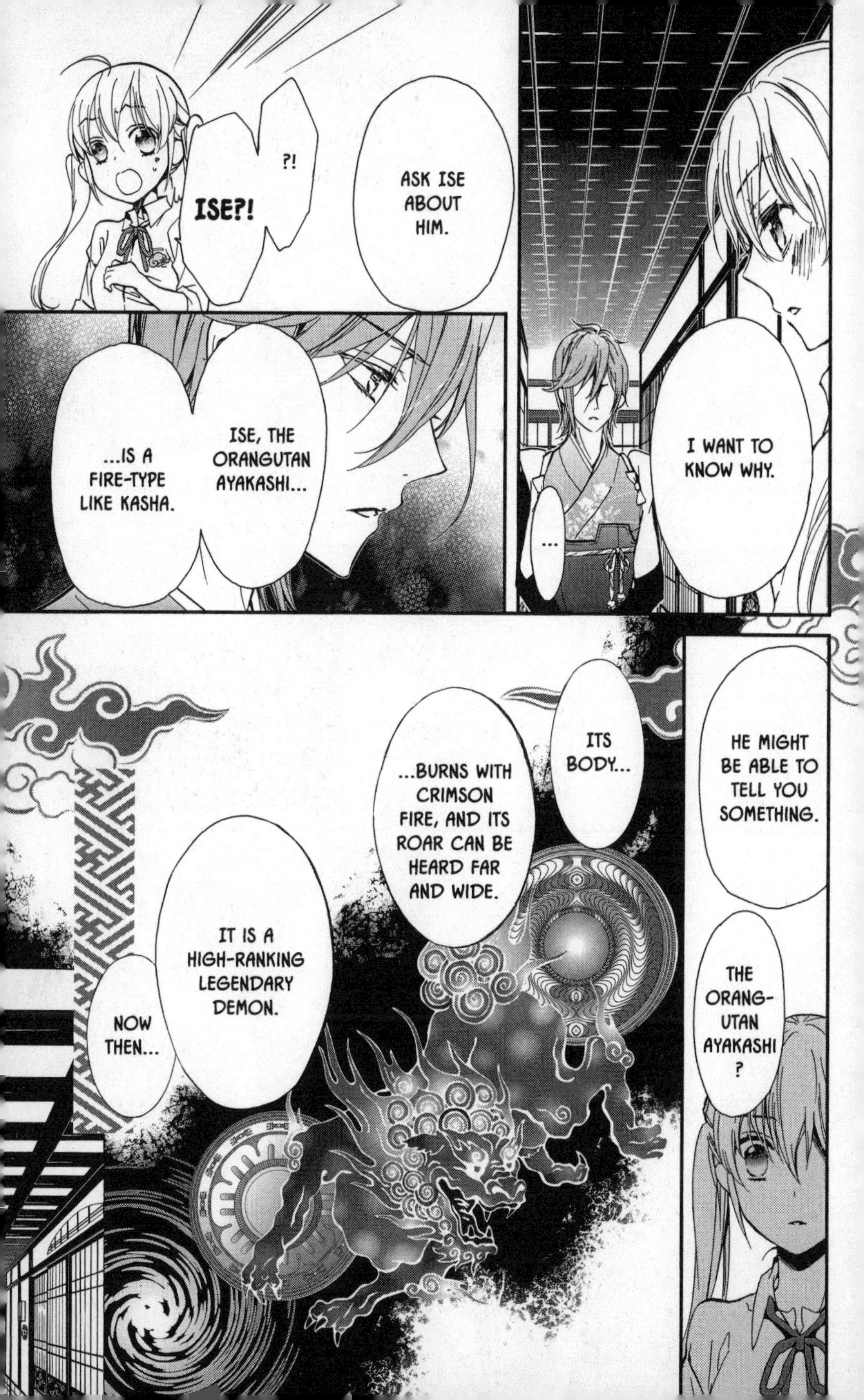
I WANT TO KNOW WHY.
...
ASK ISE ABOUT HIM.
?!
ISE?!
ISE, THE ORANGUTAN AYAKASHI...
...IS A FIRE-TYPE LIKE KASHA.
HE MIGHT BE ABLE TO TELL YOU SOMETHING.
THE ORANG-UTAN AYAKASHI?
ITS BODY...
...BURNS WITH CRIMSON FIRE, AND ITS ROAR CAN BE HEARD FAR AND WIDE.
IT IS A HIGH-RANKING LEGENDARY DEMON.
NOW THEN...

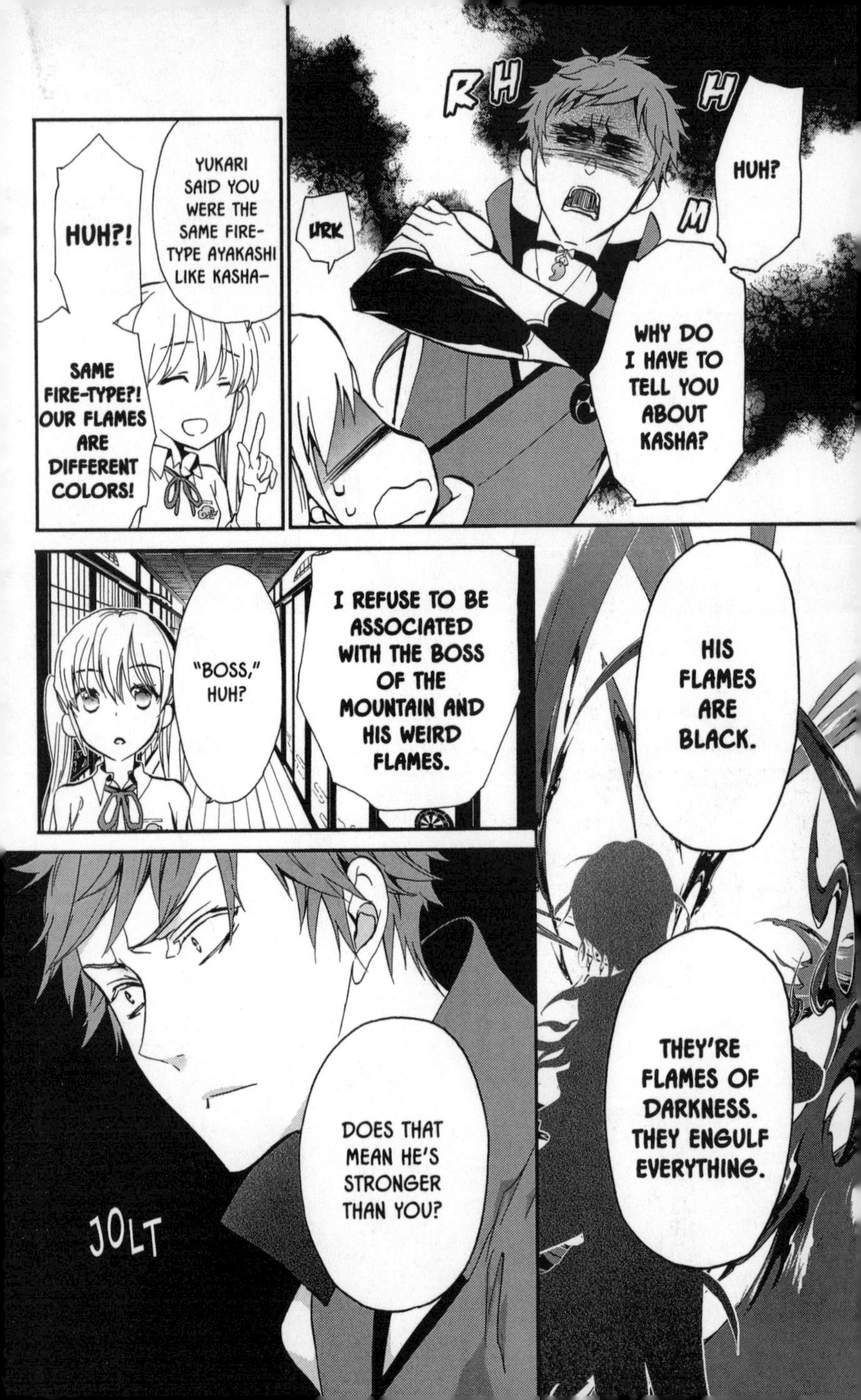
RH
H
M
HUH?
WHY DO I HAVE TO TELL YOU ABOUT KASHA?
URK
YUKARI SAID YOU WERE THE SAME FIRE-TYPE AYAKASHI LIKE KASHA—
HUH?!
SAME FIRE-TYPE?! OUR FLAMES ARE DIFFERENT COLORS!
HIS FLAMES ARE BLACK.
THEY'RE FLAMES OF DARKNESS. THEY ENGULF EVERYTHING.
I REFUSE TO BE ASSOCIATED WITH THE BOSS OF THE MOUNTAIN AND HIS WEIRD FLAMES.
"BOSS," HUH?
DOES THAT MEAN HE'S STRONGER THAN YOU?
JOLT

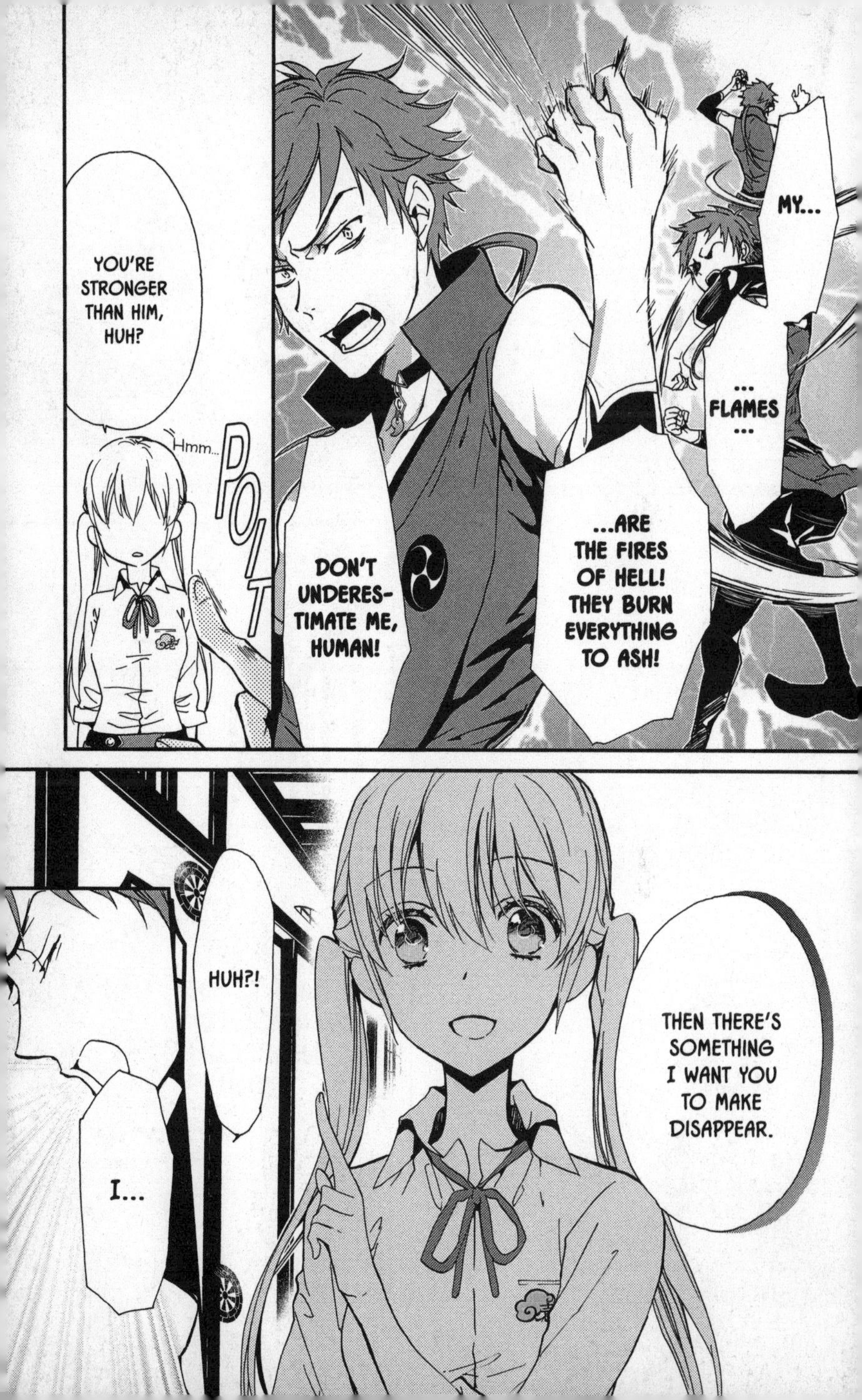
MY...
...FLAMES...
...ARE THE FIRES OF HELL! THEY BURN EVERYTHING TO ASH!
DON'T UNDERES-TIMATE ME, HUMAN!
YOU'RE STRONGER THAN HIM, HUH?
Hmm...
POIT
THEN THERE'S SOMETHING I WANT YOU TO MAKE DISAPPEAR.
HUH?!
I...

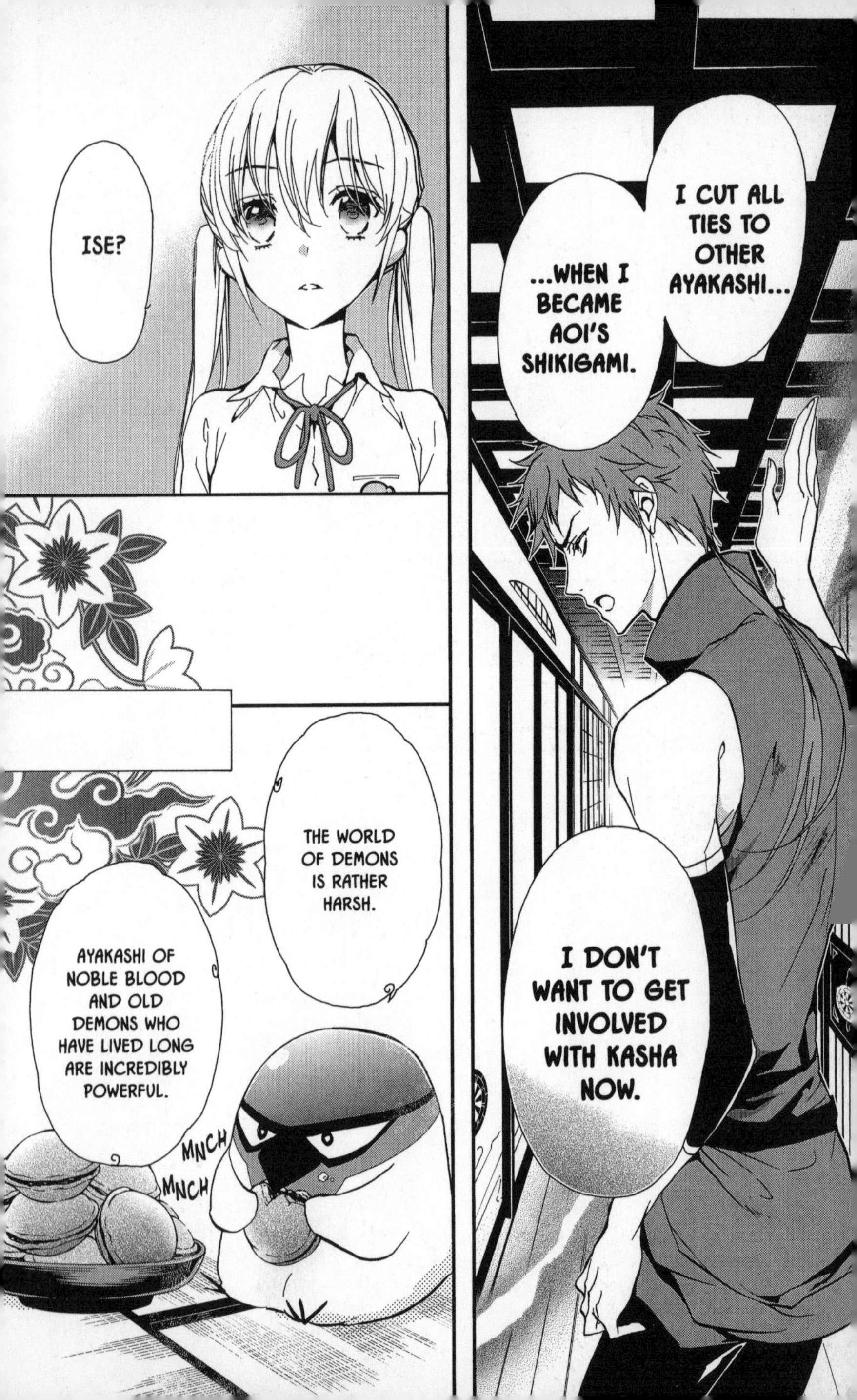
I CUT ALL TIES TO OTHER AYAKASHI...
...WHEN I BECAME AOI'S SHIKIGAMI.
I DON'T WANT TO GET INVOLVED WITH KASHA NOW.
ISE?
THE WORLD OF DEMONS IS RATHER HARSH.
AYAKASHI OF NOBLE BLOOD AND OLD DEMONS WHO HAVE LIVED LONG ARE INCREDIBLY POWERFUL.
MNCH
MNCH

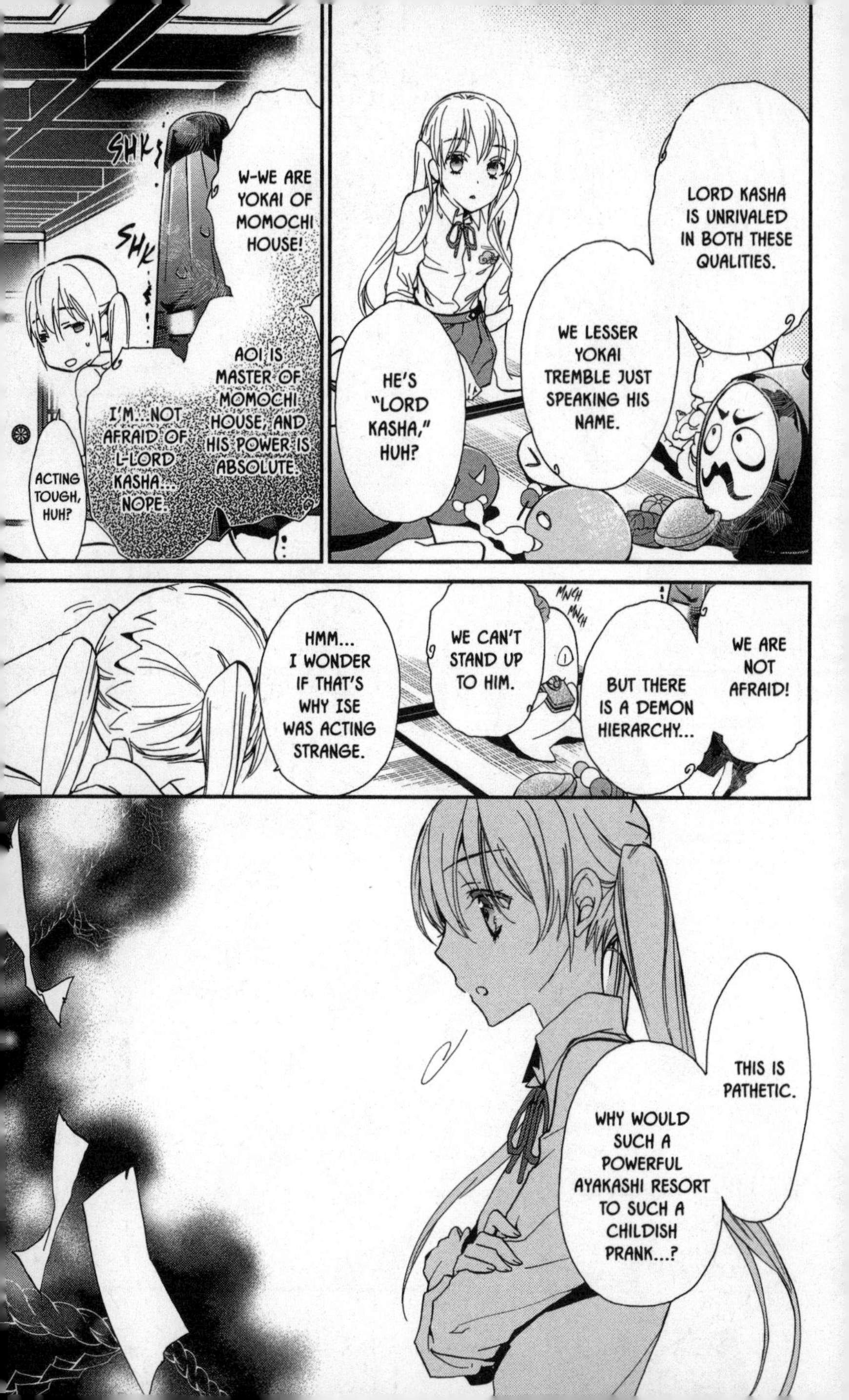
LORD KASHA IS UNRIVALED IN BOTH THESE QUALITIES.
WE LESSER YOKAI TREMBLE JUST SPEAKING HIS NAME.
HE'S "LORD KASHA," HUH?
SHK
SHK
W-WE ARE YOKAI OF MOMOCHI HOUSE!
AOI IS MASTER OF MOMOCHI HOUSE, AND HIS POWER IS ABSOLUTE.
I'M...NOT AFRAID OF L-LORD KASHA... NOPE.
ACTING TOUGH, HUH?
WE ARE NOT AFRAID!
BUT THERE IS A DEMON HIERARCHY...
MNCH MNCH
WE CAN'T STAND UP TO HIM.
HMM... I WONDER IF THAT'S WHY ISE WAS ACTING STRANGE.
THIS IS PATHETIC.
WHY WOULD SUCH A POWERFUL AYAKASHI RESORT TO SUCH A CHILDISH PRANK...?

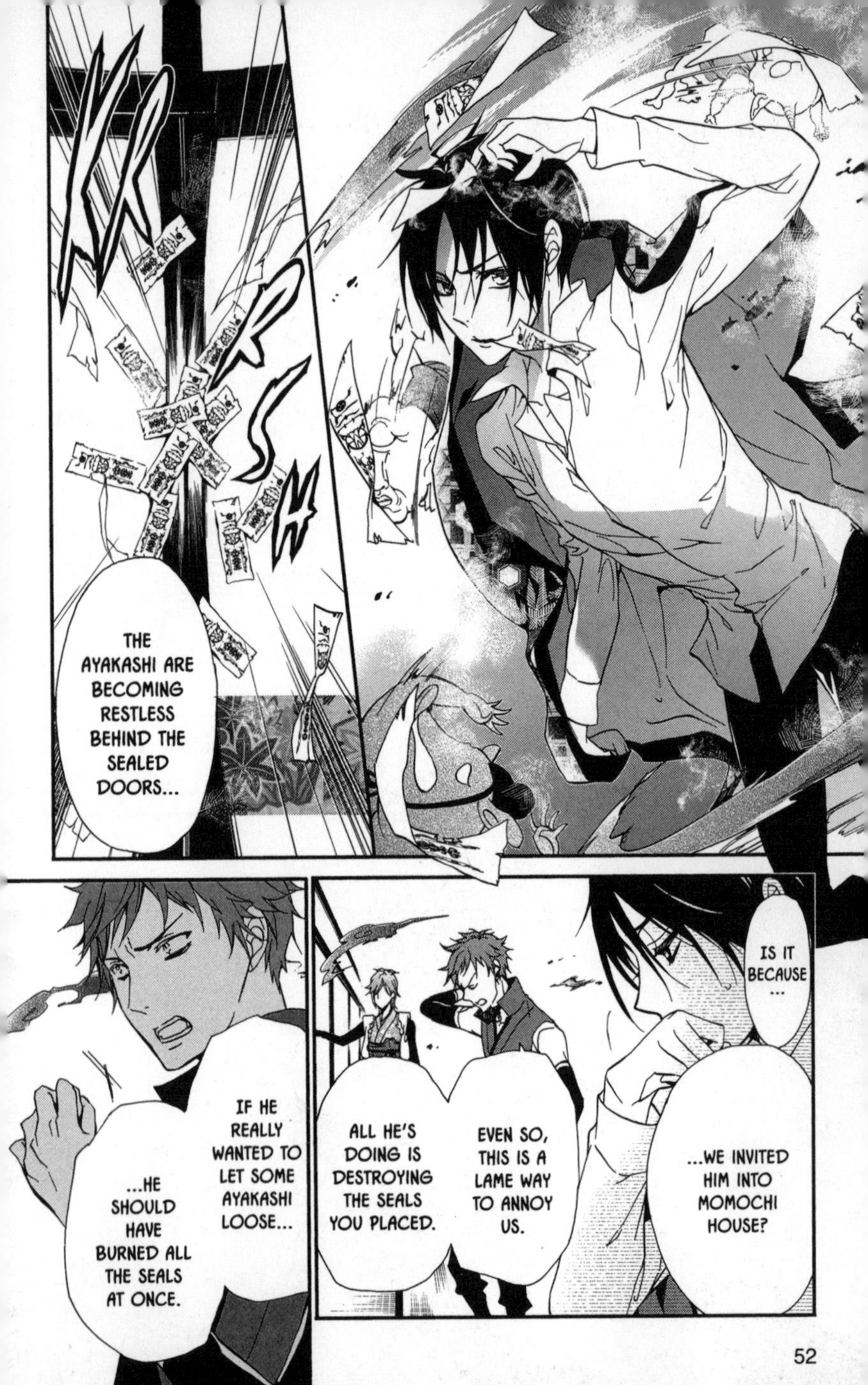
THE AYAKASHI ARE BECOMING RESTLESS BEHIND THE SEALED DOORS...
IS IT BECAUSE...
...WE INVITED HIM INTO MOMOCHI HOUSE?
EVEN SO, THIS IS A LAME WAY TO ANNOY US.
ALL HE'S DOING IS DESTROYING THE SEALS YOU PLACED.
IF HE REALLY WANTED TO LET SOME AYAKASHI LOOSE...
...HE SHOULD HAVE BURNED ALL THE SEALS AT ONCE.

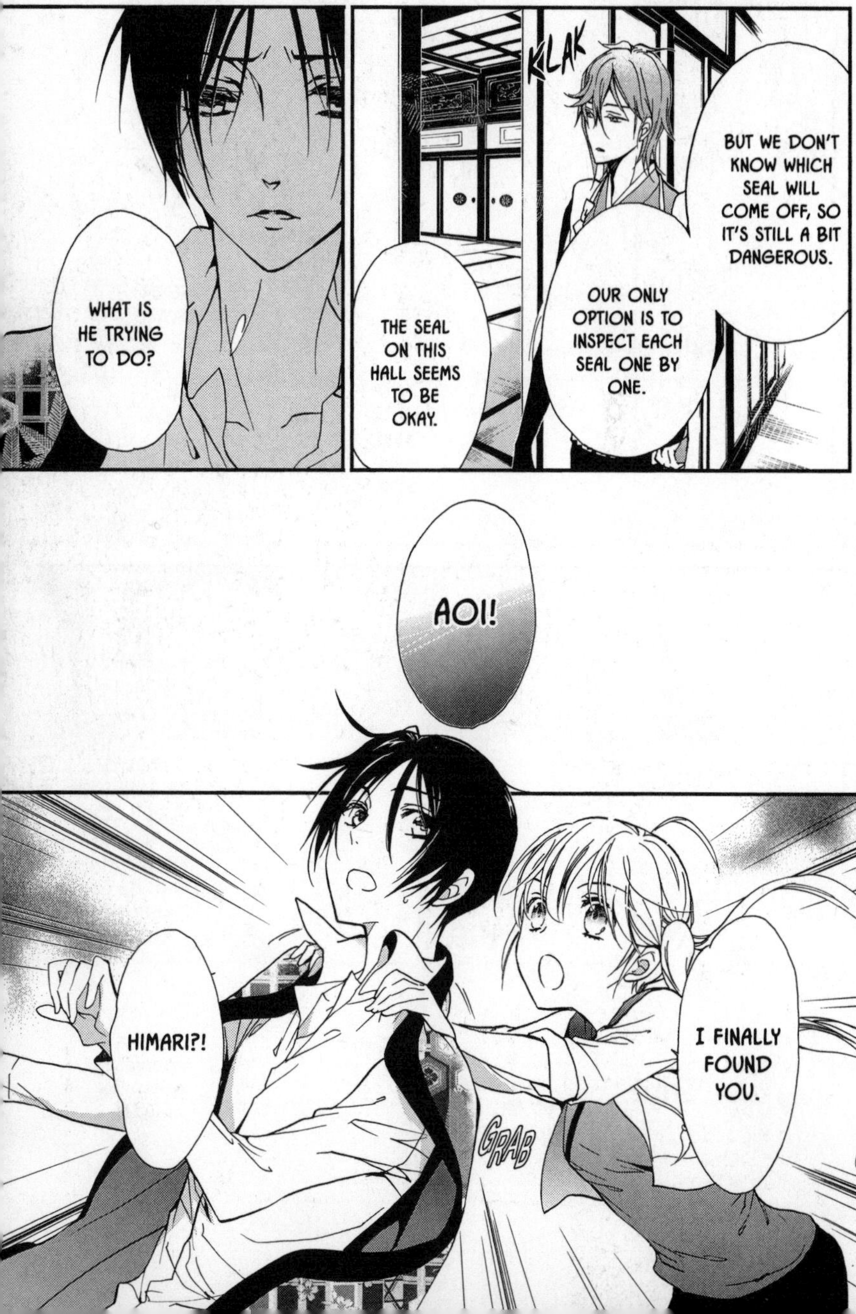
KLAK
BUT WE DON'T KNOW WHICH SEAL WILL COME OFF, SO IT'S STILL A BIT DANGEROUS.
OUR ONLY OPTION IS TO INSPECT EACH SEAL ONE BY ONE.
THE SEAL ON THIS HALL SEEMS TO BE OKAY.
WHAT IS HE TRYING TO DO?
AOI!
I FINALLY FOUND YOU.
HIMARI?!
GRAB

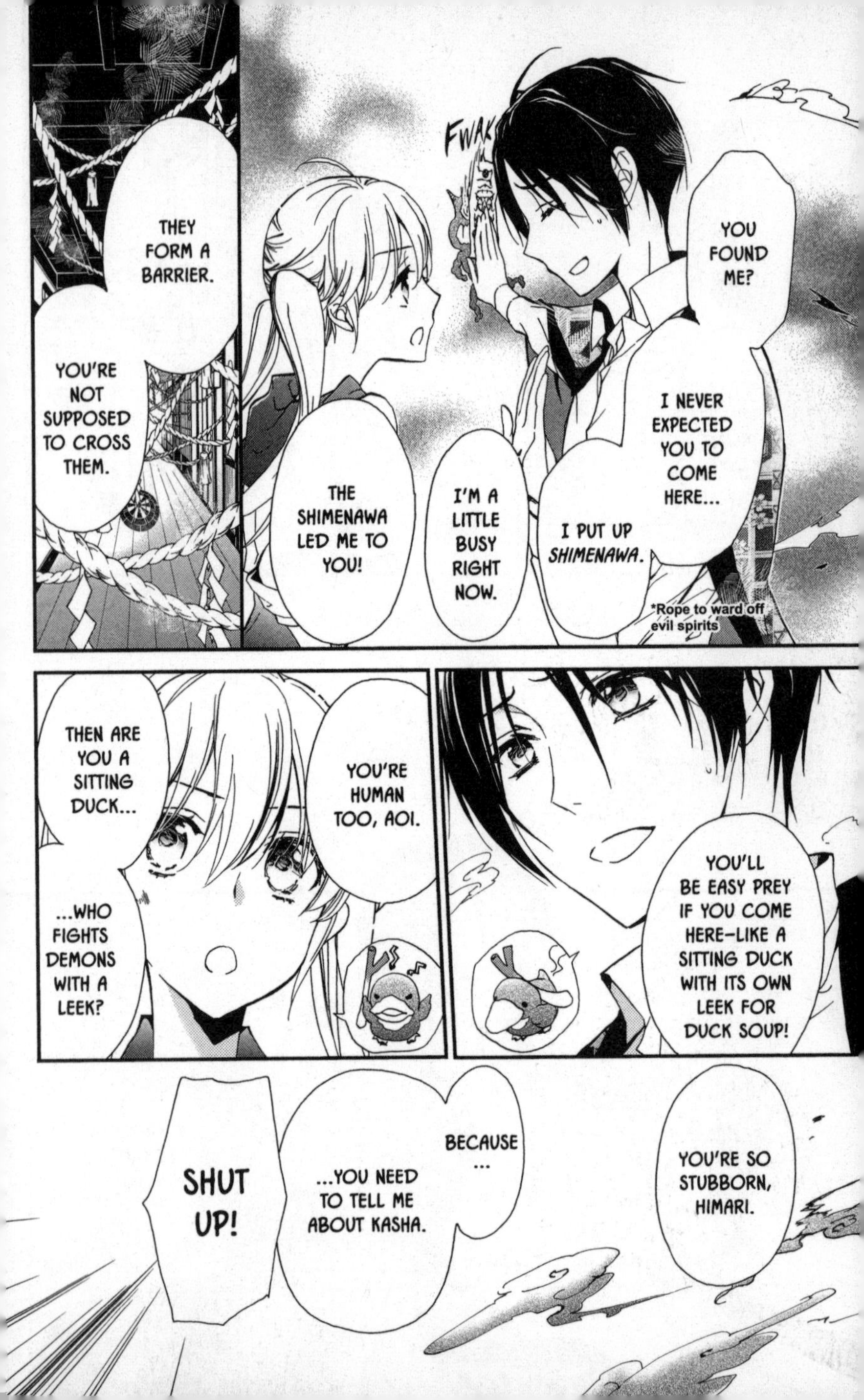
FWAK
YOU FOUND ME?
I NEVER EXPECTED YOU TO COME HERE...
I PUT UP SHIMENAWA.
*Rope to ward off evil spirits
I'M A LITTLE BUSY RIGHT NOW.
THE SHIMENAWA LED ME TO YOU!
THEY FORM A BARRIER.
YOU'RE NOT SUPPOSED TO CROSS THEM.
YOU'LL BE EASY PREY IF YOU COME HERE—LIKE A SITTING DUCK WITH ITS OWN LEEK FOR DUCK SOUP!
YOU'RE HUMAN TOO, AOI.
THEN ARE YOU A SITTING DUCK...
...WHO FIGHTS DEMONS WITH A LEEK?
YOU'RE SO STUBBORN, HIMARI.
BECAUSE...
...YOU NEED TO TELL ME ABOUT KASHA.
SHUT UP!

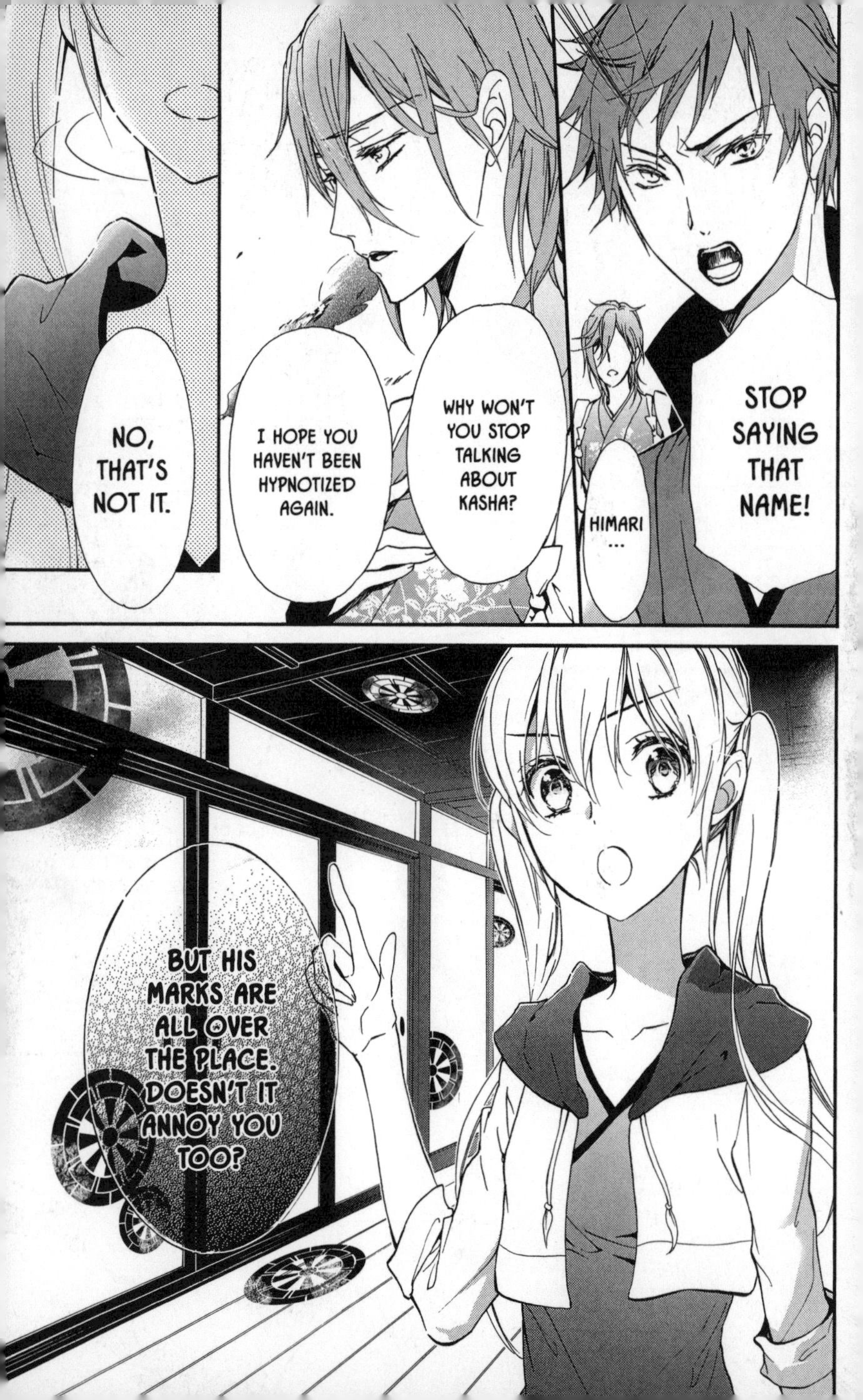
STOP SAYING THAT NAME!
HIMARI...
WHY WON'T YOU STOP TALKING ABOUT KASHA?
I HOPE YOU HAVEN'T BEEN HYPNOTIZED AGAIN.
NO, THAT'S NOT IT.
BUT HIS MARKS ARE ALL OVER THE PLACE. DOESN'T IT ANNOY YOU TOO?

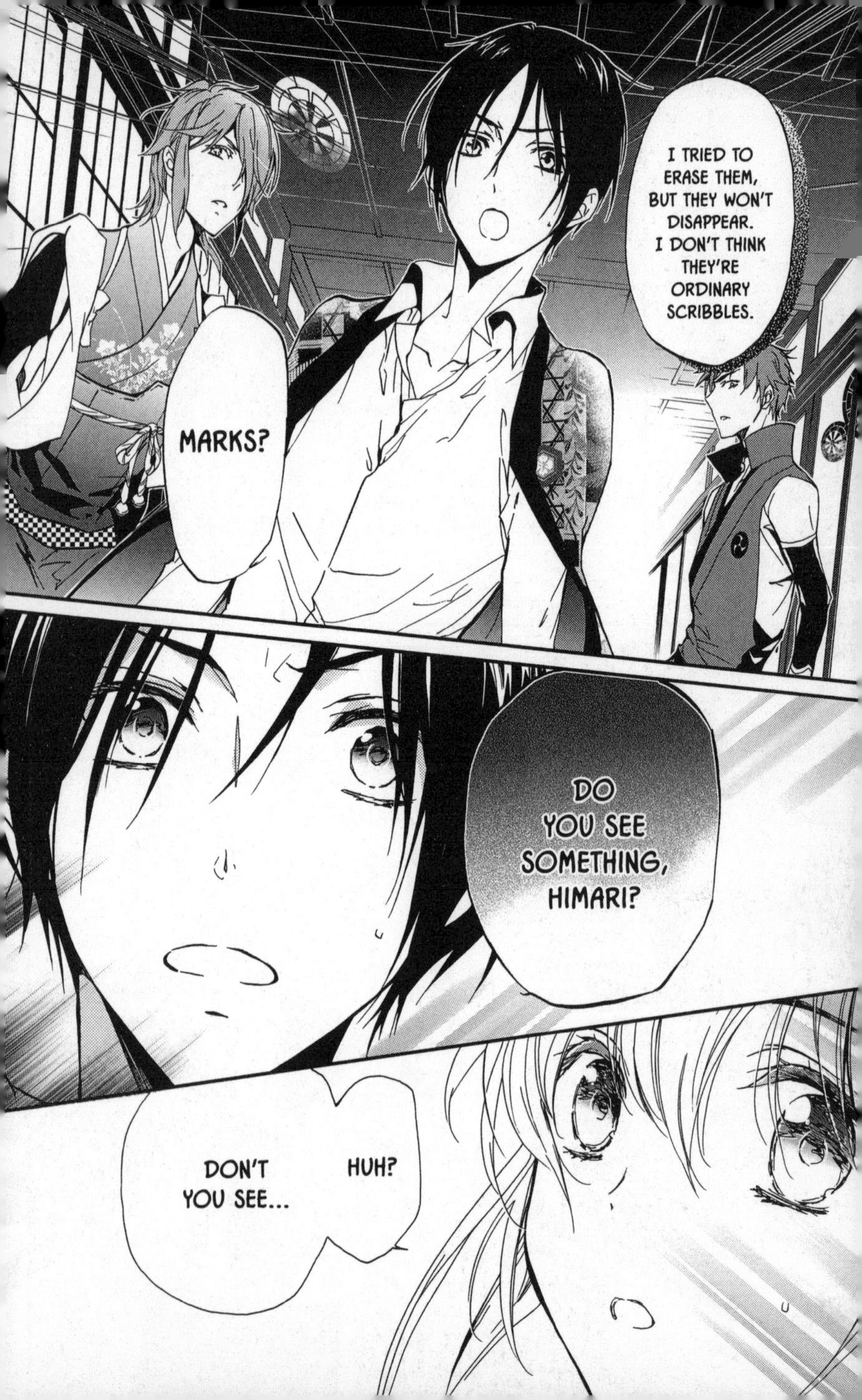
I TRIED TO ERASE THEM, BUT THEY WON'T DISAPPEAR. I DON'T THINK THEY'RE ORDINARY SCRIBBLES.
MARKS?
DO YOU SEE SOMETHING, HIMARI?
HUH?
DON'T YOU SEE...

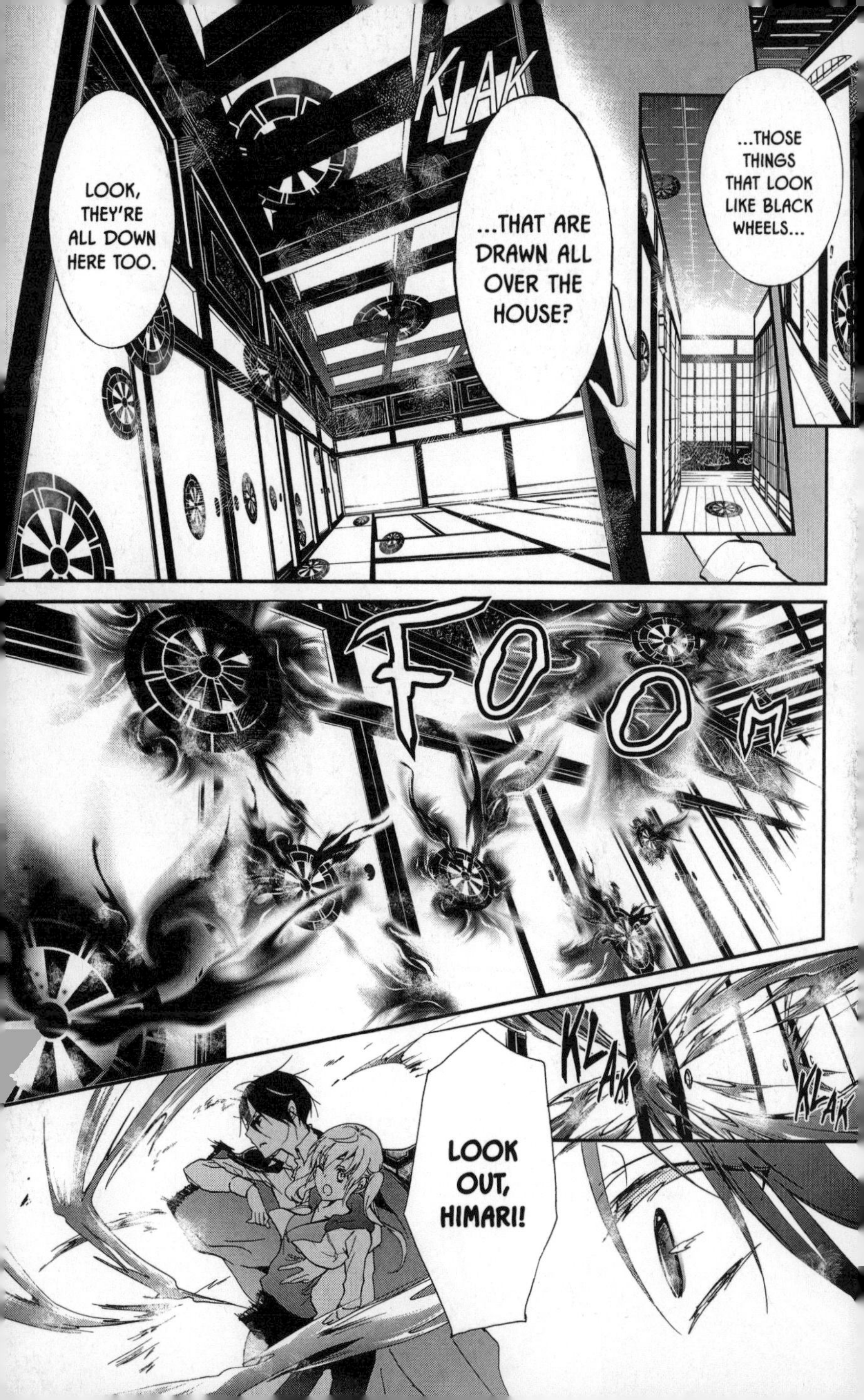
...THOSE THINGS THAT LOOK LIKE BLACK WHEELS...
KLAK
...THAT ARE DRAWN ALL OVER THE HOUSE?
LOOK, THEY'RE ALL DOWN HERE TOO.
FOOOM
KLAK KLAK
KLAK KLAK
LOOK OUT, HIMARI!

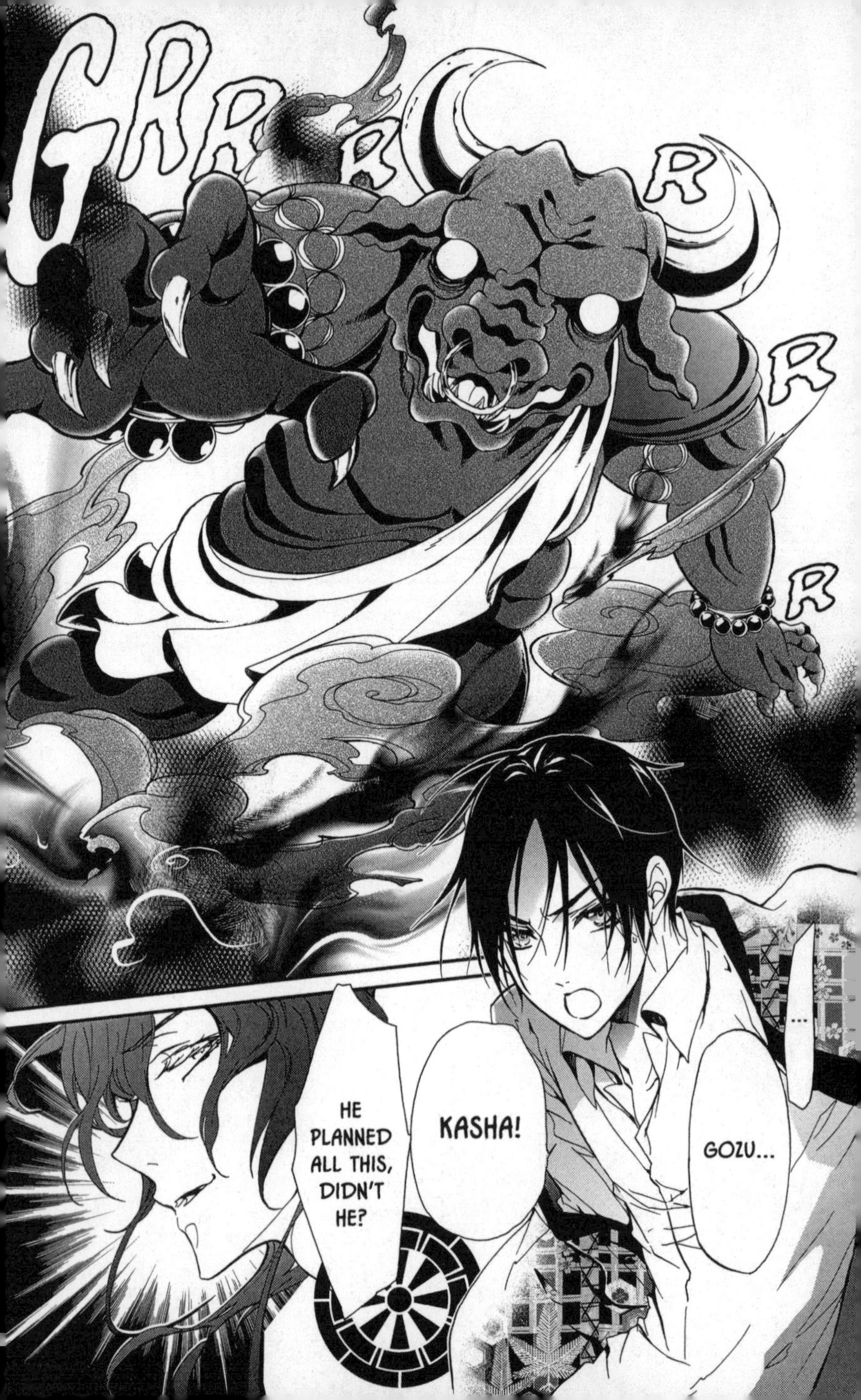
GRRRRRR
...
GOZU...
KASHA!
HE PLANNED ALL THIS, DIDN'T HE?

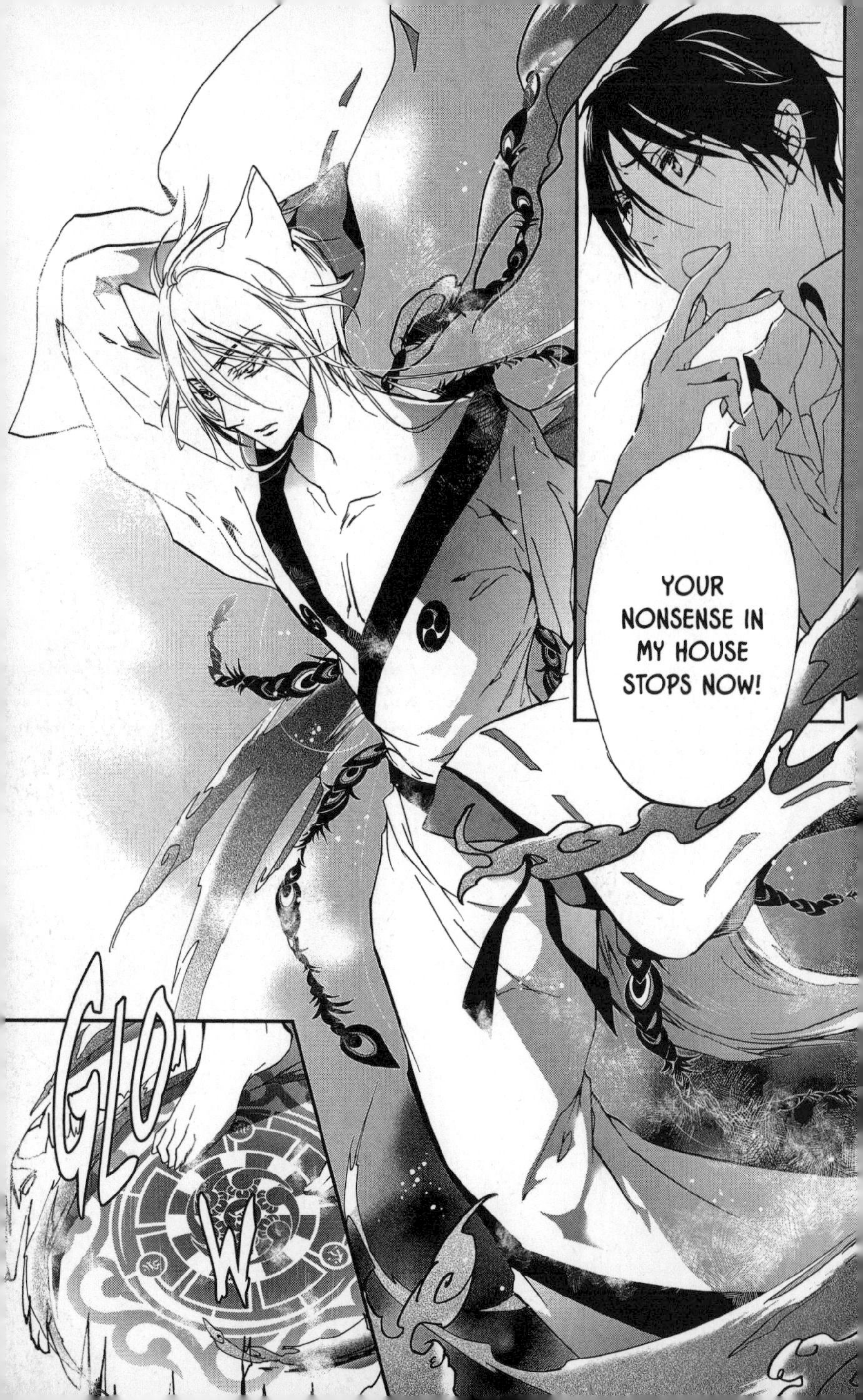
YOUR NONSENSE IN MY HOUSE STOPS NOW!
GLOW

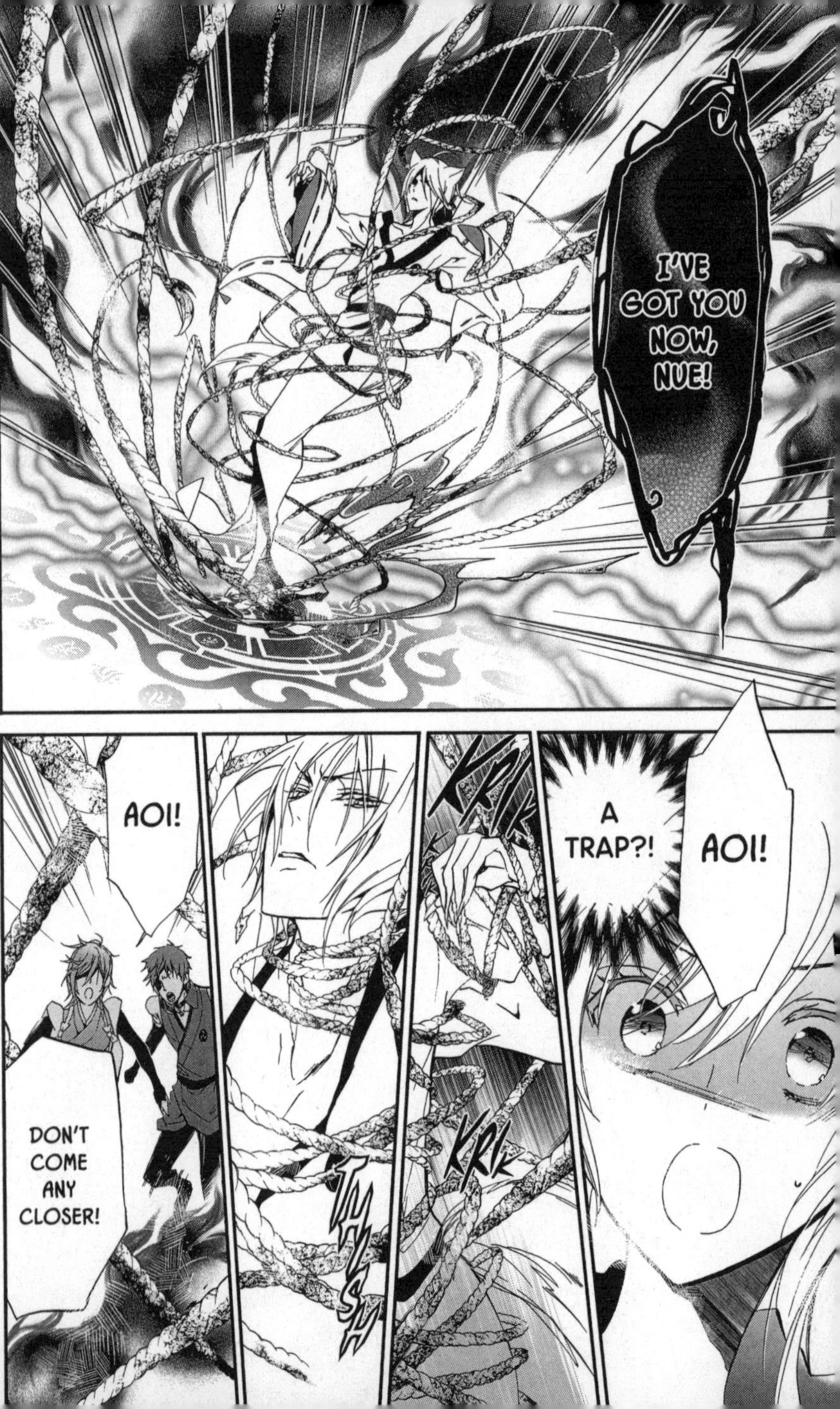
I'VE GOT YOU NOW, NUE!
AOI!
A TRAP?!
KRIK
KRIK
AOI!
DON'T COME ANY CLOSER!

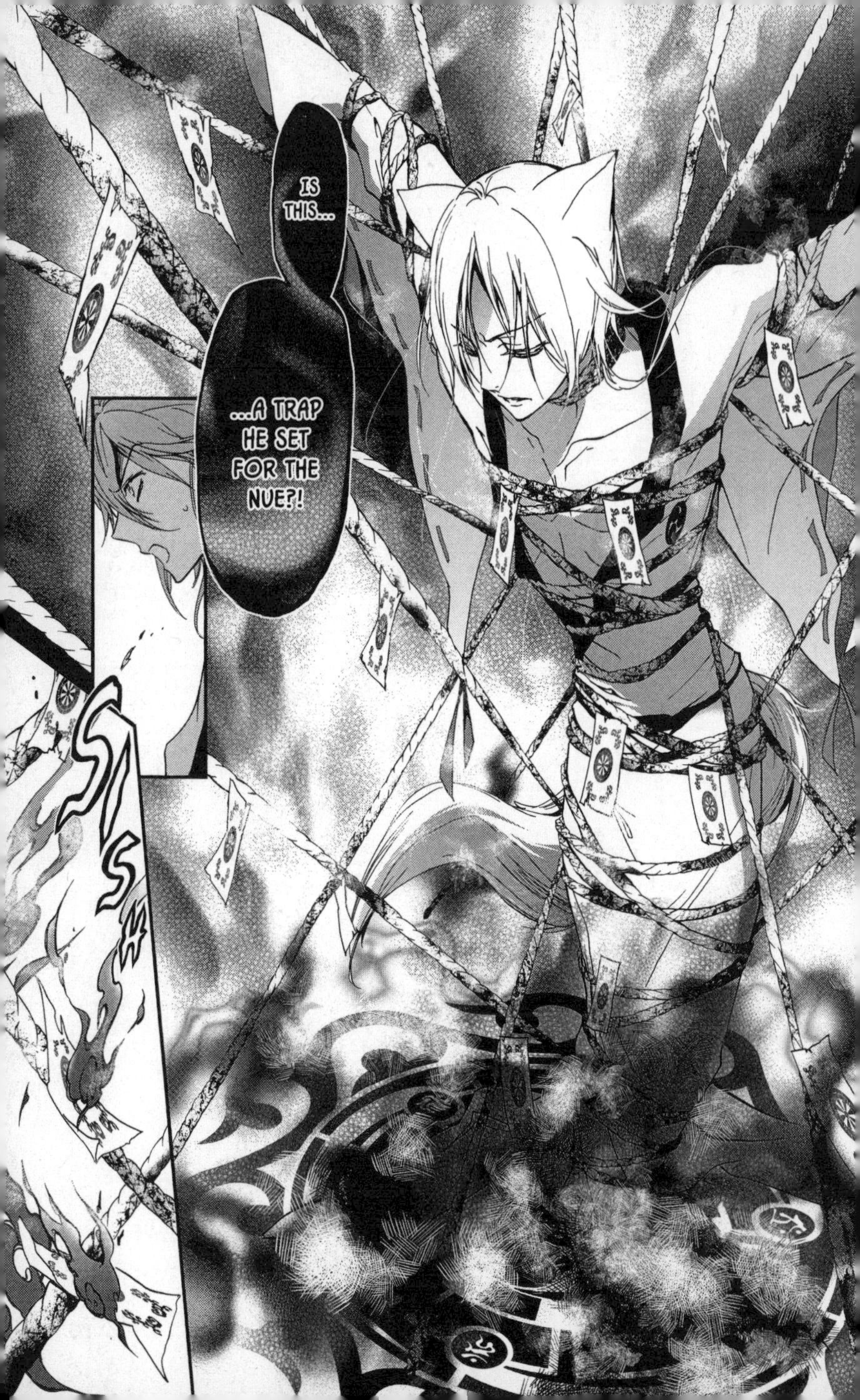
IS THIS...
...A TRAP HE SET FOR THE NUE?!
SSSH

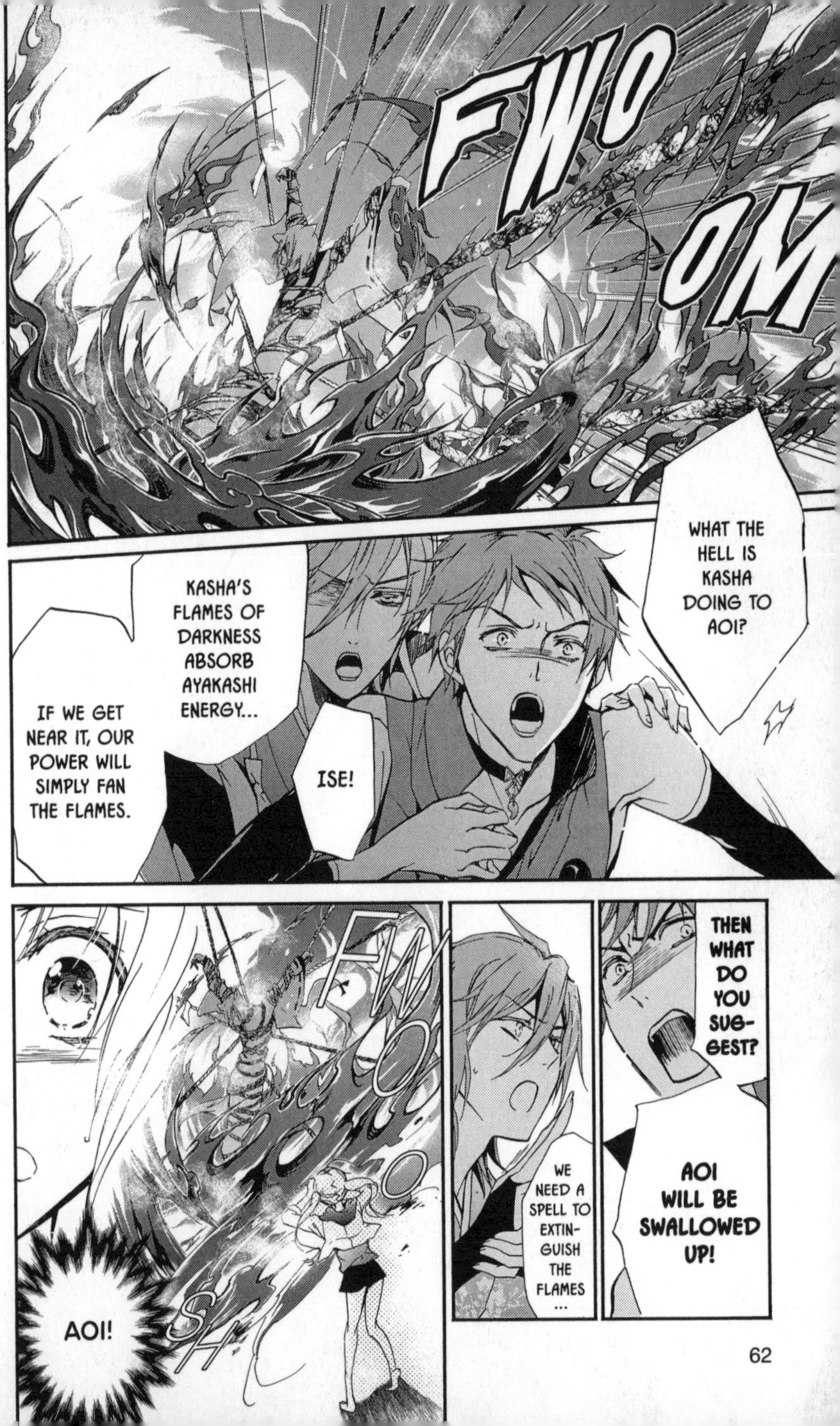
FWOOM
WHAT THE HELL IS KASHA DOING TO AOI?
ISE!
KASHA'S FLAMES OF DARKNESS ABSORB AYAKASHI ENERGY...
IF WE GET NEAR IT, OUR POWER WILL SIMPLY FAN THE FLAMES.
THEN WHAT DO YOU SUG-GEST?
AOI WILL BE SWALLOWED UP!
WE NEED A SPELL TO EXTIN-GUISH THE FLAMES...
FWOOOO
SH
AOI!

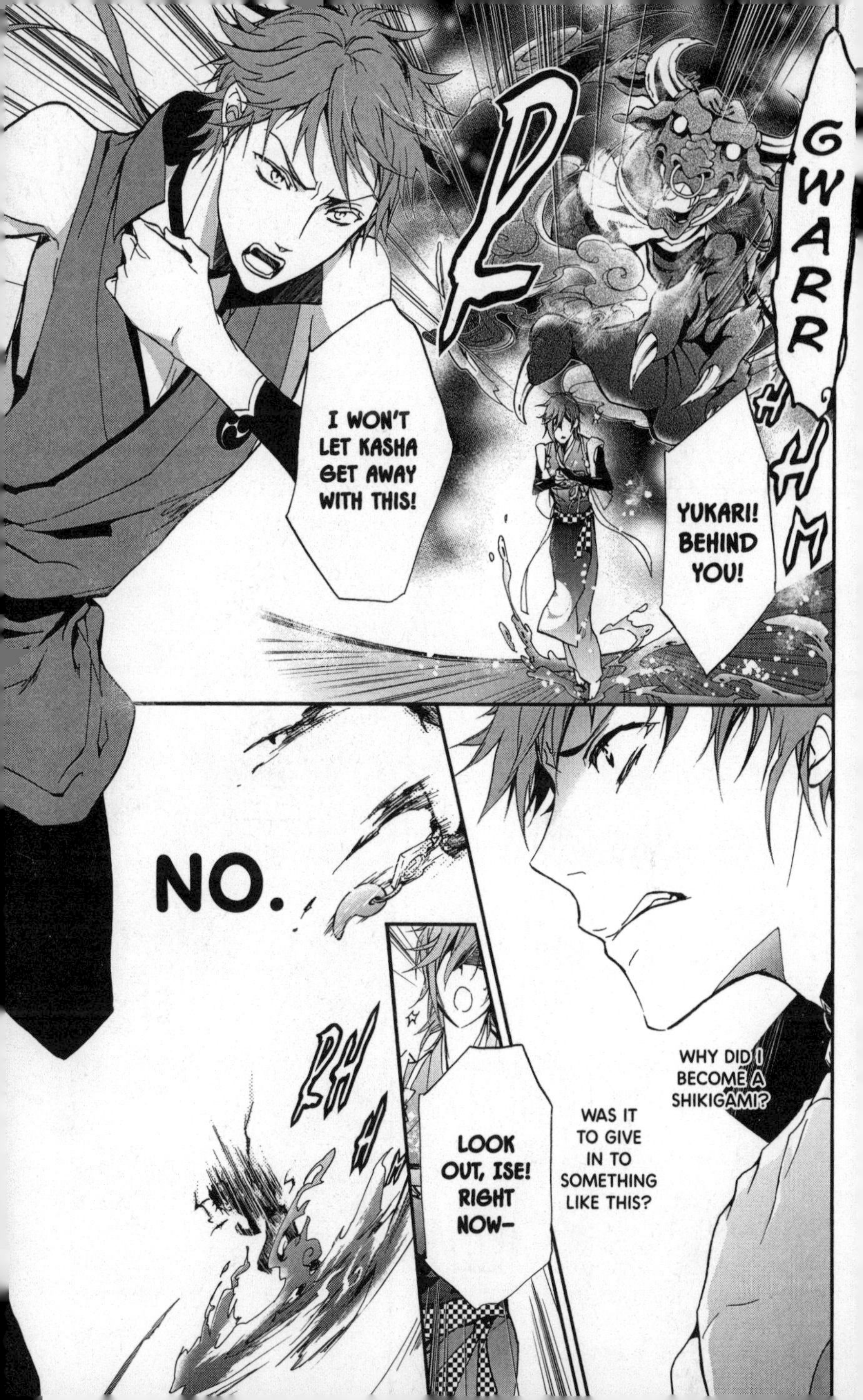
GWARRHHM
YUKARI! BEHIND YOU!
I WON'T LET KASHA GET AWAY WITH THIS!
WHY DID I BECOME A SHIKIGAMI?
WAS IT TO GIVE IN TO SOMETHING LIKE THIS?
LOOK OUT, ISE! RIGHT NOW–
NO.

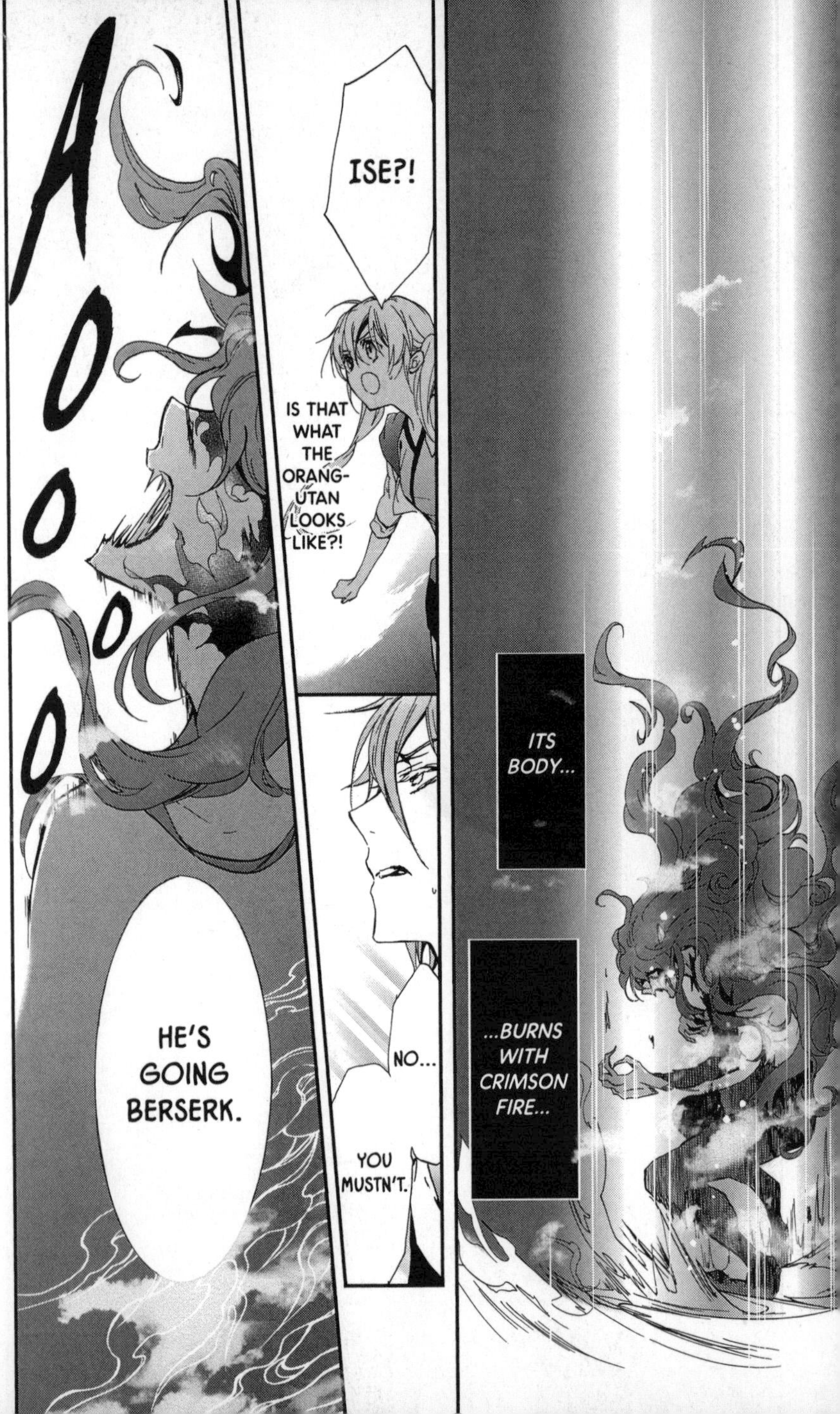
ITS BODY...
...BURNS WITH CRIMSON FIRE...
ISE?!
IS THAT WHAT THE ORANG-UTAN LOOKS LIKE?!
NO...
YOU MUSTN'T.
AOOOO
HE'S GOING BERSERK.

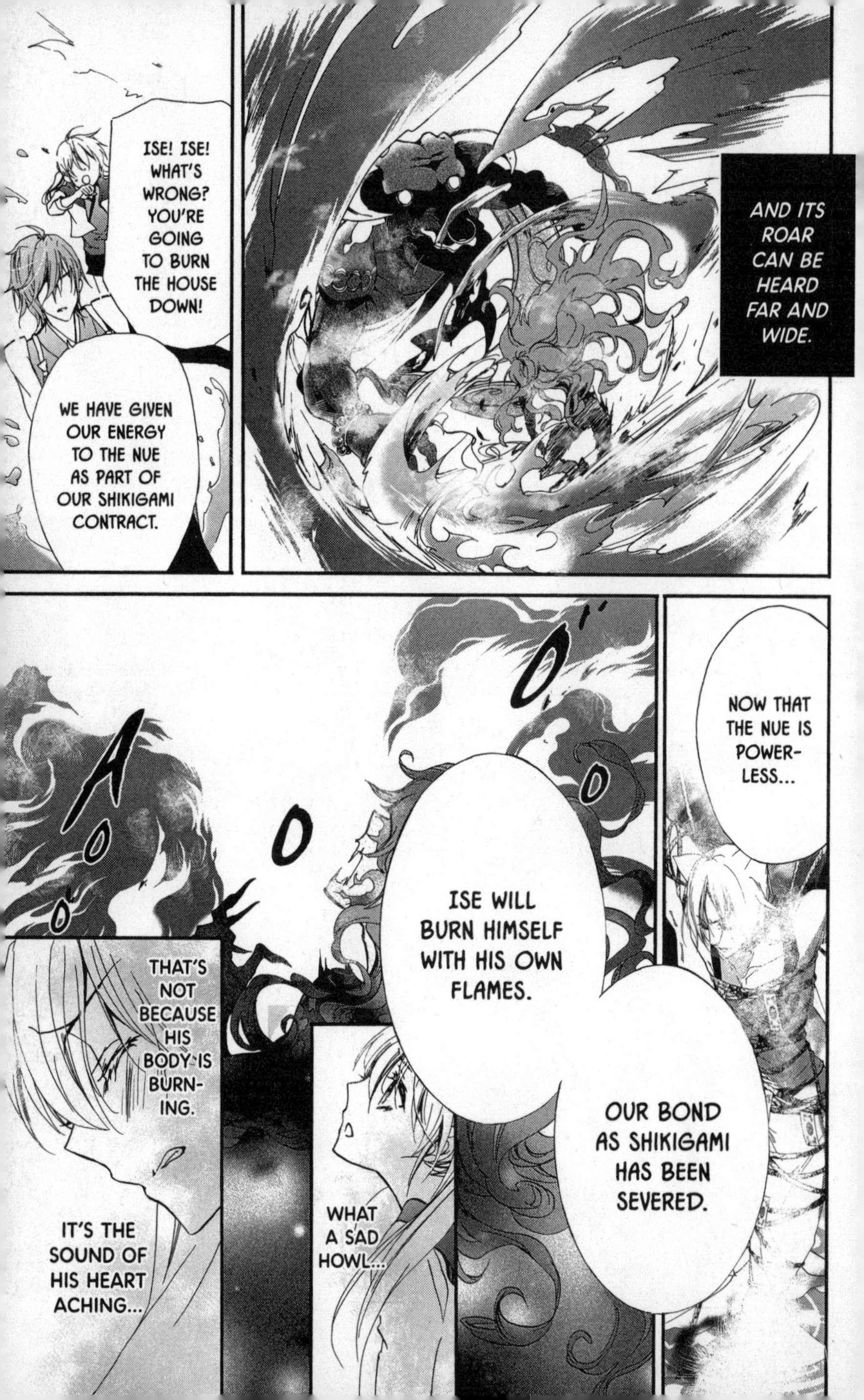
AND ITS ROAR CAN BE HEARD FAR AND WIDE.
ISE! ISE! WHAT'S WRONG? YOU'RE GOING TO BURN THE HOUSE DOWN!
WE HAVE GIVEN OUR ENERGY TO THE NUE AS PART OF OUR SHIKIGAMI CONTRACT.
NOW THAT THE NUE IS POWER-LESS...
ISE WILL BURN HIMSELF WITH HIS OWN FLAMES.
OUR BOND AS SHIKIGAMI HAS BEEN SEVERED.
AOOOOO
WHAT A SAD HOWL...
THAT'S NOT BECAUSE HIS BODY IS BURN-ING.
IT'S THE SOUND OF HIS HEART ACHING...

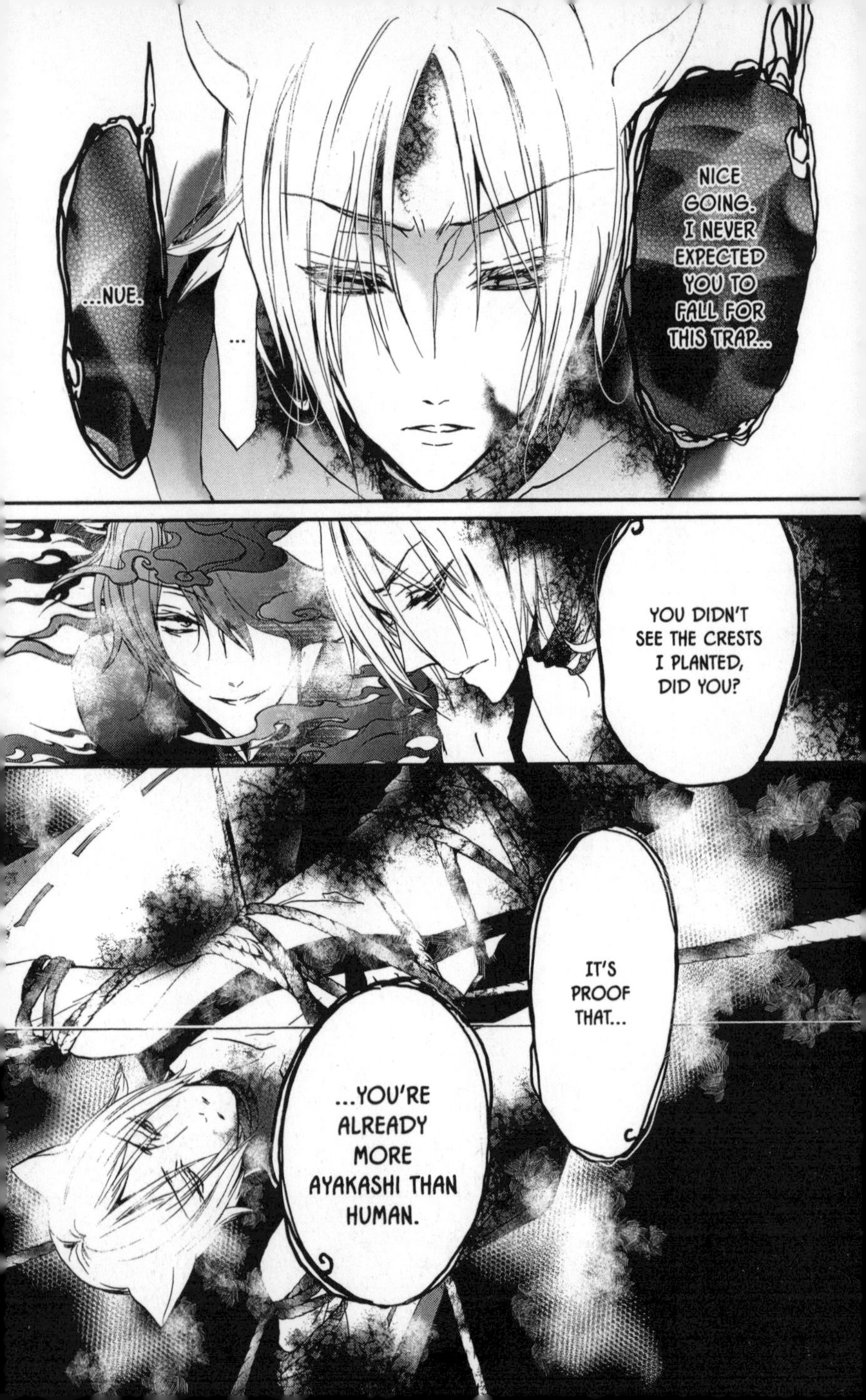
NICE GOING. I NEVER EXPECTED YOU TO FALL FOR THIS TRAP...
...
...NUE.
YOU DIDN'T SEE THE CRESTS I PLANTED, DID YOU?
IT'S PROOF THAT...
...YOU'RE ALREADY MORE AYAKASHI THAN HUMAN.

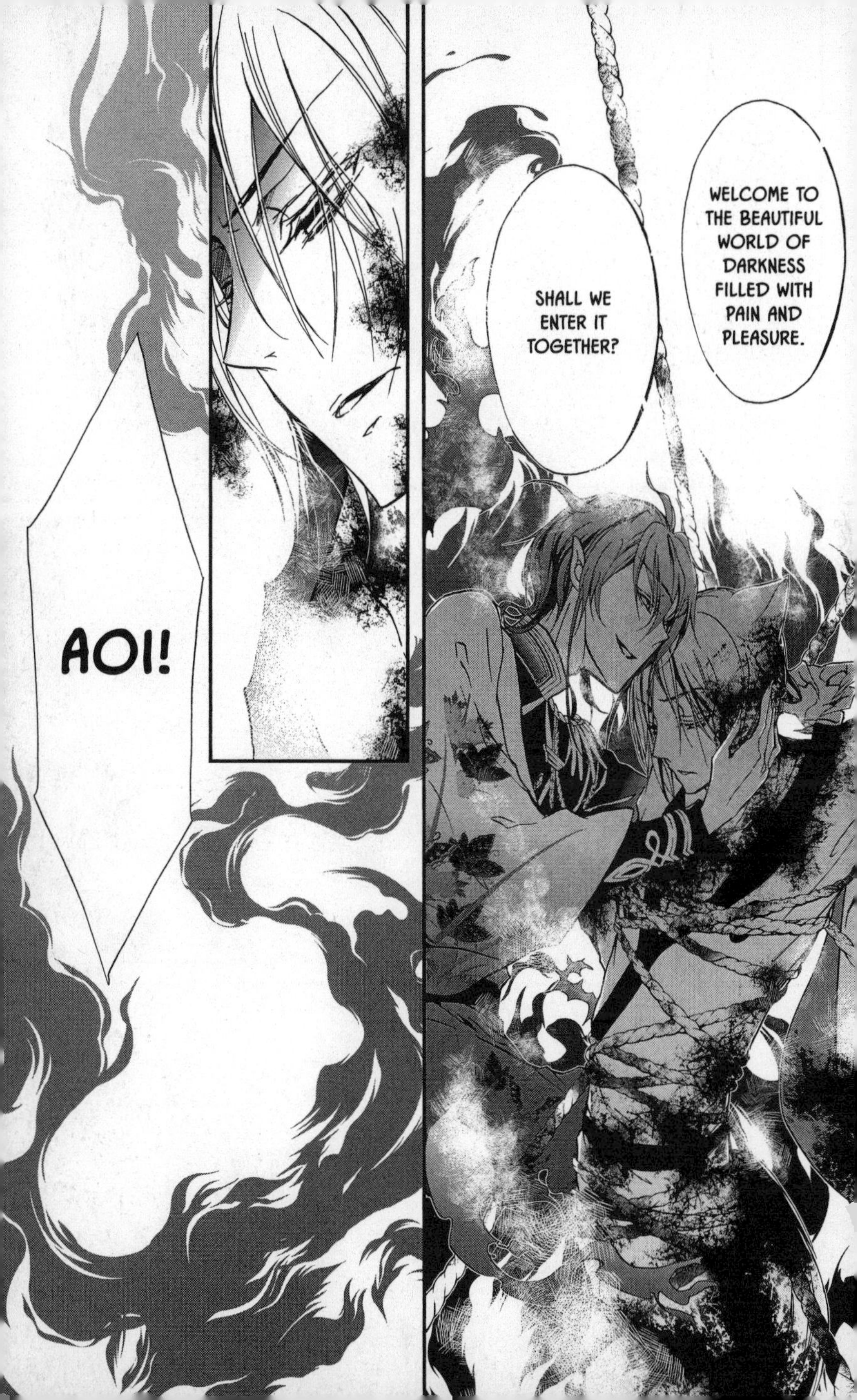
WELCOME TO THE BEAUTIFUL WORLD OF DARKNESS FILLED WITH PAIN AND PLEASURE.
SHALL WE ENTER IT TOGETHER?
AOI!

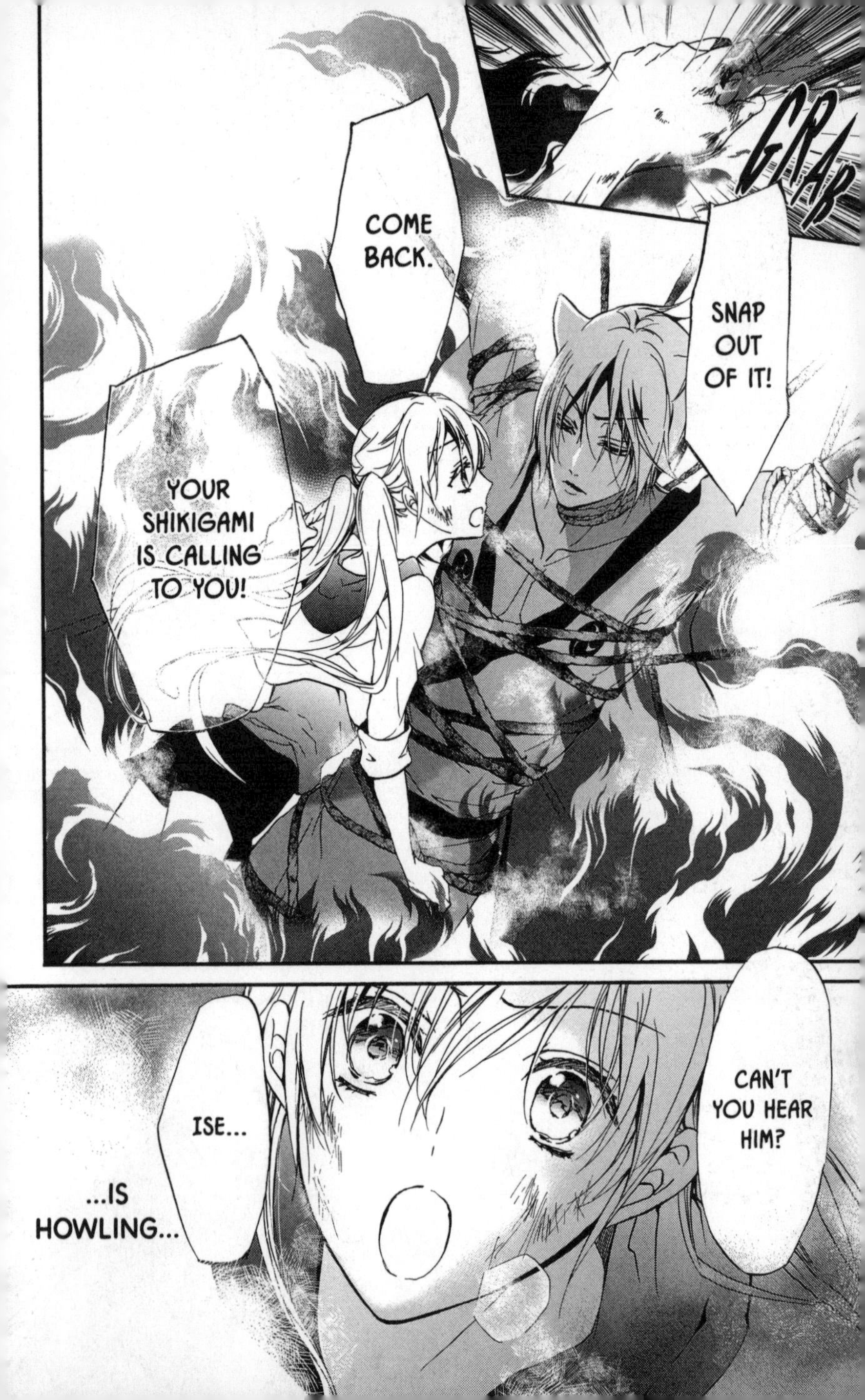
GRAB
SNAP OUT OF IT!
COME BACK.
YOUR SHIKIGAMI IS CALLING TO YOU!
CAN'T YOU HEAR HIM?
ISE...
...IS HOWLING...

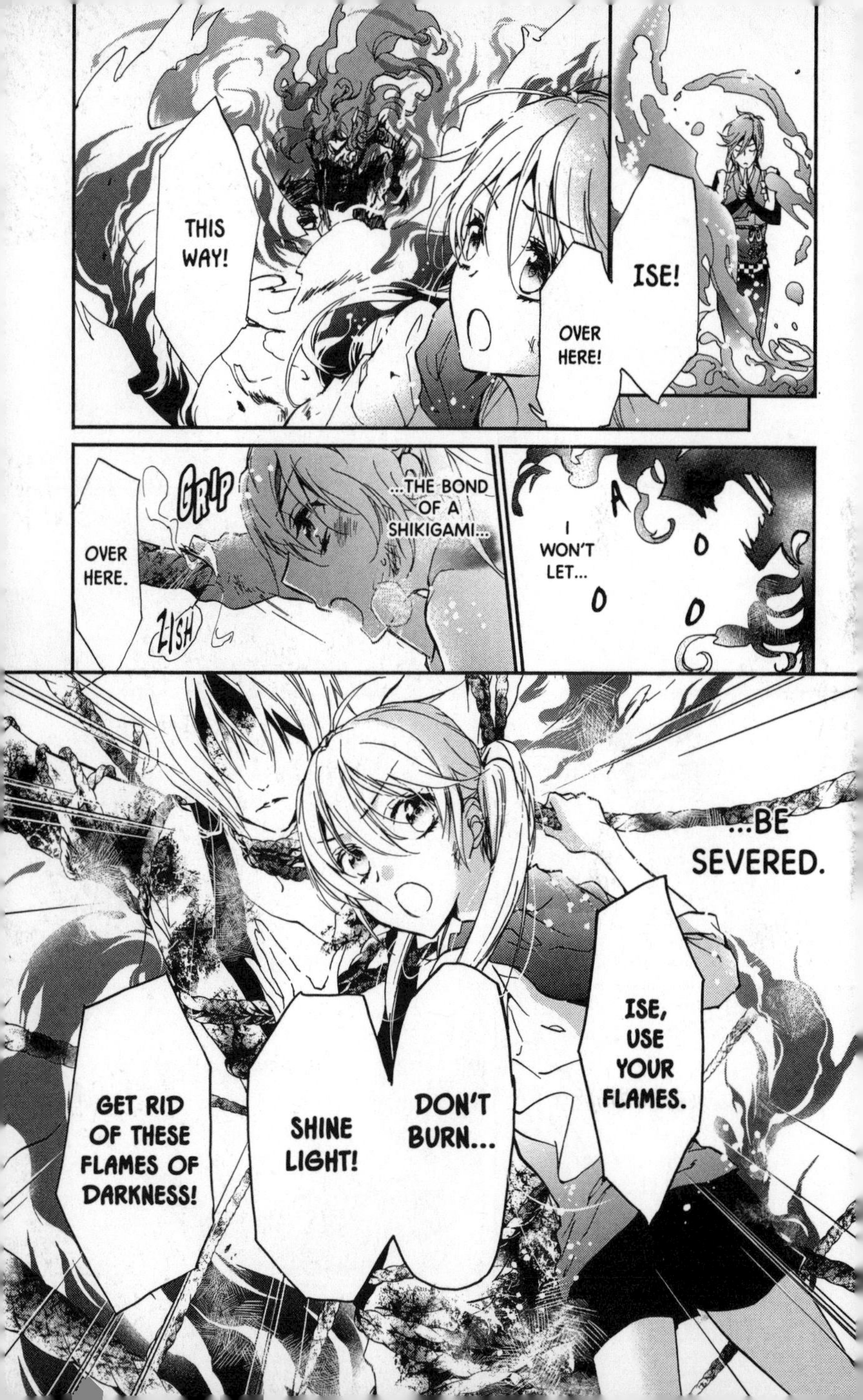
ISE!
OVER HERE!
THIS WAY!
I WON'T LET...
AOOO
...THE BOND OF A SHIKIGAMI...
GRIP
OVER HERE.
ZISH
...BE SEVERED.
ISE, USE YOUR FLAMES.
DON'T BURN...
SHINE LIGHT!
GET RID OF THESE FLAMES OF DARKNESS!

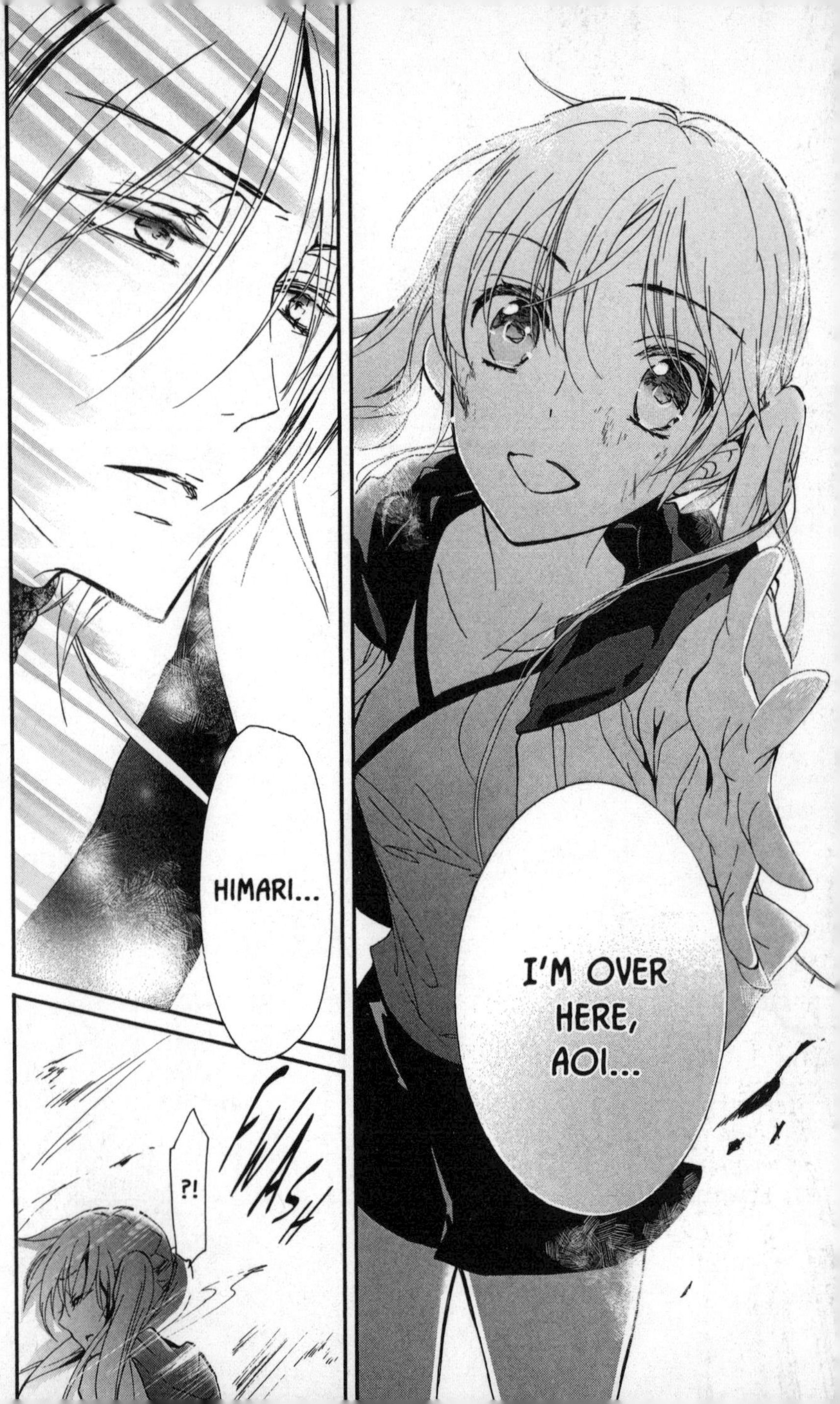
I'M OVER HERE, AOI...
HIMARI...
FWASH
?!

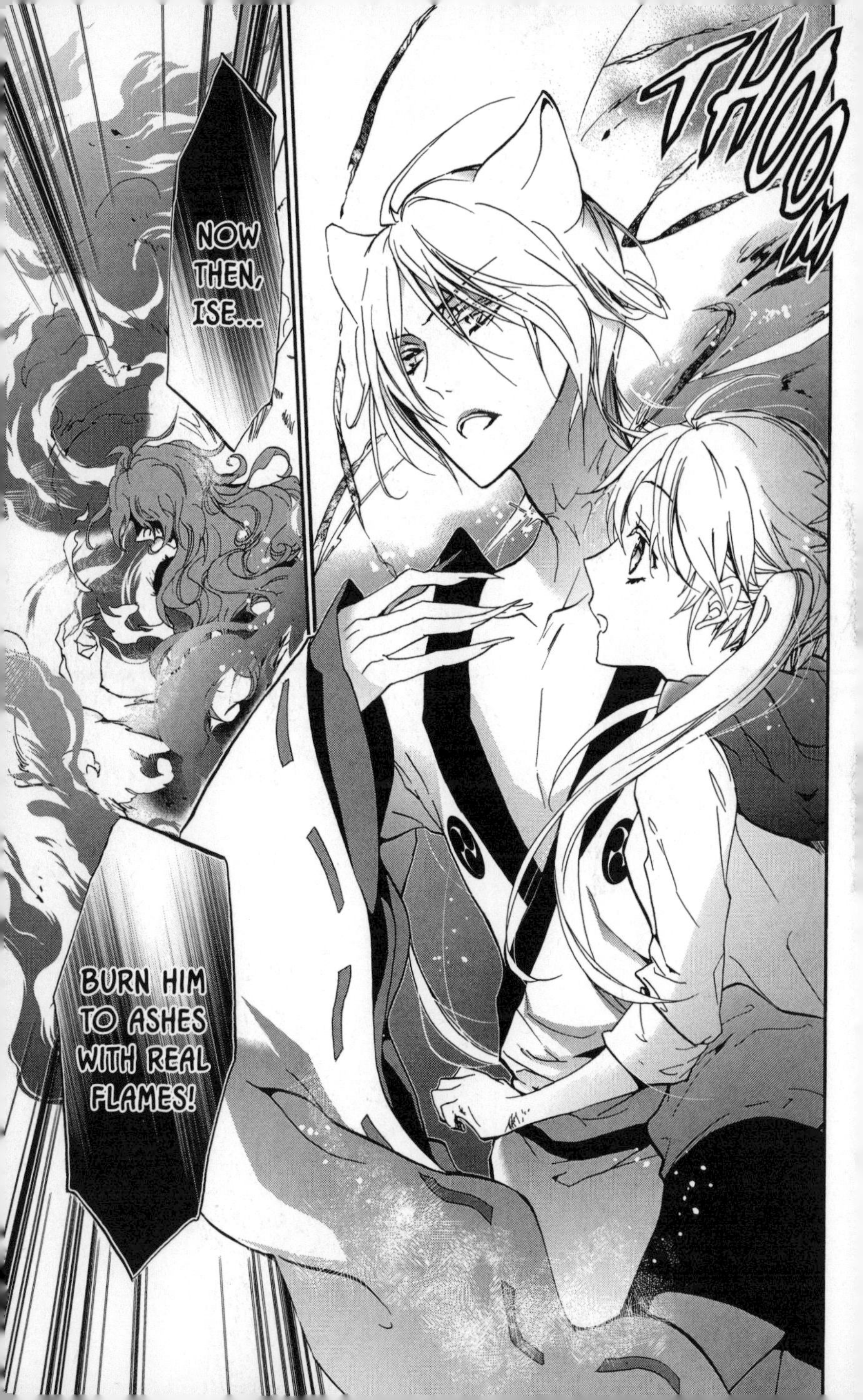
THOOM
NOW THEN, ISE...
BURN HIM TO ASHES WITH REAL FLAMES!

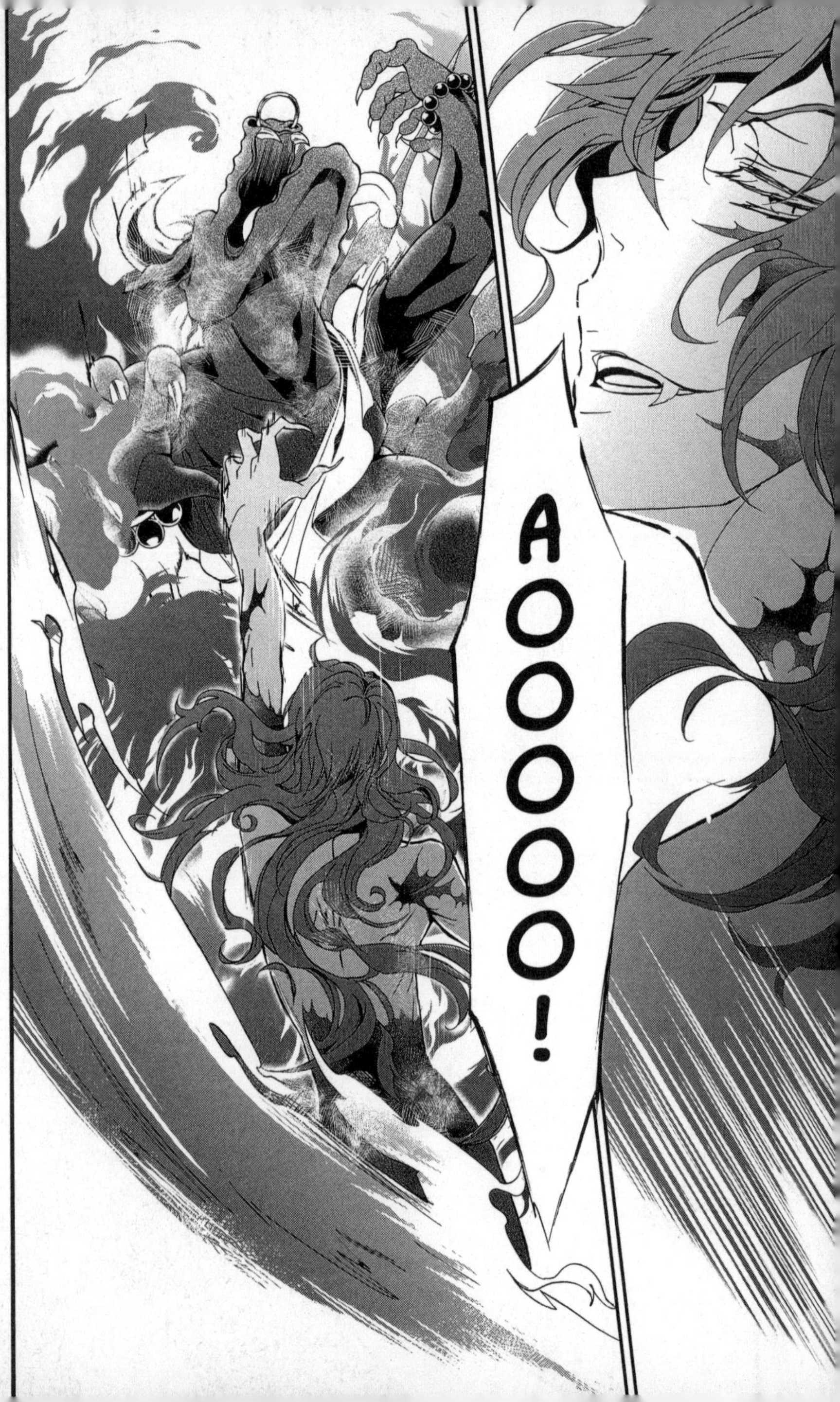
AOOOOO!

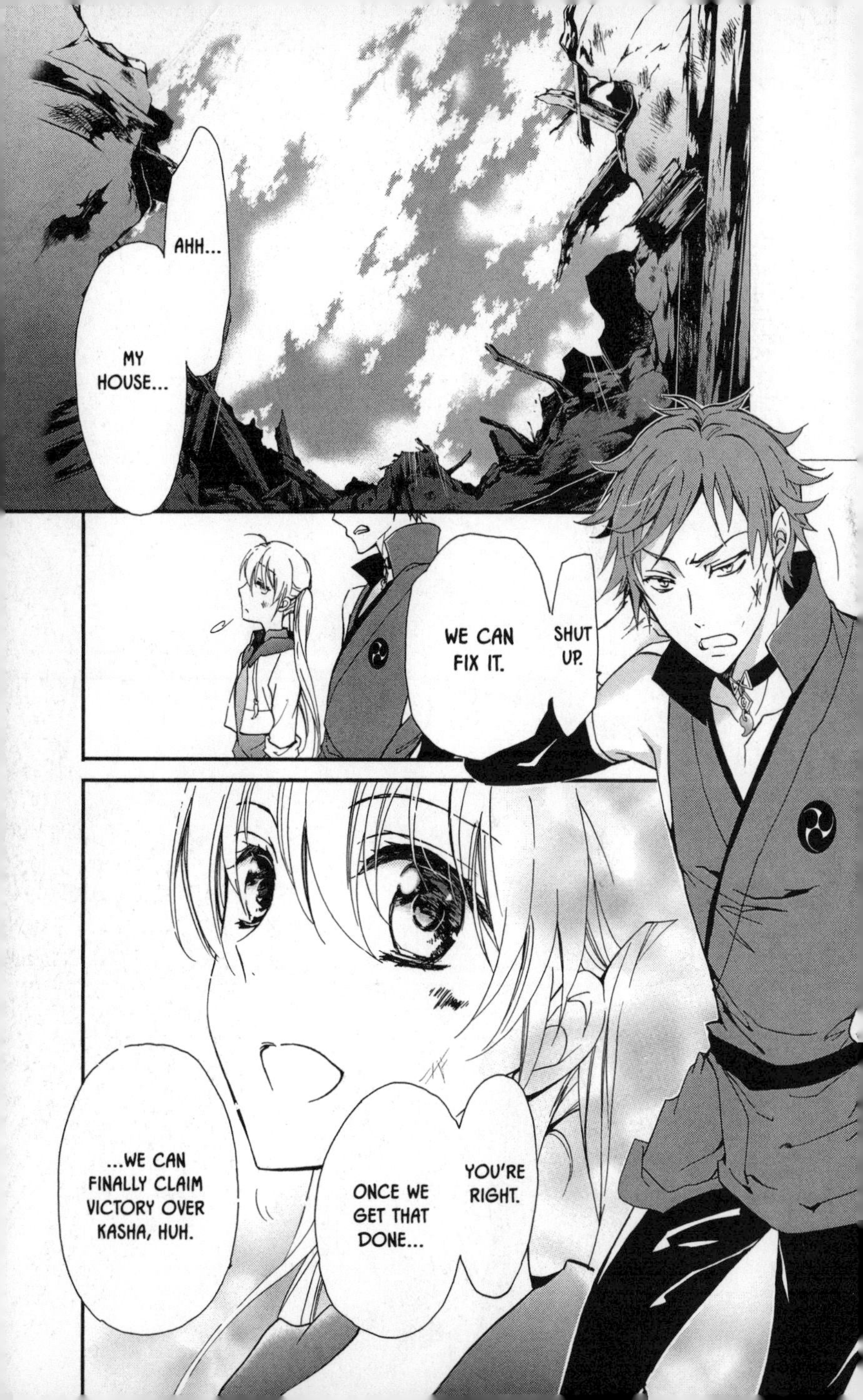
AHH...
MY HOUSE...
SHUT UP.
WE CAN FIX IT.
YOU'RE RIGHT.
ONCE WE GET THAT DONE...
...WE CAN FINALLY CLAIM VICTORY OVER KASHA, HUH.

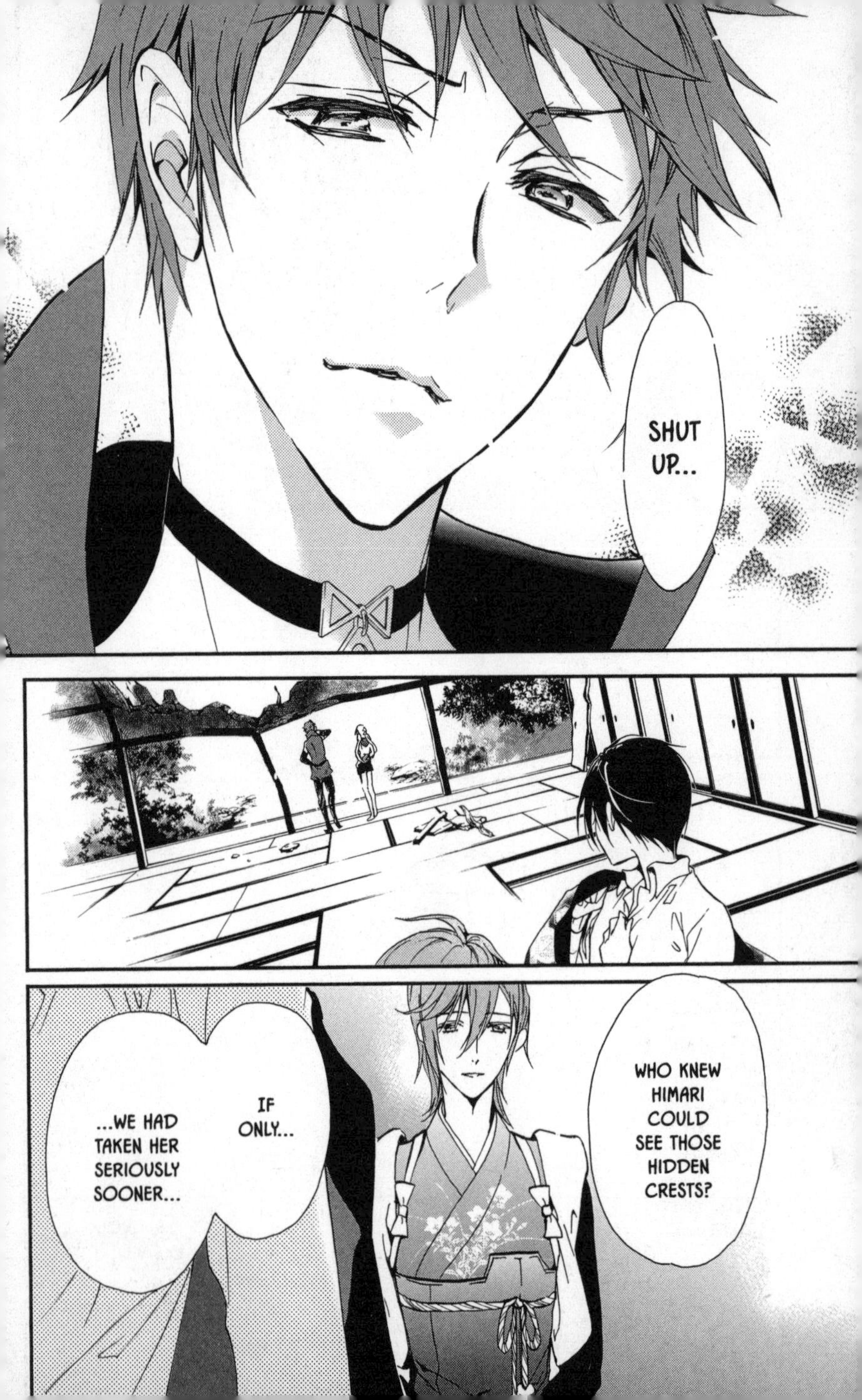
SHUT UP...
WHO KNEW HIMARI COULD SEE THOSE HIDDEN CRESTS?
IF ONLY...
...WE HAD TAKEN HER SERIOUSLY SOONER...

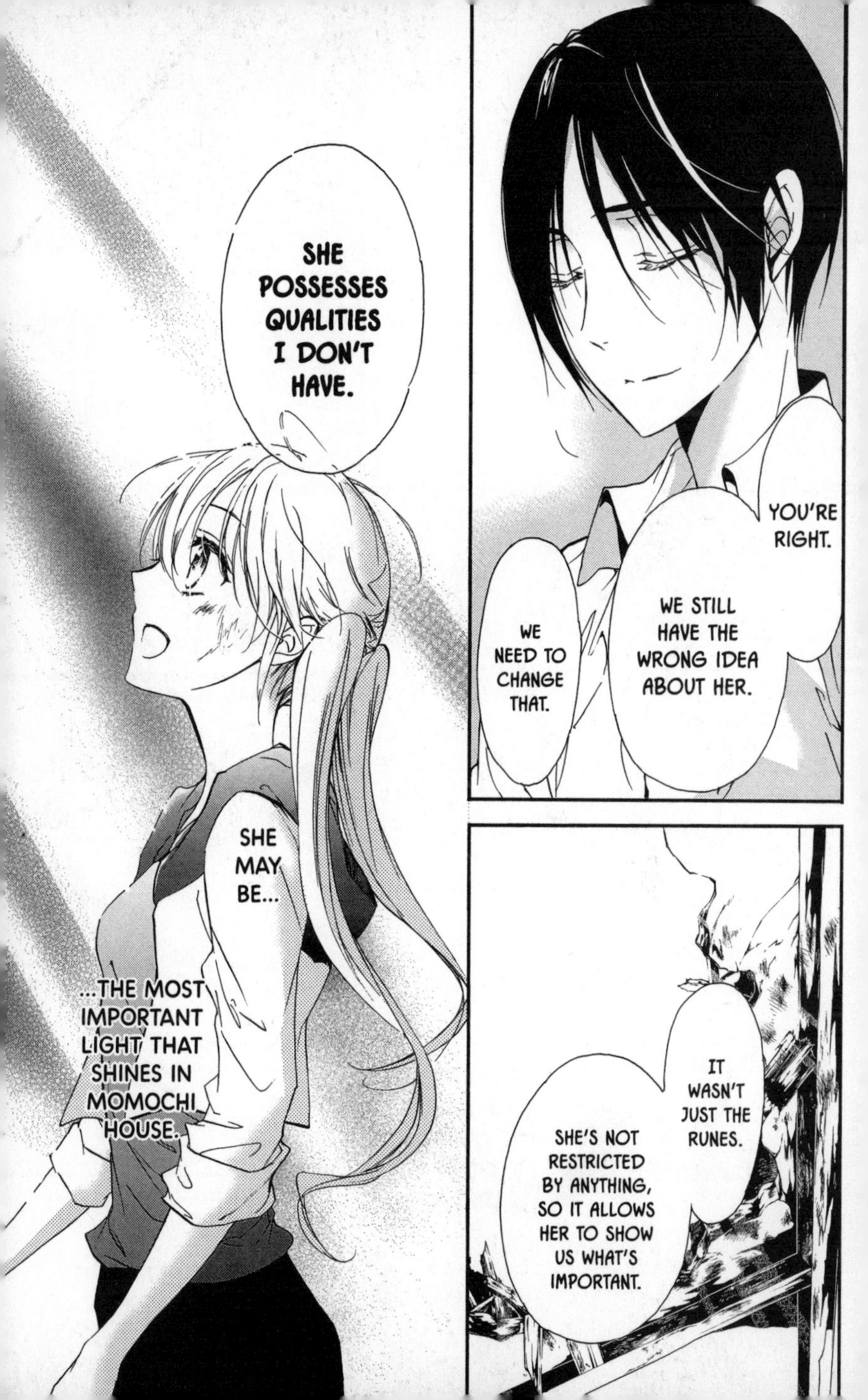
YOU'RE RIGHT.
WE STILL HAVE THE WRONG IDEA ABOUT HER.
WE NEED TO CHANGE THAT.
IT WASN'T JUST THE RUNES.
SHE'S NOT RESTRICTED BY ANYTHING, SO IT ALLOWS HER TO SHOW US WHAT'S IMPORTANT.
SHE POSSESSES QUALITIES I DON'T HAVE.
SHE MAY BE...
...THE MOST IMPORTANT LIGHT THAT SHINES IN MOMOCHI HOUSE.

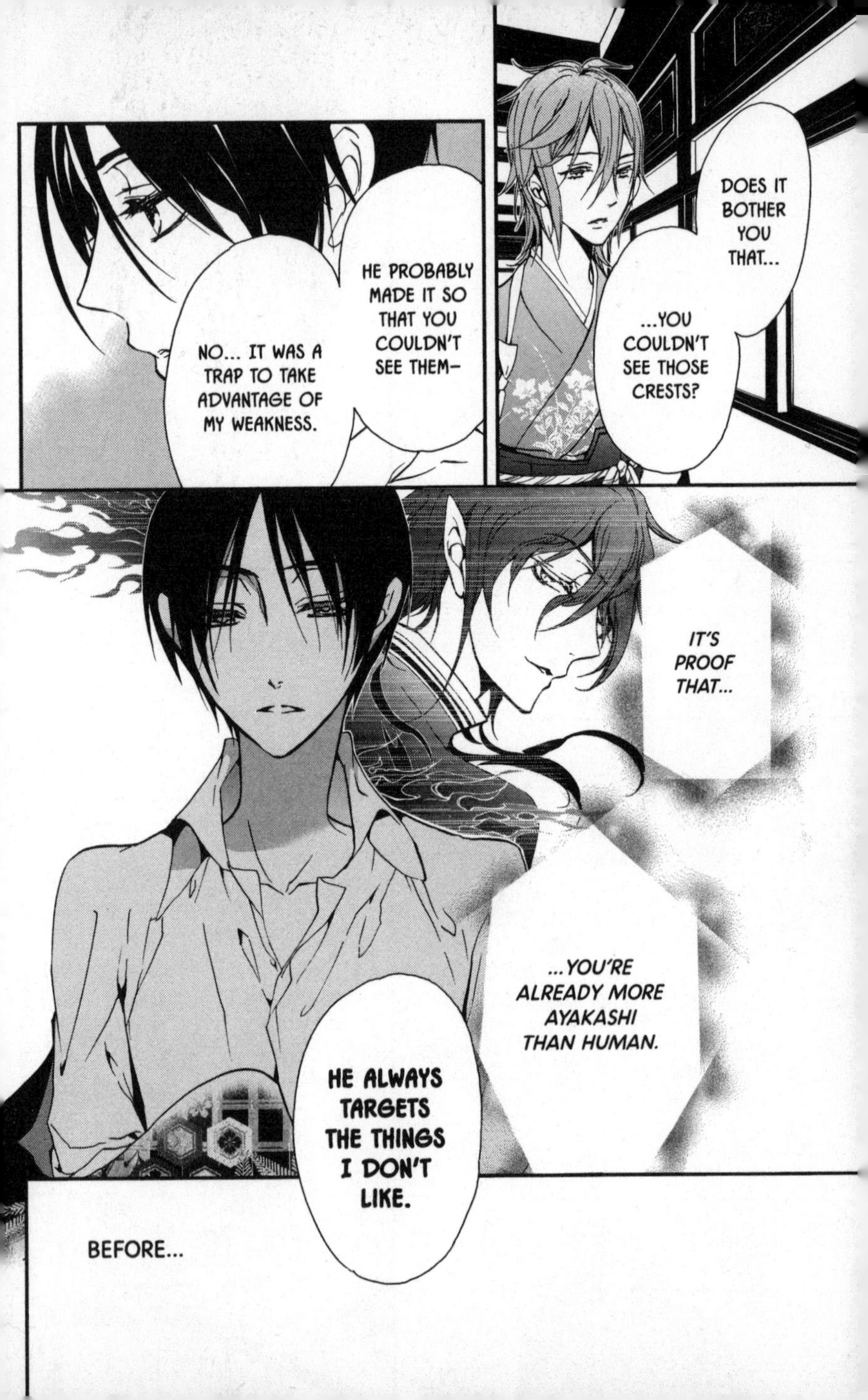
DOES IT BOTHER YOU THAT...
...YOU COULDN'T SEE THOSE CRESTS?
HE PROBABLY MADE IT SO THAT YOU COULDN'T SEE THEM—
NO... IT WAS A TRAP TO TAKE ADVANTAGE OF MY WEAKNESS.
IT'S PROOF THAT...
...YOU'RE ALREADY MORE AYAKASHI THAN HUMAN.
HE ALWAYS TARGETS THE THINGS I DON'T LIKE.
BEFORE...

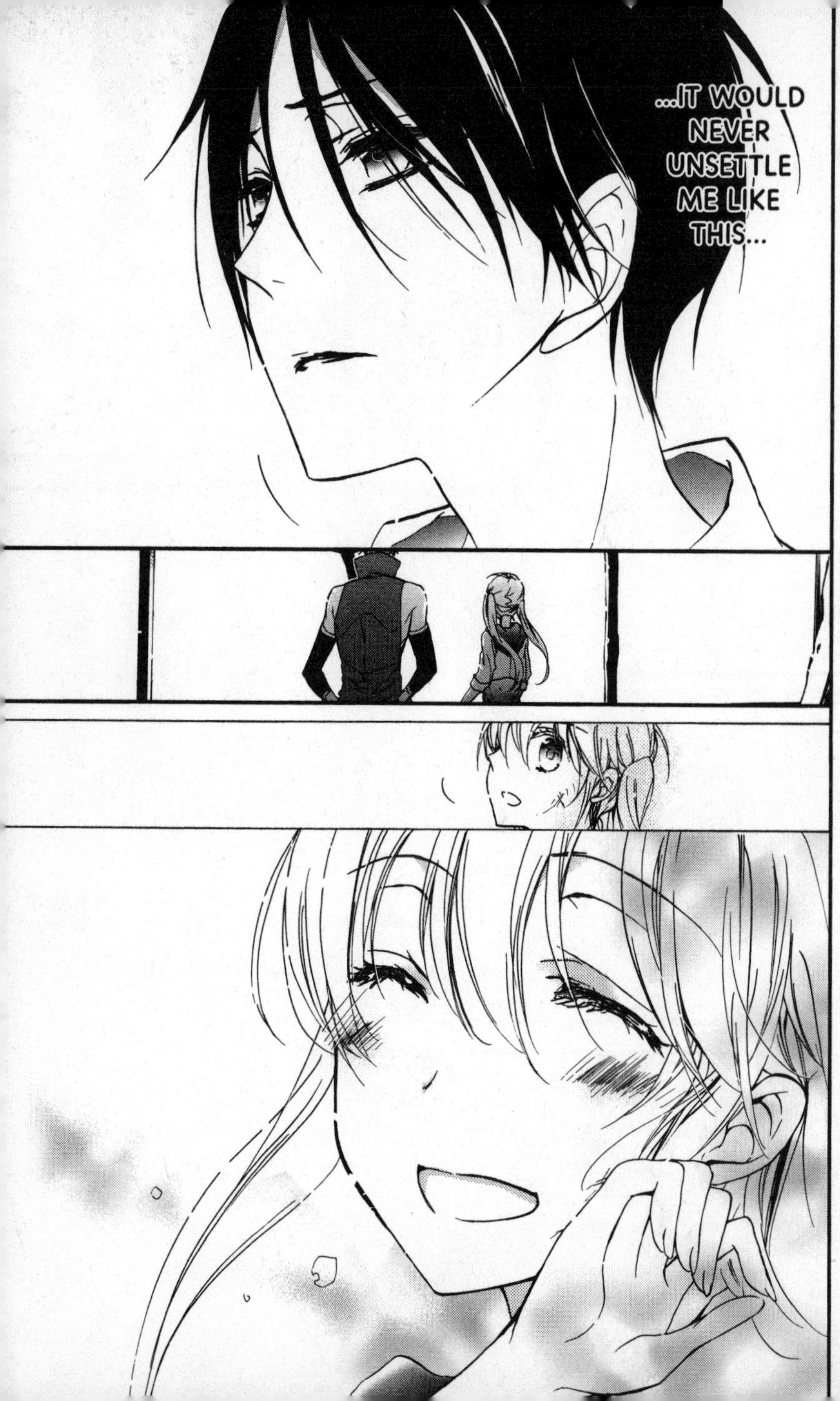
...IT WOULD NEVER UNSETTLE ME LIKE THIS...

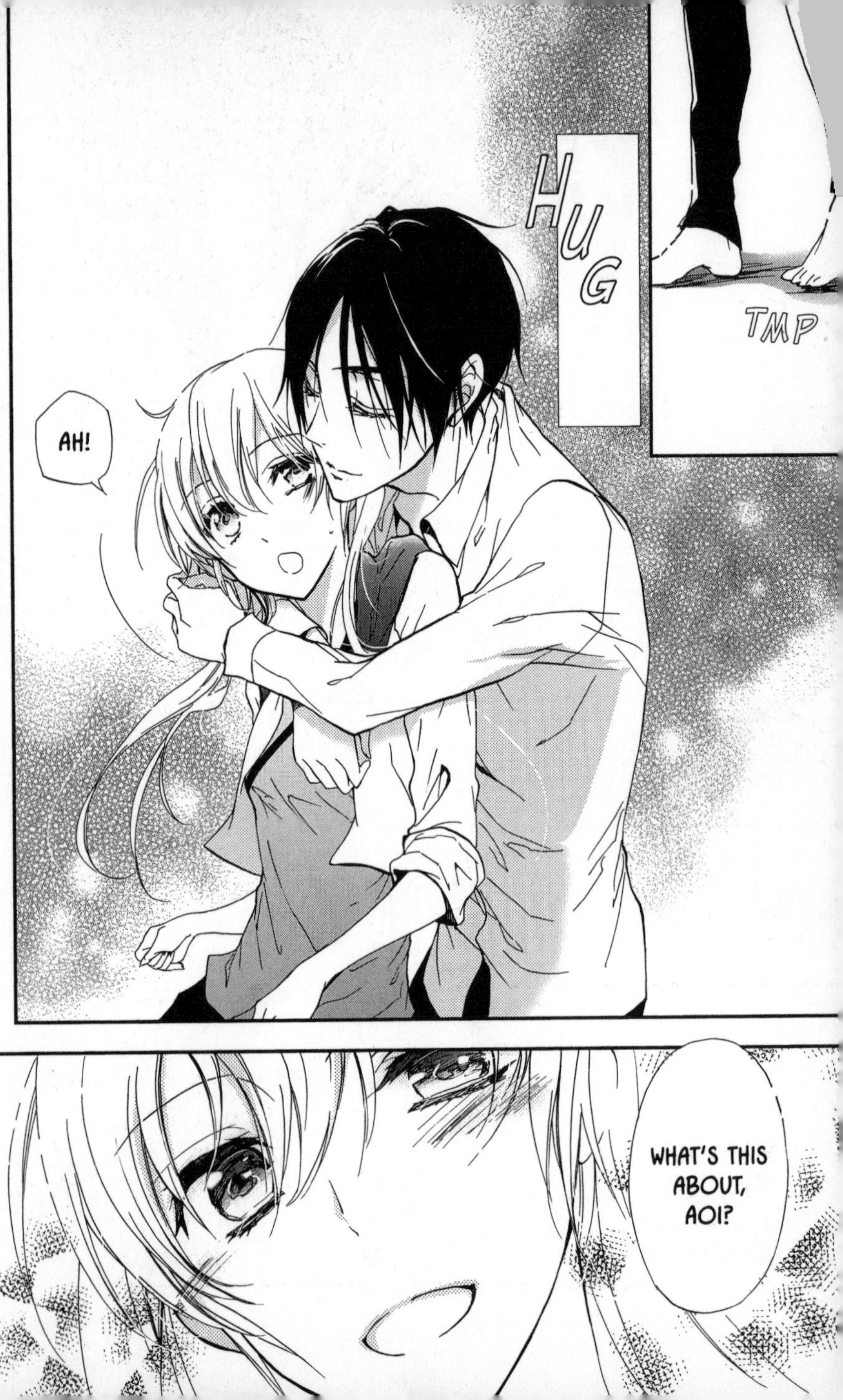
TMP
HUG
AH!
WHAT'S THIS ABOUT, AOI?

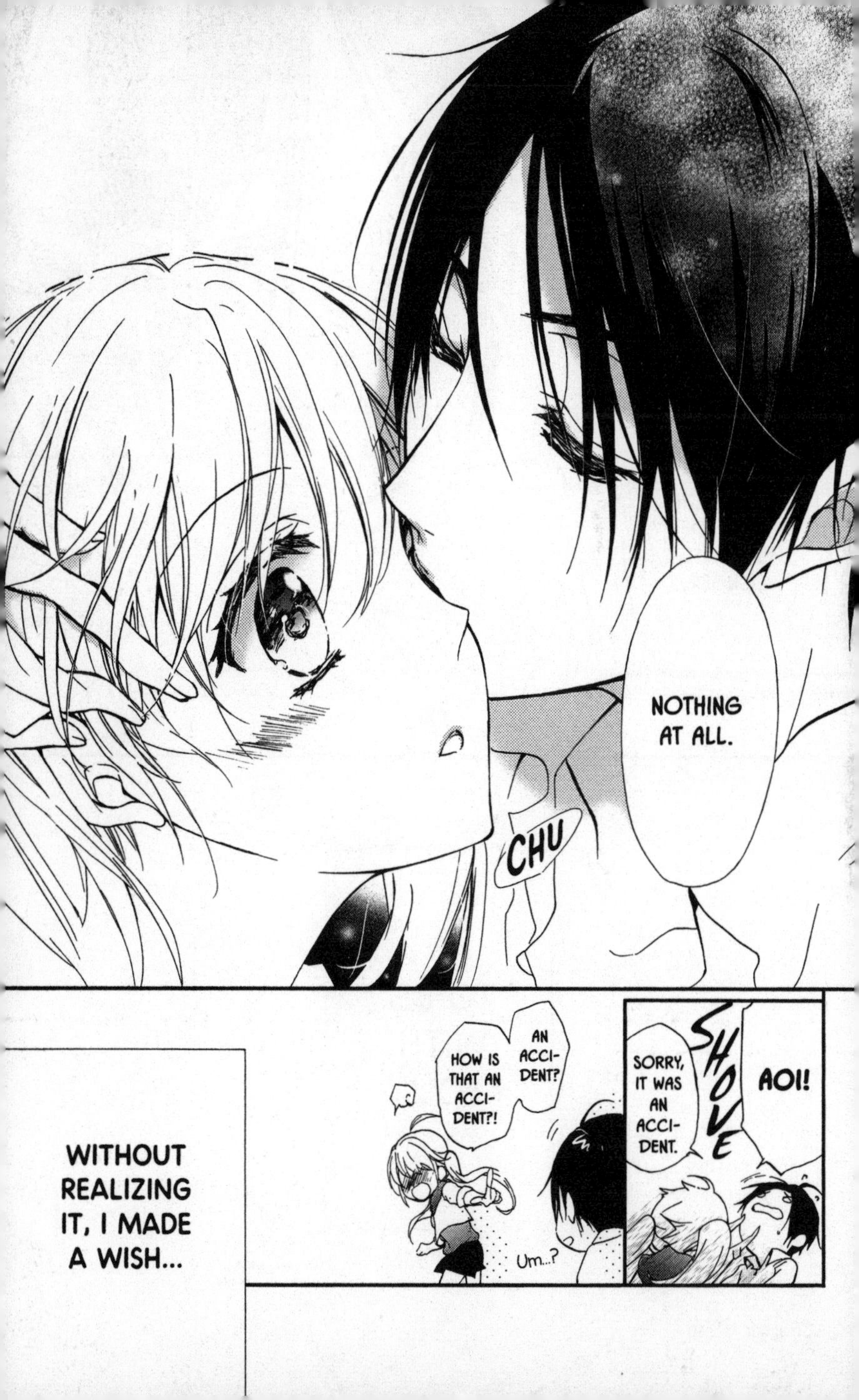
NOTHING AT ALL.
CHU
AOI!
SHOVE
SORRY, IT WAS AN ACCIDENT.
AN ACCIDENT?
HOW IS THAT AN ACCIDENT?!
Um...?
WITHOUT REALIZING IT, I MADE A WISH...

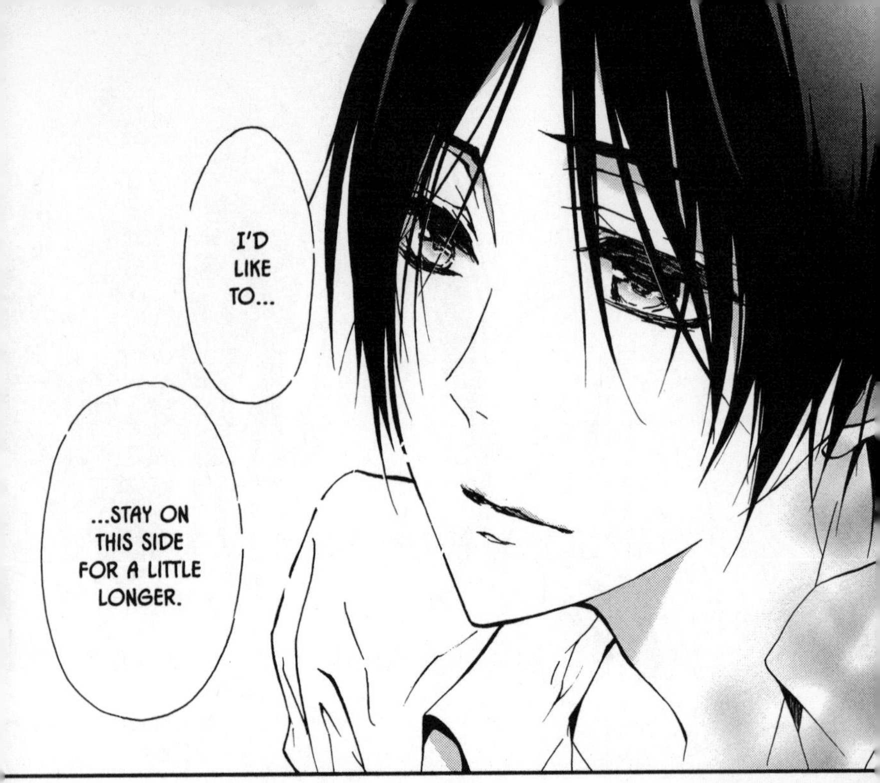
I'D LIKE TO...
...STAY ON THIS SIDE FOR A LITTLE LONGER.

TO BE WITH YOU.

Chapter 9/End

the
DEMON
PRINCE
of MOMOCHI
HOUSE

The
DEMON
PRINCE
of MOMOCHI
HOUSE

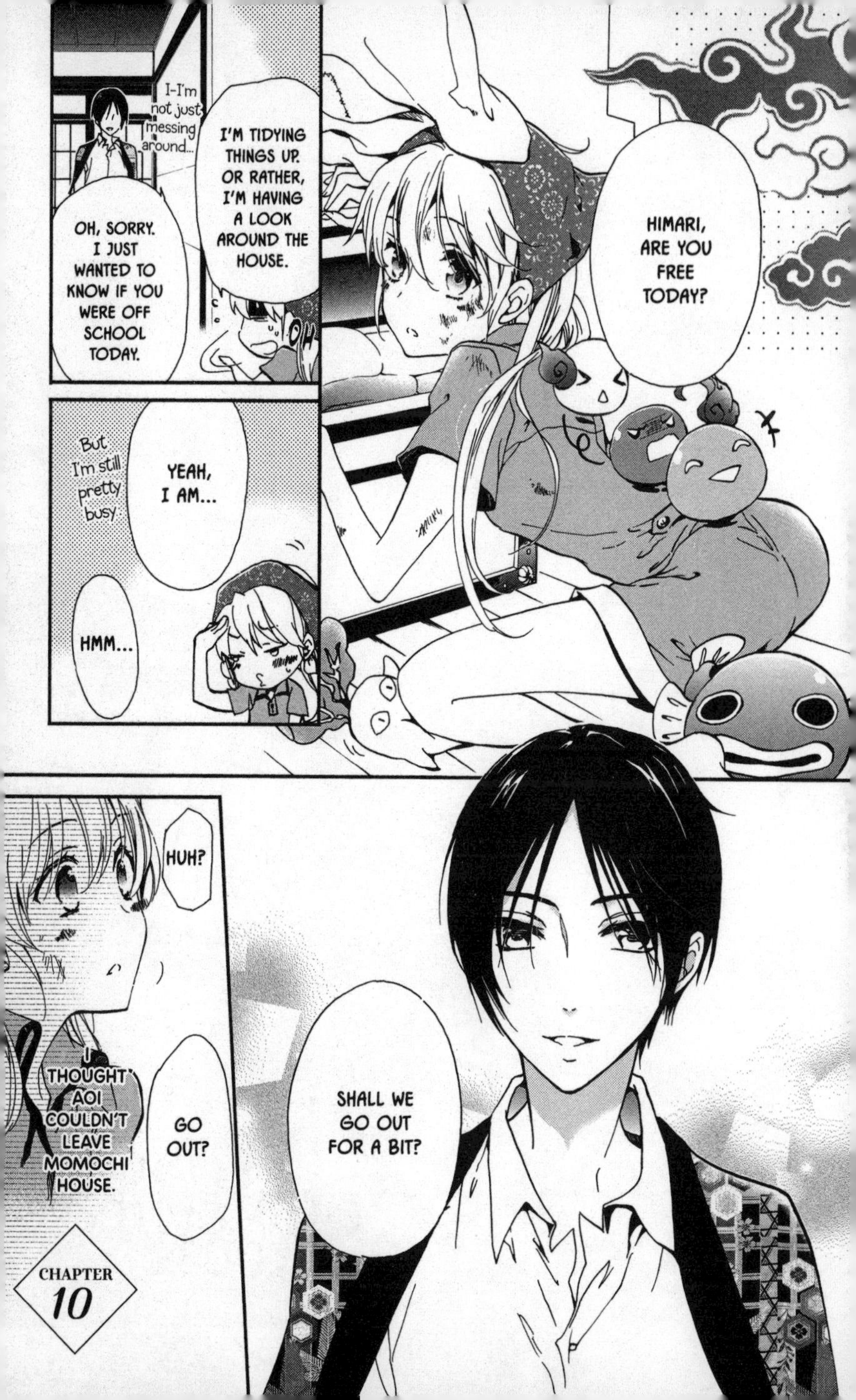
HIMARI, ARE YOU FREE TODAY?
I'M TIDYING THINGS UP. OR RATHER, I'M HAVING A LOOK AROUND THE HOUSE.
I-I'm not just messing around...
OH
OH, SORRY. I JUST WANTED TO KNOW IF YOU WERE OFF SCHOOL TODAY.
YEAH, I AM...
But I'm still pretty busy.
HMM...
SHALL WE GO OUT FOR A BIT?
HUH?
GO OUT?
I THOUGHT AOI COULDN'T LEAVE MOMOCHI HOUSE.
CHAPTER 10

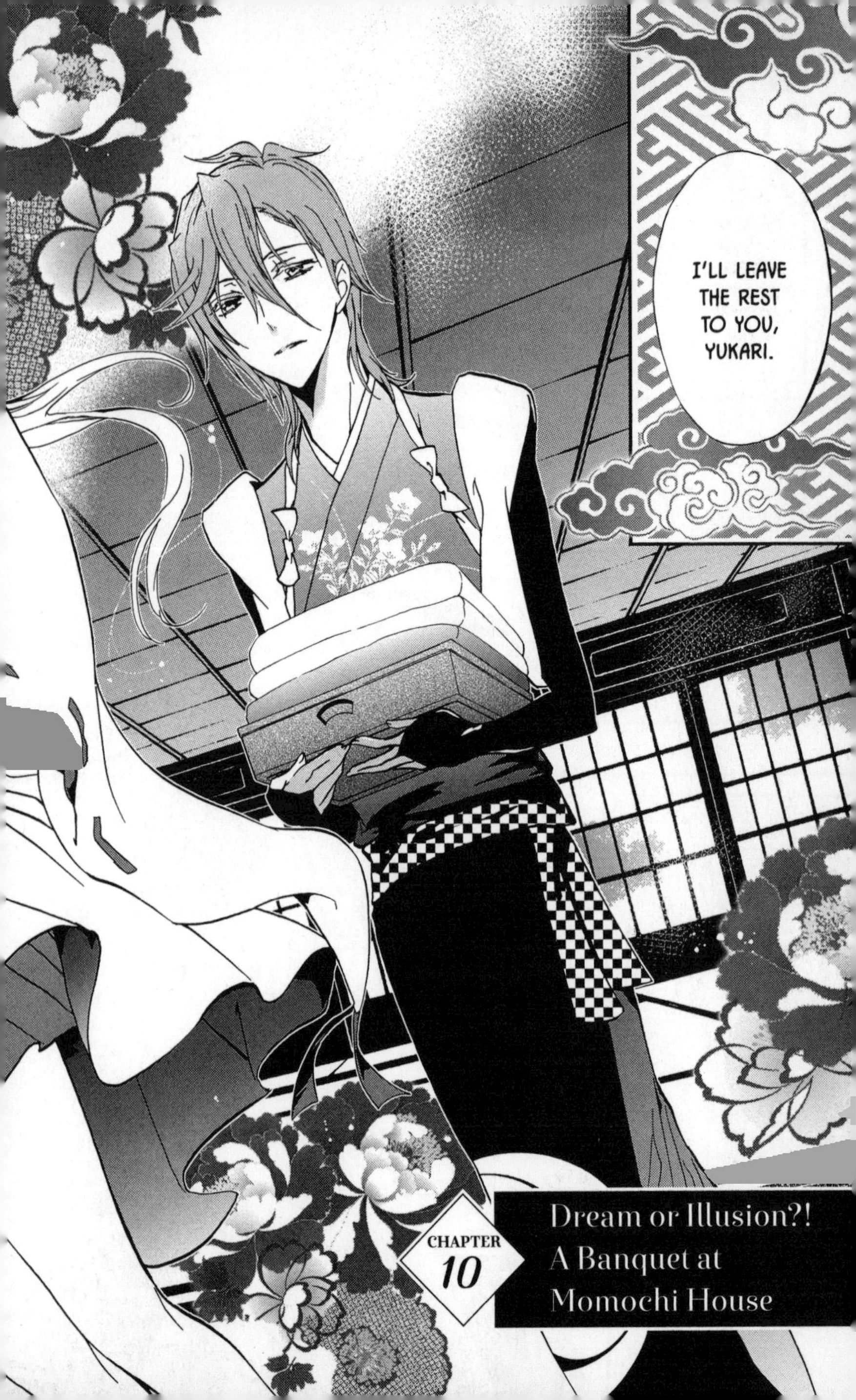
I'LL LEAVE THE REST TO YOU, YUKARI.
CHAPTER 10
Dream or Illusion?! A Banquet at Momochi House

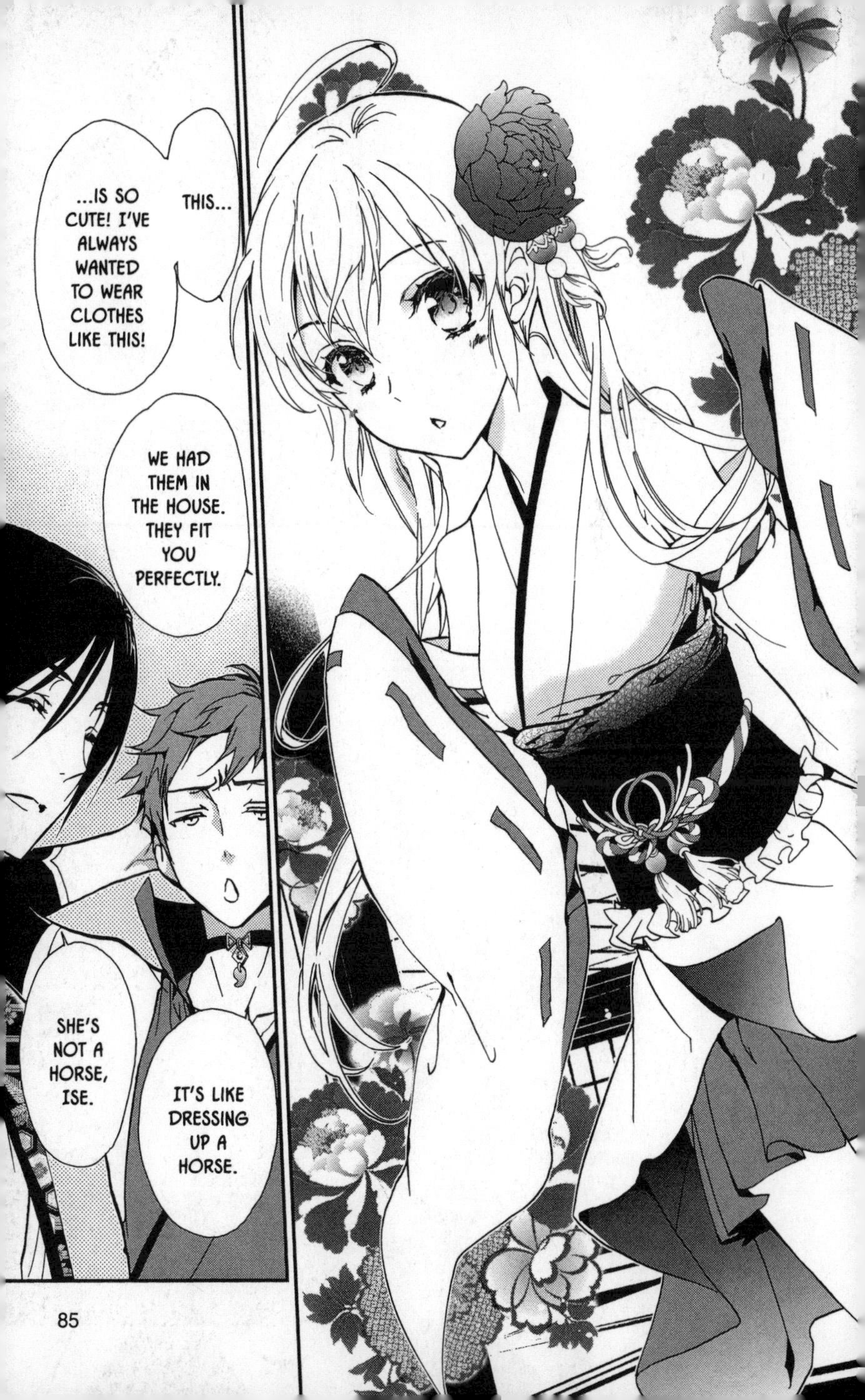
THIS...
...IS SO CUTE! I'VE ALWAYS WANTED TO WEAR CLOTHES LIKE THIS!
WE HAD THEM IN THE HOUSE. THEY FIT YOU PERFECTLY.
IT'S LIKE DRESSING UP A HORSE.
SHE'S NOT A HORSE, ISE.

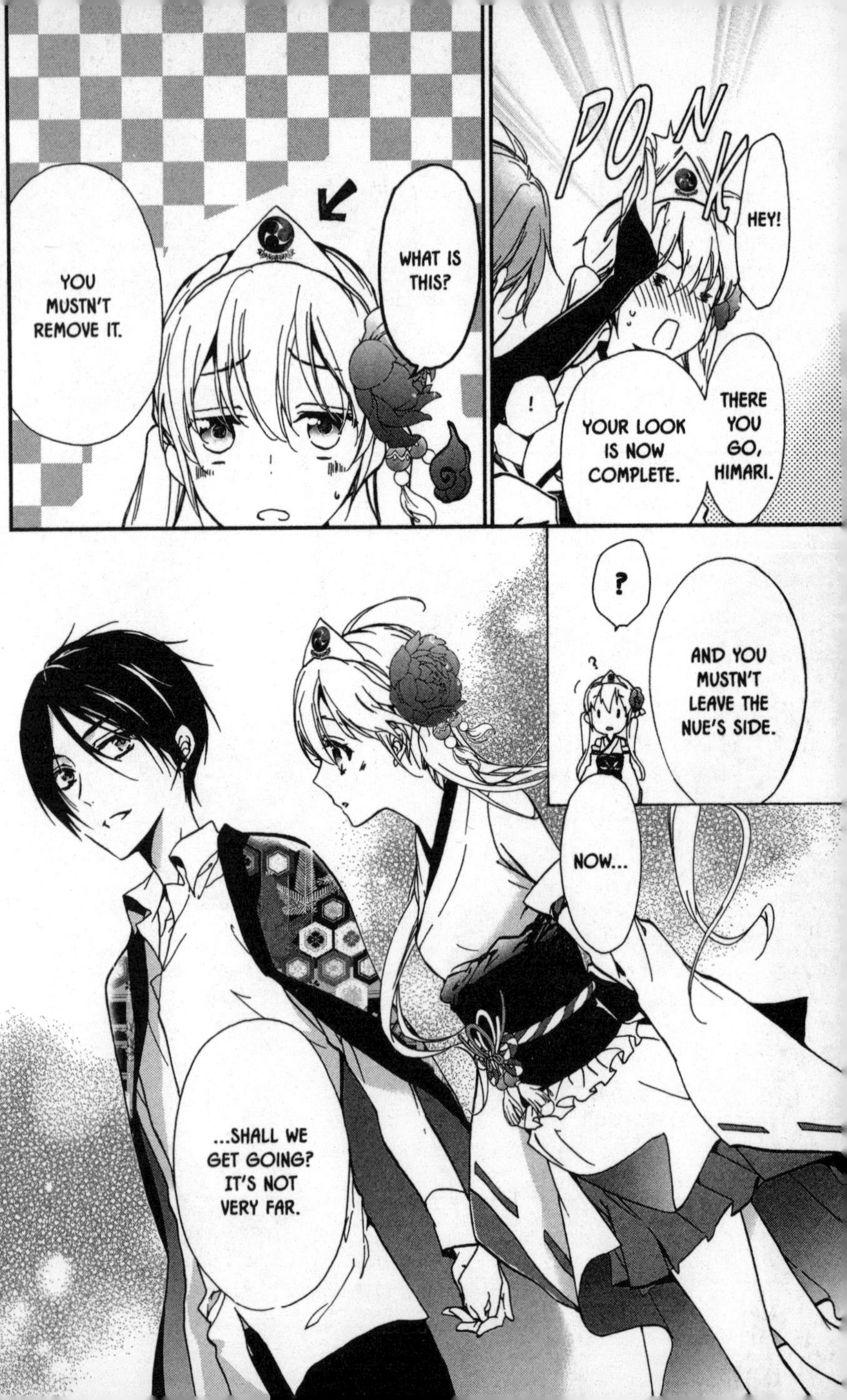
PONK
HEY!
THERE YOU GO, HIMARI.
YOUR LOOK IS NOW COMPLETE.
!
WHAT IS THIS?
YOU MUSTN'T REMOVE IT.
?
AND YOU MUSTN'T LEAVE THE NUE'S SIDE.
NOW...
...SHALL WE GET GOING? IT'S NOT VERY FAR.

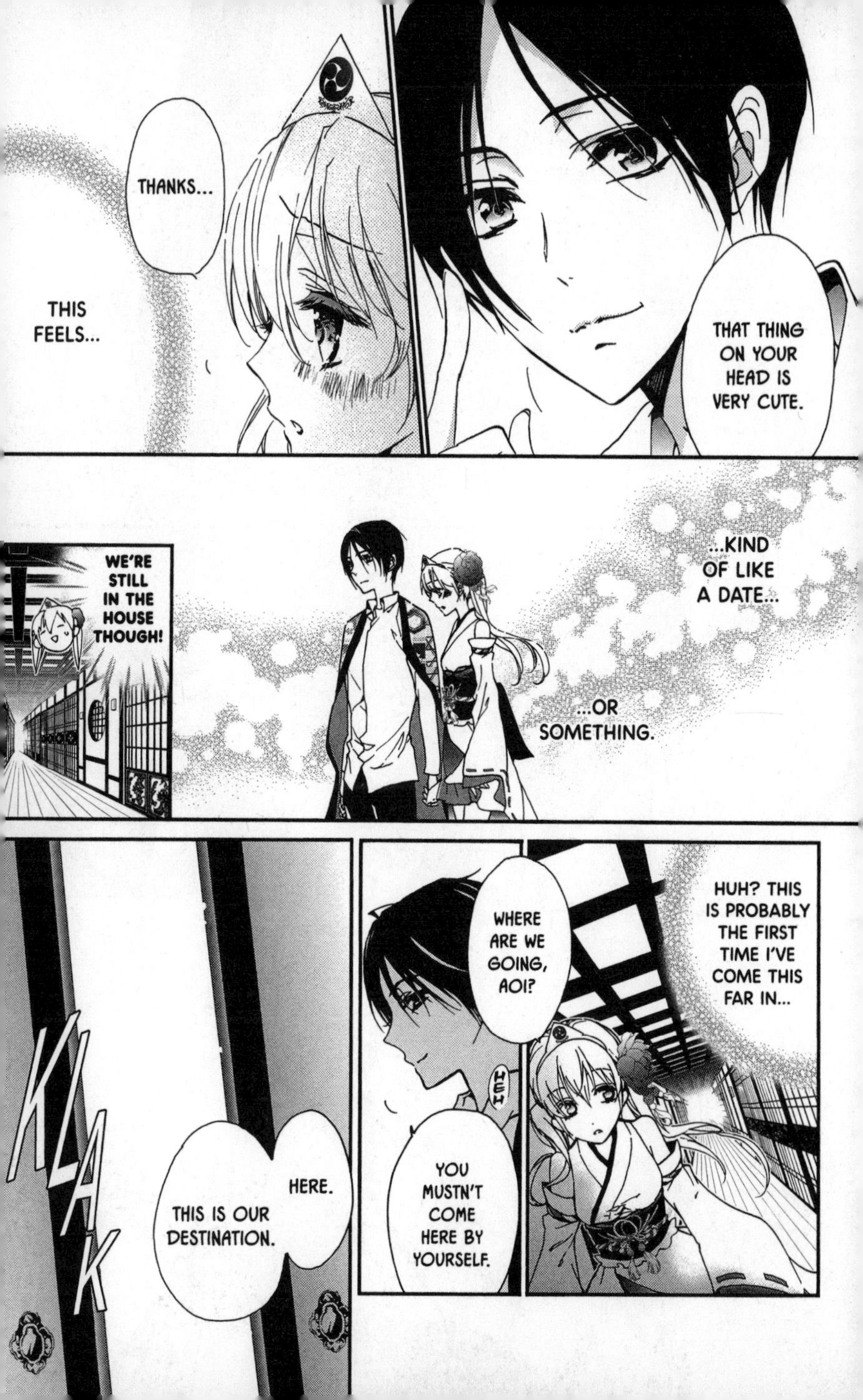
THAT THING ON YOUR HEAD IS VERY CUTE.
THANKS...
THIS FEELS...
...KIND OF LIKE A DATE...
...OR SOMETHING.
WE'RE STILL IN THE HOUSE THOUGH!
HUH? THIS IS PROBABLY THE FIRST TIME I'VE COME THIS FAR IN...
WHERE ARE WE GOING, AOI?
HEH
YOU MUSTN'T COME HERE BY YOURSELF.
HERE.
THIS IS OUR DESTINATION.
KLAK

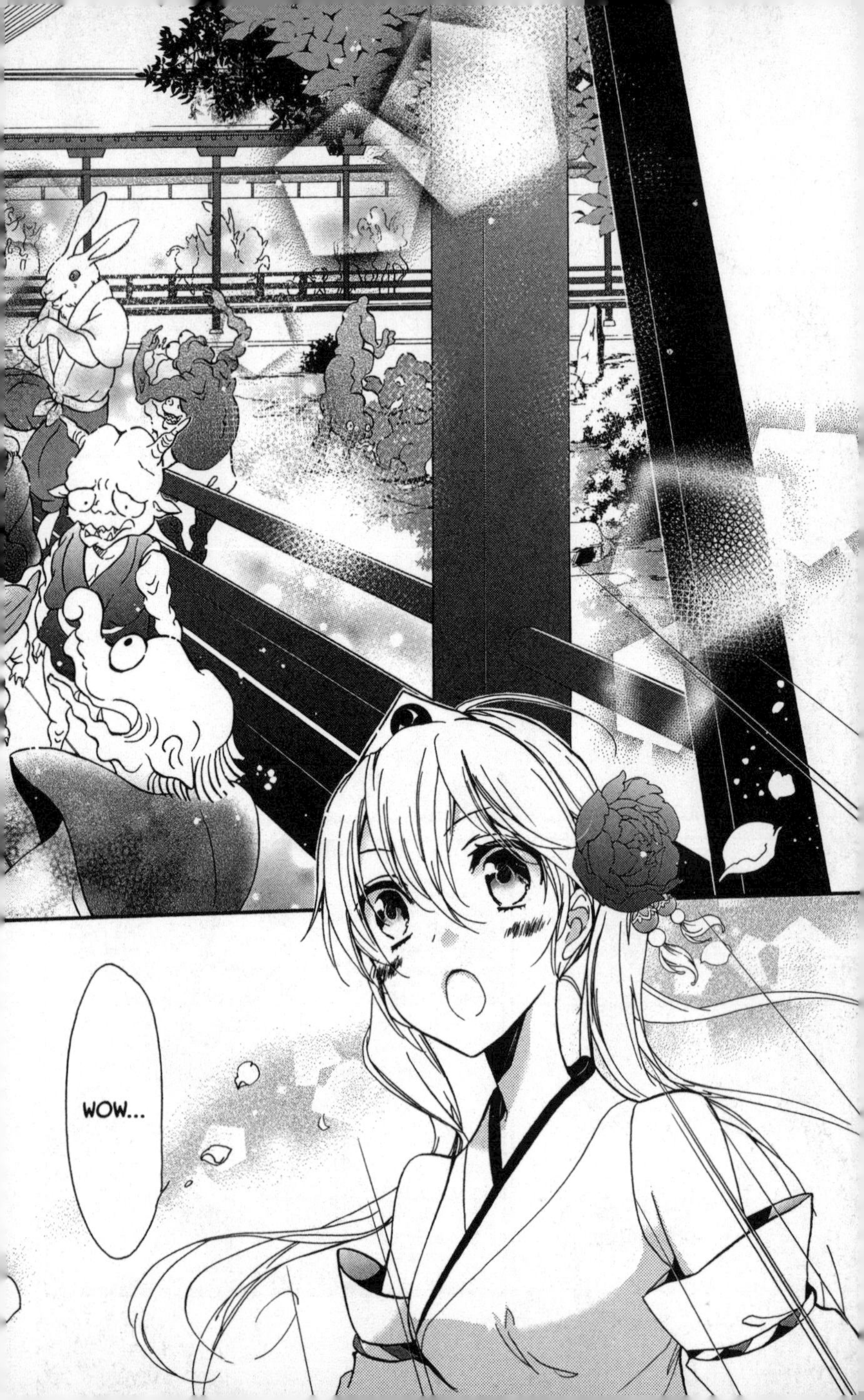
WOW...

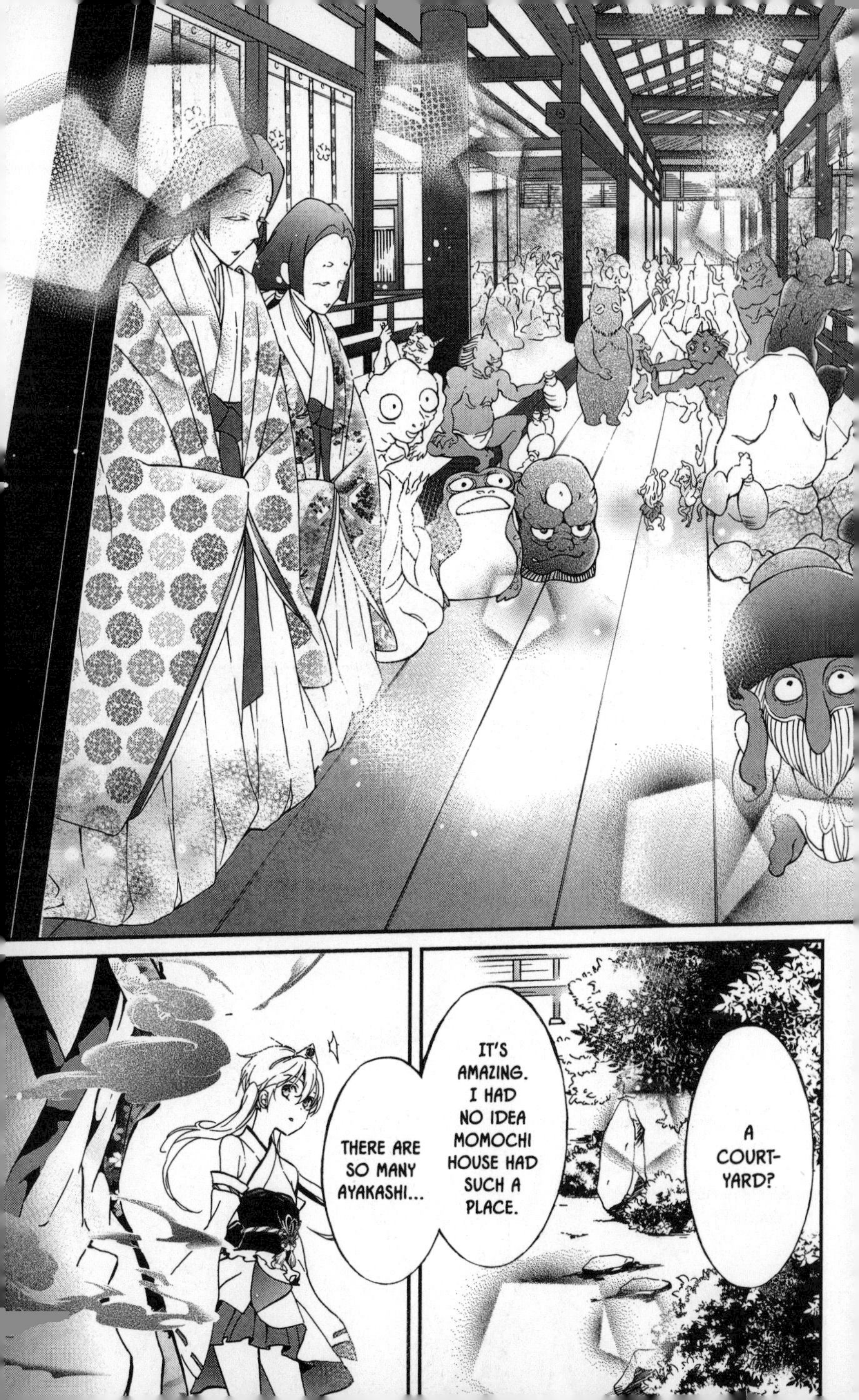
A COURTYARD?
IT'S AMAZING. I HAD NO IDEA MOMOCHI HOUSE HAD SUCH A PLACE.
THERE ARE SO MANY AYAKASHI...

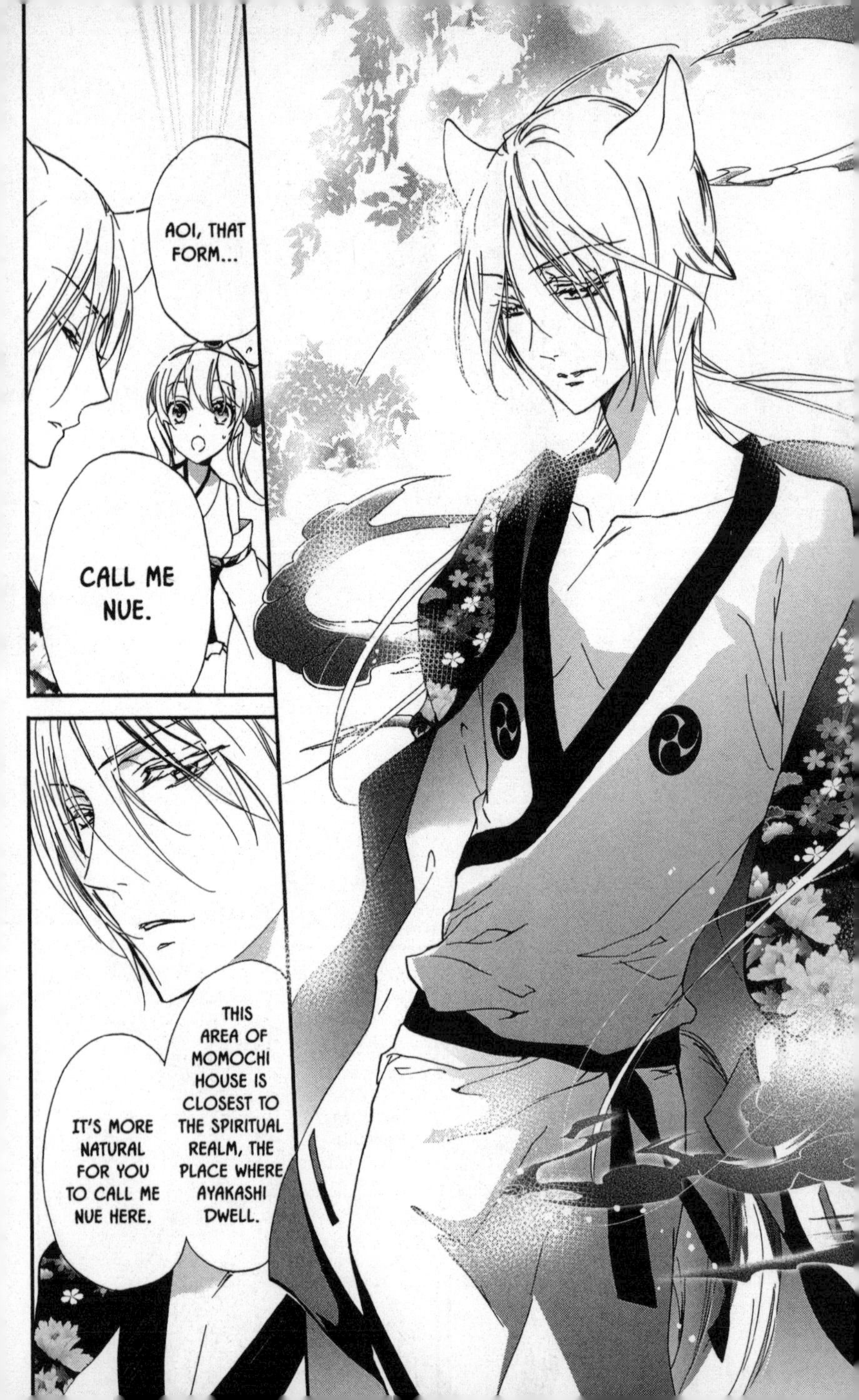
AOI, THAT FORM...
CALL ME NUE.
THIS AREA OF MOMOCHI HOUSE IS CLOSEST TO THE SPIRITUAL REALM, THE PLACE WHERE AYAKASHI DWELL.
IT'S MORE NATURAL FOR YOU TO CALL ME NUE HERE.

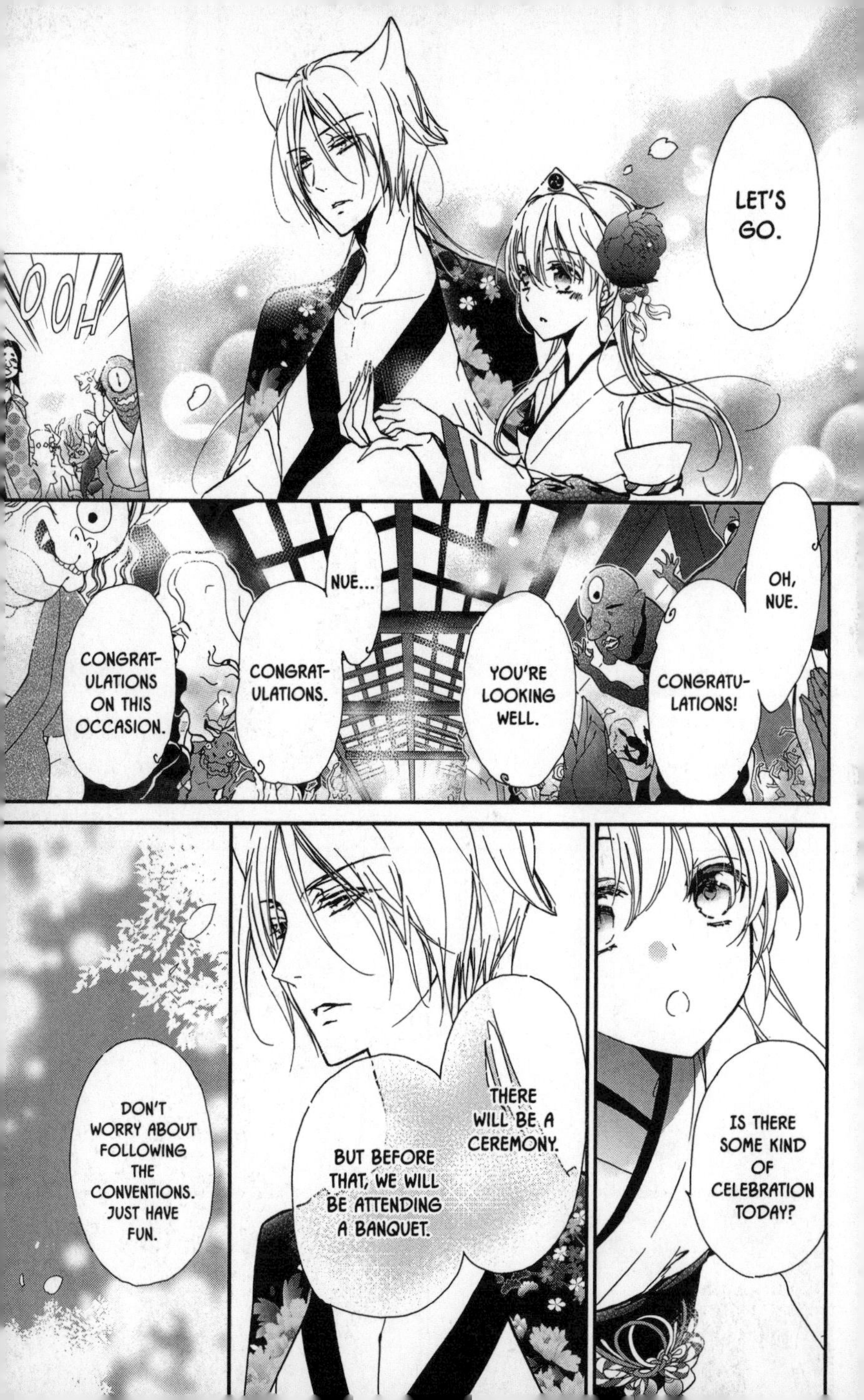
LET'S GO.
OOH
OH, NUE.
CONGRATU-LATIONS!
YOU'RE LOOKING WELL.
NUE...
CONGRAT-ULATIONS.
CONGRAT-ULATIONS ON THIS OCCASION.
IS THERE SOME KIND OF CELEBRATION TODAY?
THERE WILL BE A CEREMONY.
BUT BEFORE THAT, WE WILL BE ATTENDING A BANQUET.
DON'T WORRY ABOUT FOLLOWING THE CONVENTIONS. JUST HAVE FUN.

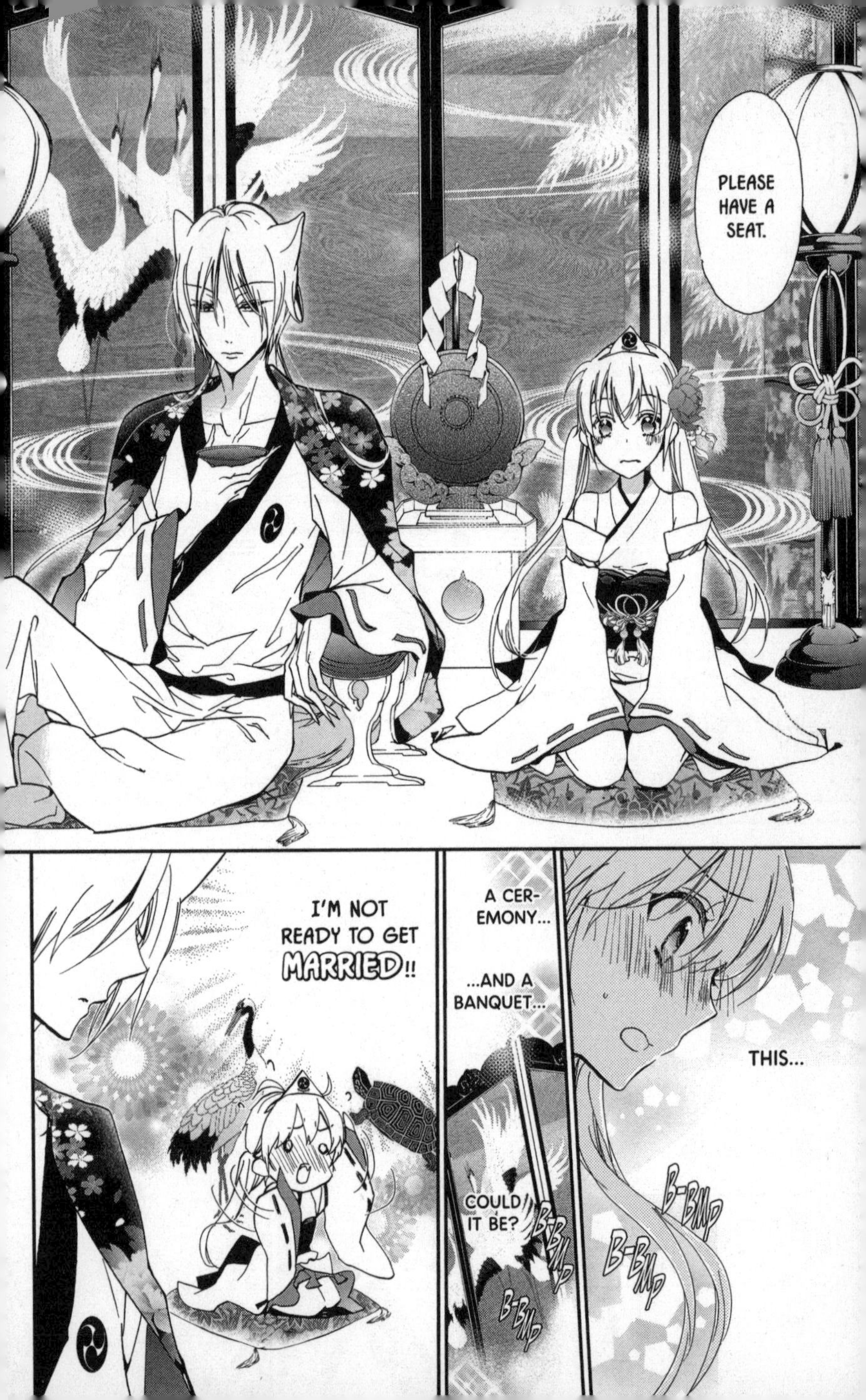
PLEASE HAVE A SEAT.
THIS...
B-BMP
B-BMP
A CER-EMONY...
...AND A BANQUET...
COULD IT BE?
B-BMP
B-BMP
I'M NOT READY TO GET MARRIED!!

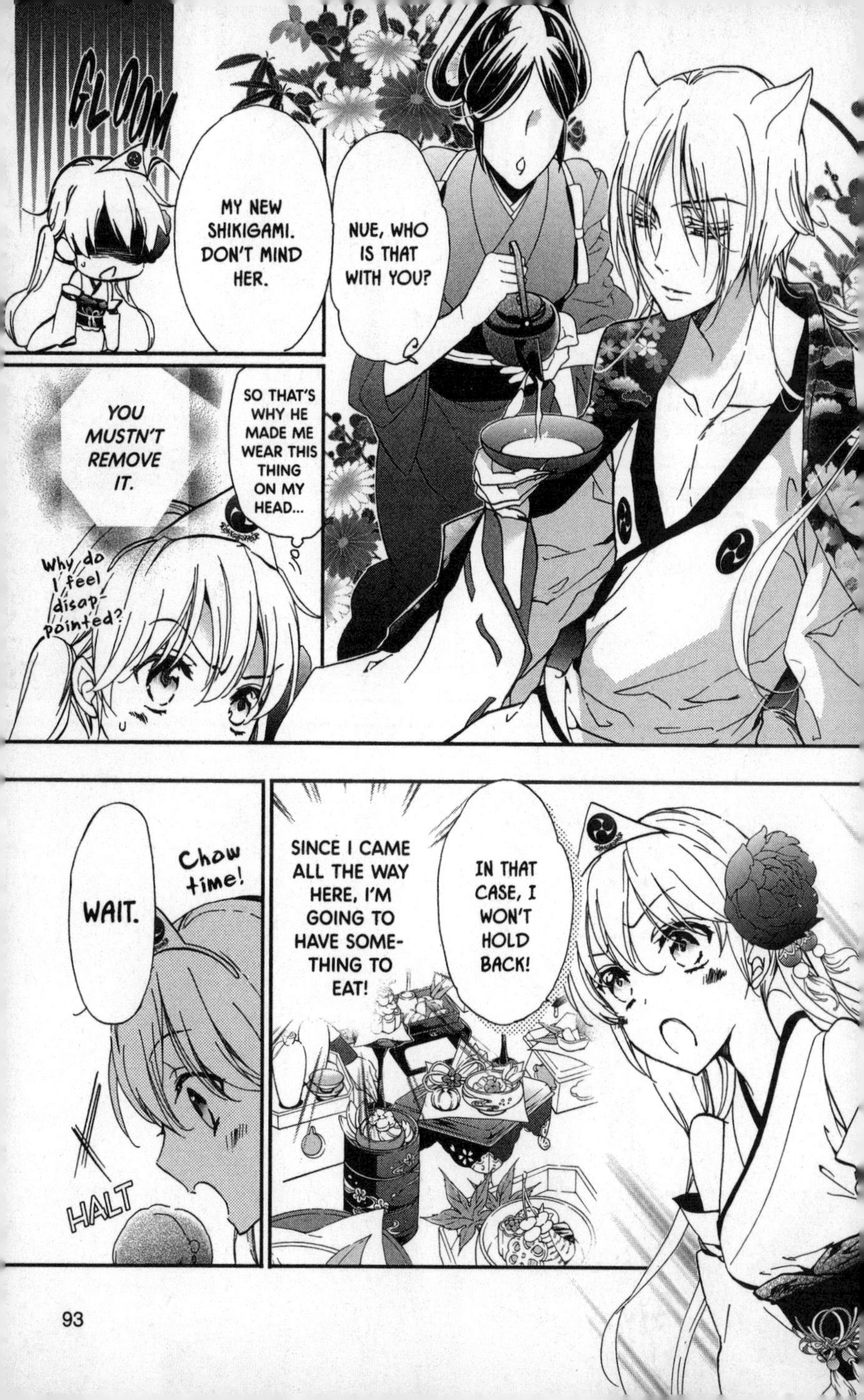
NUE, WHO IS THAT WITH YOU?
MY NEW SHIKIGAMI. DON'T MIND HER.
GLOOM
SO THAT'S WHY HE MADE ME WEAR THIS THING ON MY HEAD...
YOU MUSTN'T REMOVE IT.
Why do I feel disappointed?
IN THAT CASE, I WON'T HOLD BACK!
SINCE I CAME ALL THE WAY HERE, I'M GOING TO HAVE SOME-THING TO EAT!
Chow time!
WAIT.
HALT

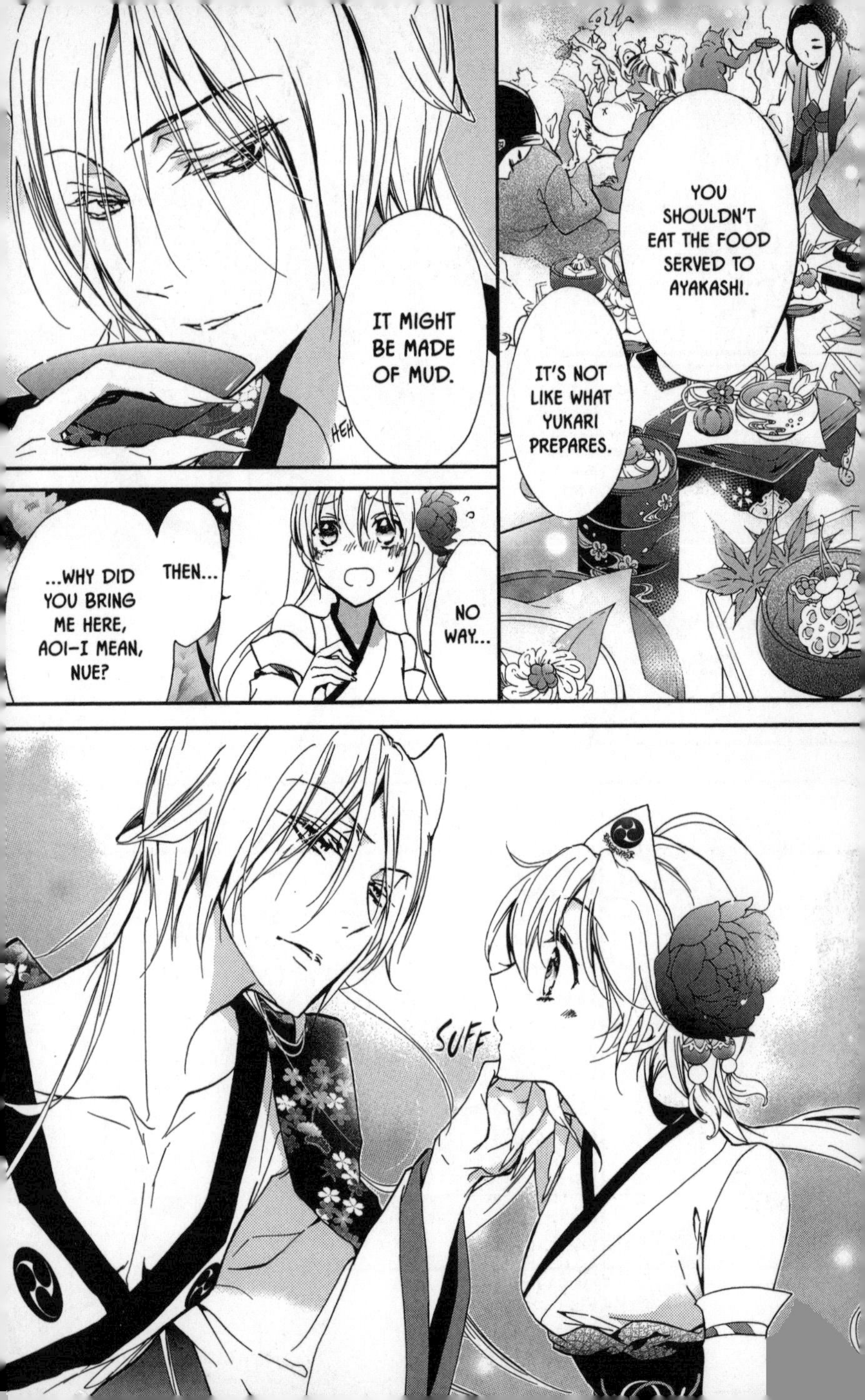
YOU SHOULDN'T EAT THE FOOD SERVED TO AYAKASHI.
IT'S NOT LIKE WHAT YUKARI PREPARES.
HEH
IT MIGHT BE MADE OF MUD.
NO WAY...
THEN...
...WHY DID YOU BRING ME HERE, AOI—I MEAN, NUE?
SUFF

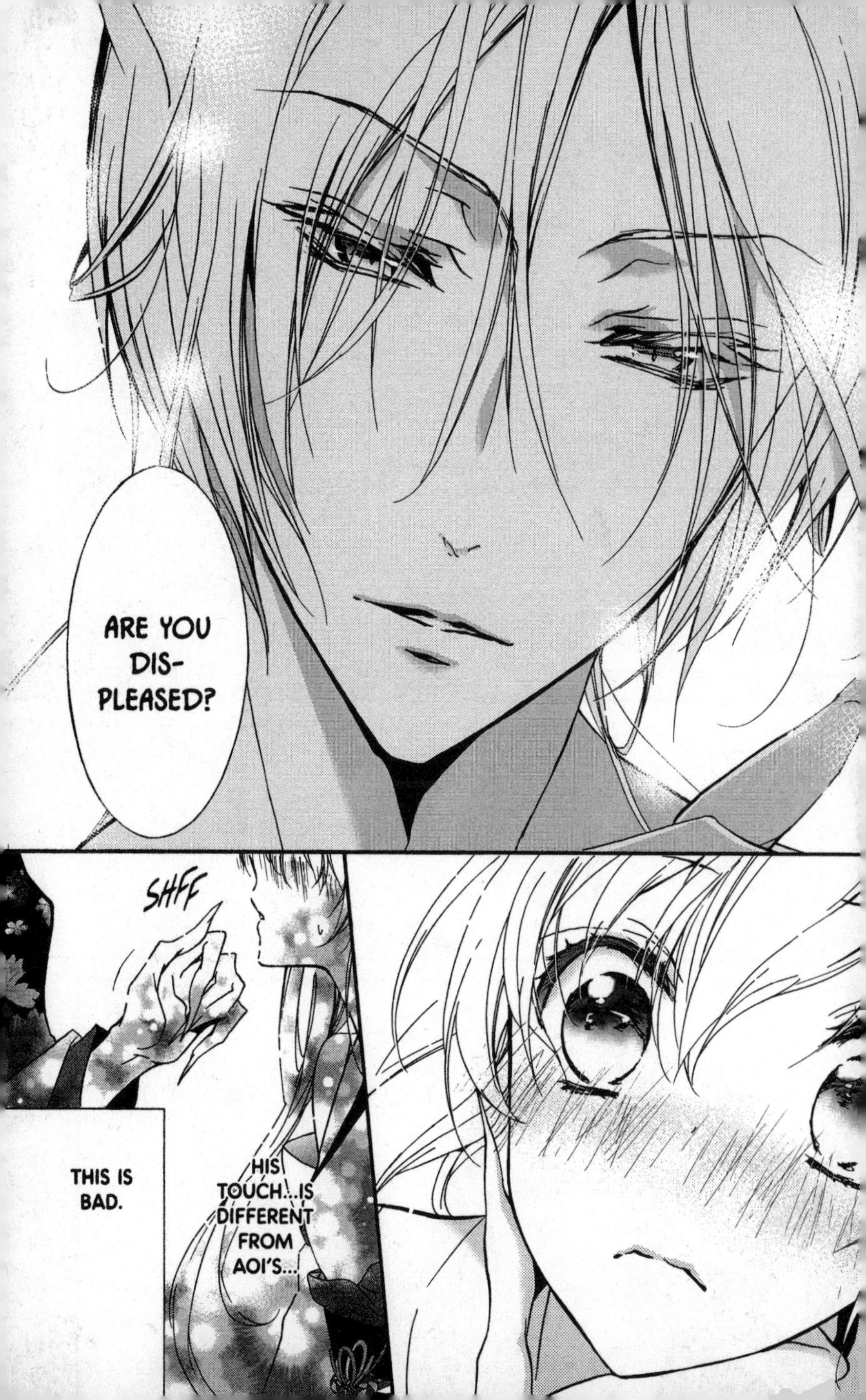
ARE YOU DIS-PLEASED?
SHFF
HIS TOUCH...IS DIFFERENT FROM AOI'S...
THIS IS BAD.

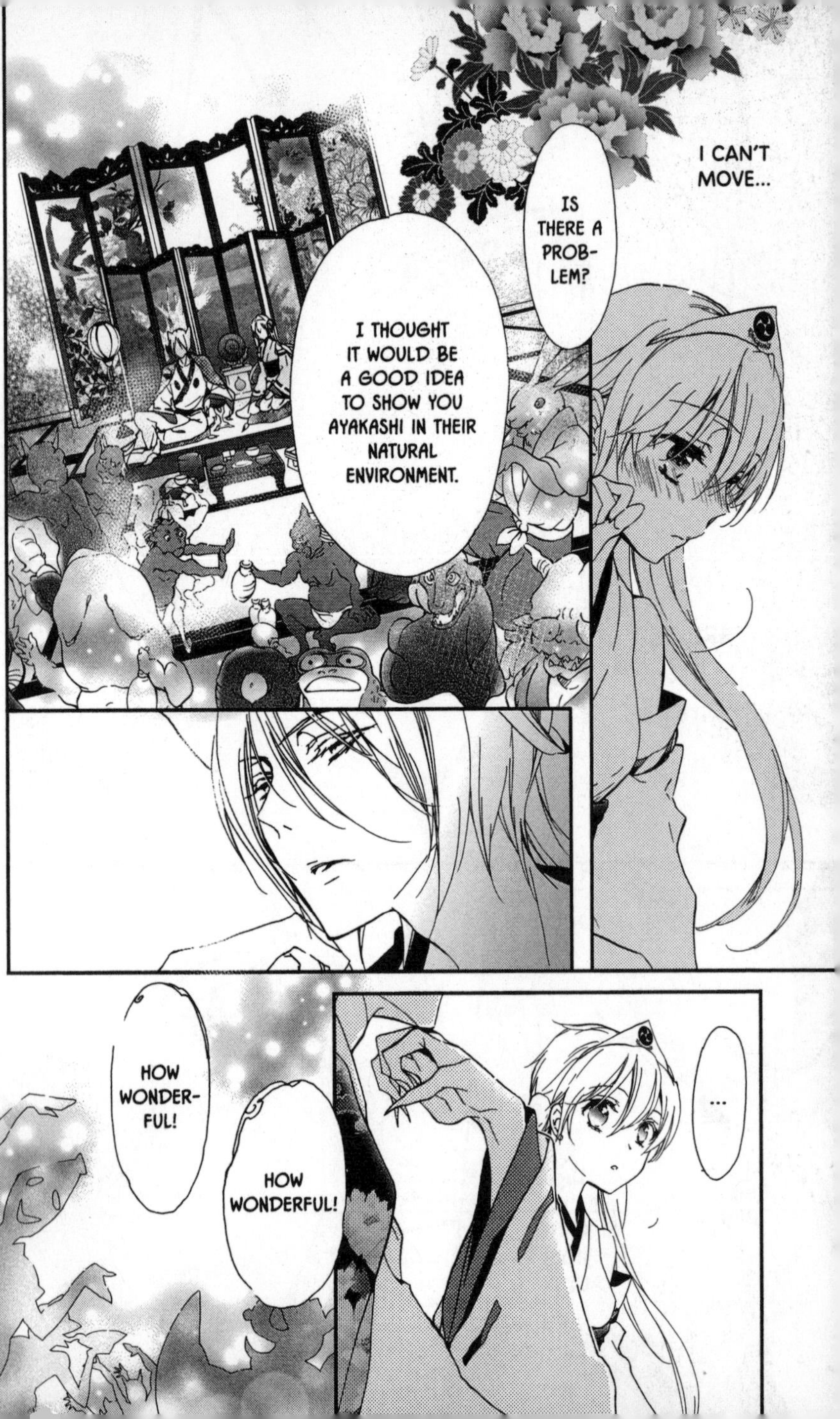
I CAN'T MOVE...
IS THERE A PROB-LEM?
I THOUGHT IT WOULD BE A GOOD IDEA TO SHOW YOU AYAKASHI IN THEIR NATURAL ENVIRONMENT.
...
HOW WONDERFUL!
HOW WONDER-FUL!

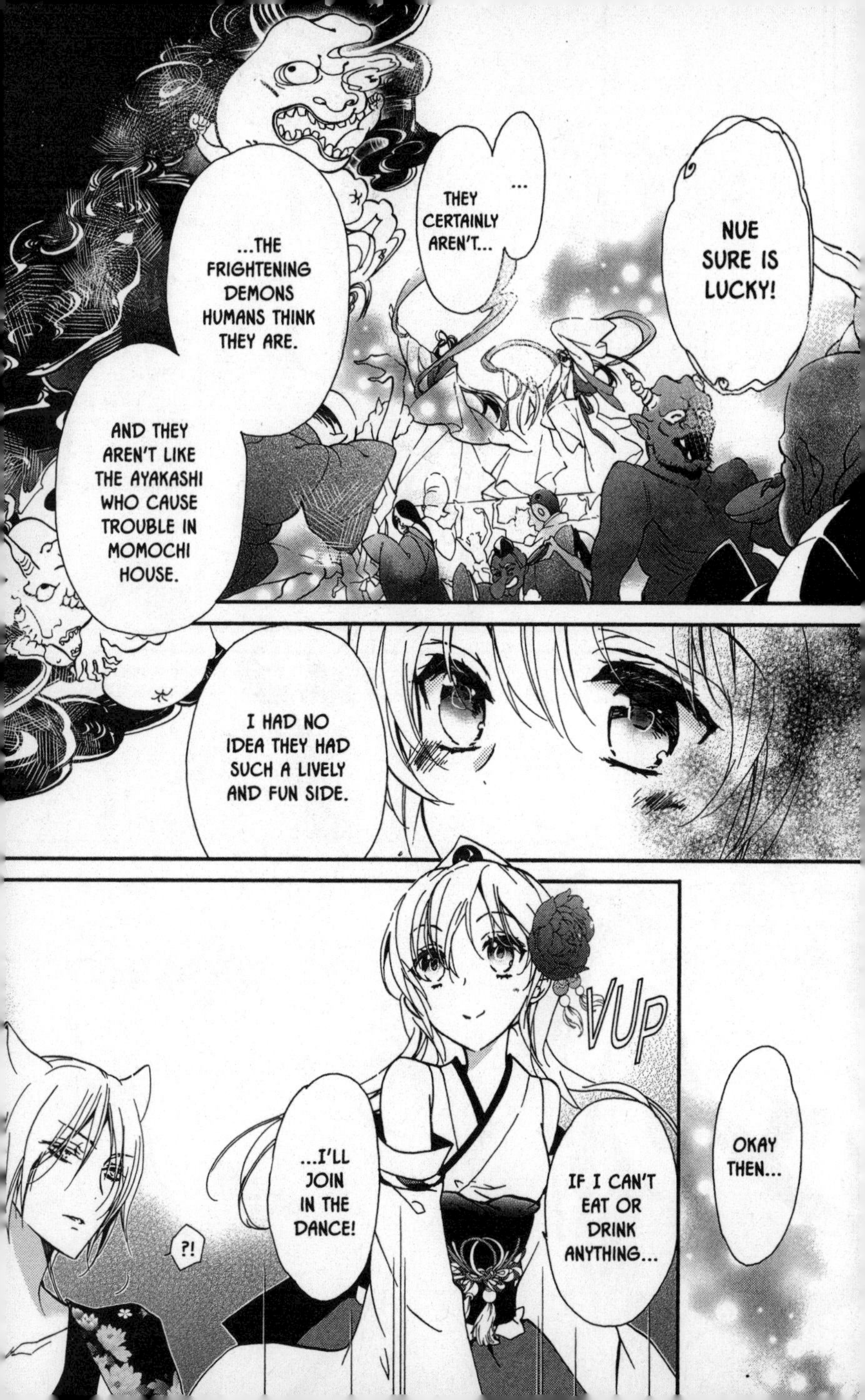
NUE SURE IS LUCKY!
... THEY CERTAINLY AREN'T...
...THE FRIGHTENING DEMONS HUMANS THINK THEY ARE.
AND THEY AREN'T LIKE THE AYAKASHI WHO CAUSE TROUBLE IN MOMOCHI HOUSE.
I HAD NO IDEA THEY HAD SUCH A LIVELY AND FUN SIDE.
OKAY THEN...
IF I CAN'T EAT OR DRINK ANYTHING...
VUP
...I'LL JOIN IN THE DANCE!
?!

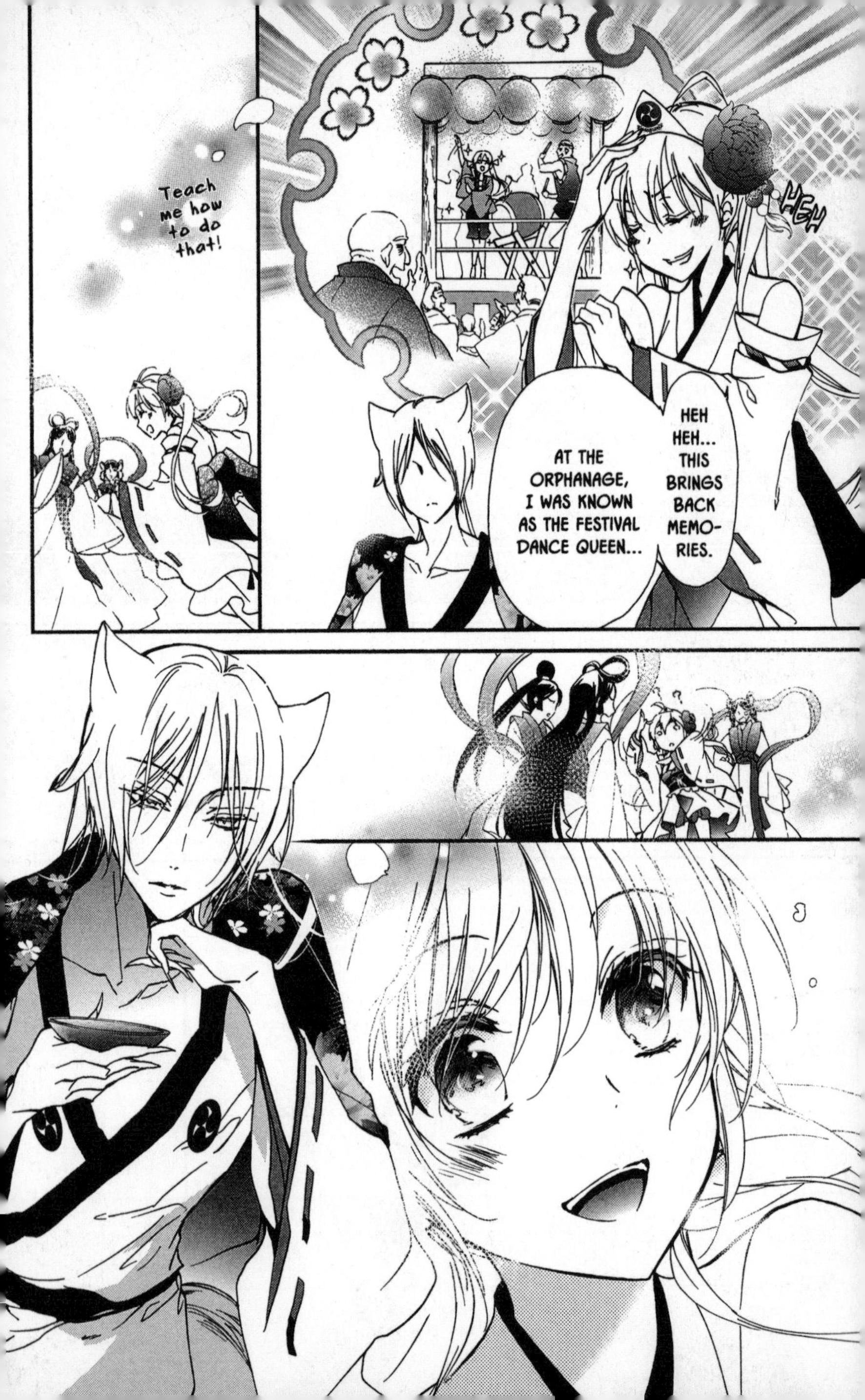
HEH
HEH HEH... THIS BRINGS BACK MEMORIES.
AT THE ORPHANAGE, I WAS KNOWN AS THE FESTIVAL DANCE QUEEN...
Teach me how to do that!

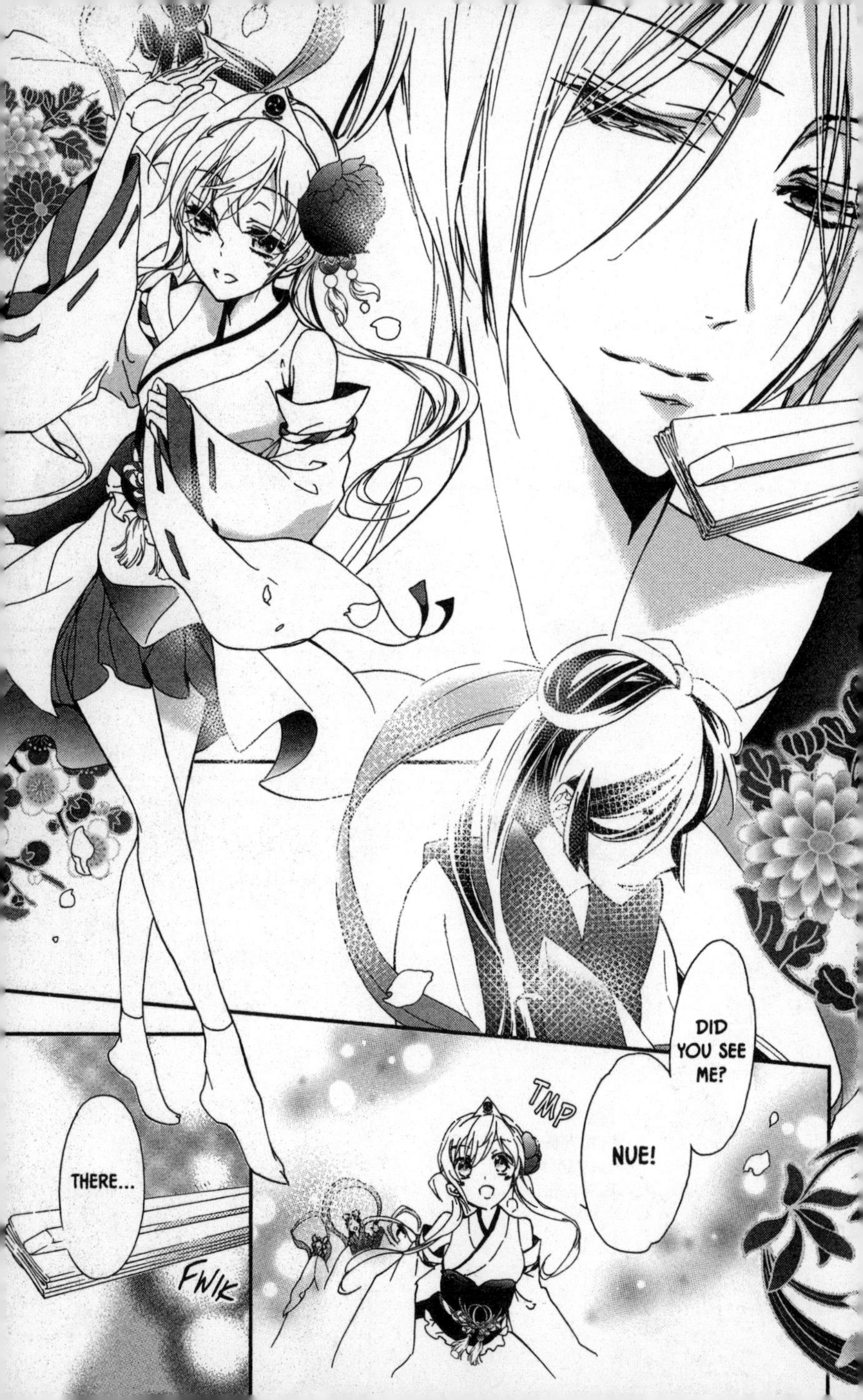
DID YOU SEE ME?
TMP
NUE!
THERE...
FWIK

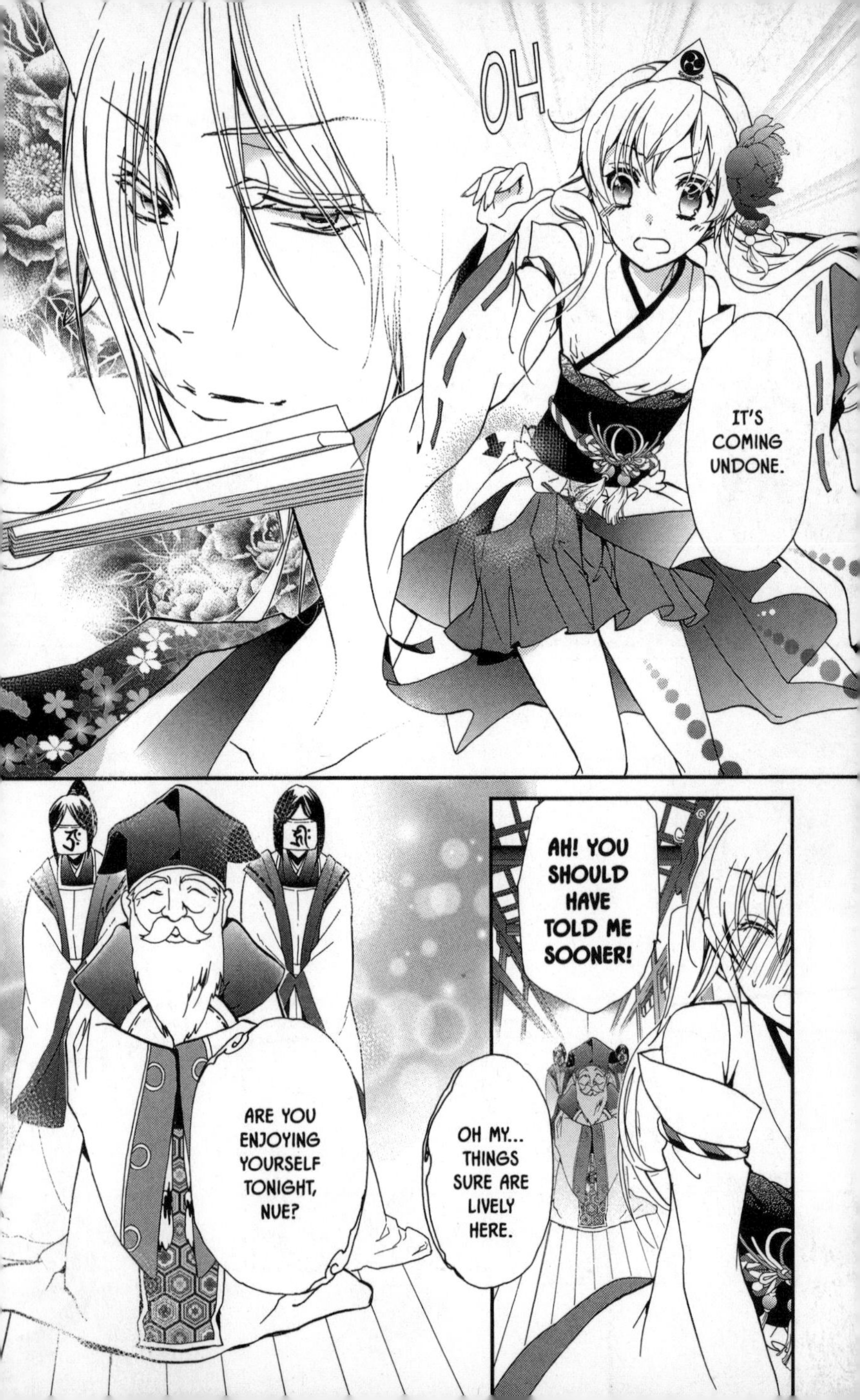
OH
IT'S COMING UNDONE.
AH! YOU SHOULD HAVE TOLD ME SOONER!
OH MY... THINGS SURE ARE LIVELY HERE.
ARE YOU ENJOYING YOURSELF TONIGHT, NUE?

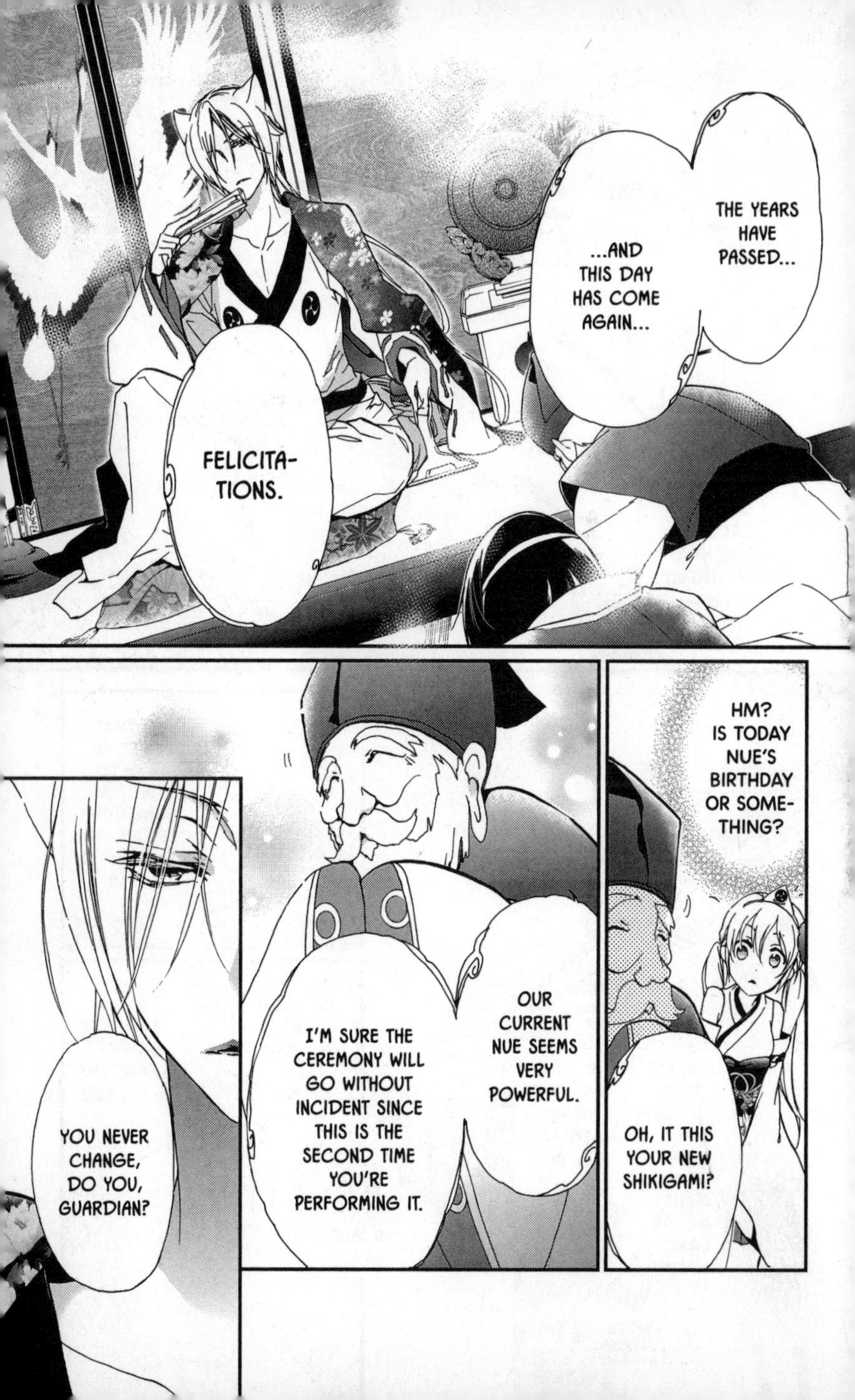
THE YEARS HAVE PASSED...
...AND THIS DAY HAS COME AGAIN...
FELICITA-TIONS.
HM? IS TODAY NUE'S BIRTHDAY OR SOME-THING?
OH, IT THIS YOUR NEW SHIKIGAMI?
OUR CURRENT NUE SEEMS VERY POWERFUL.
I'M SURE THE CEREMONY WILL GO WITHOUT INCIDENT SINCE THIS IS THE SECOND TIME YOU'RE PERFORMING IT.
YOU NEVER CHANGE, DO YOU, GUARDIAN?

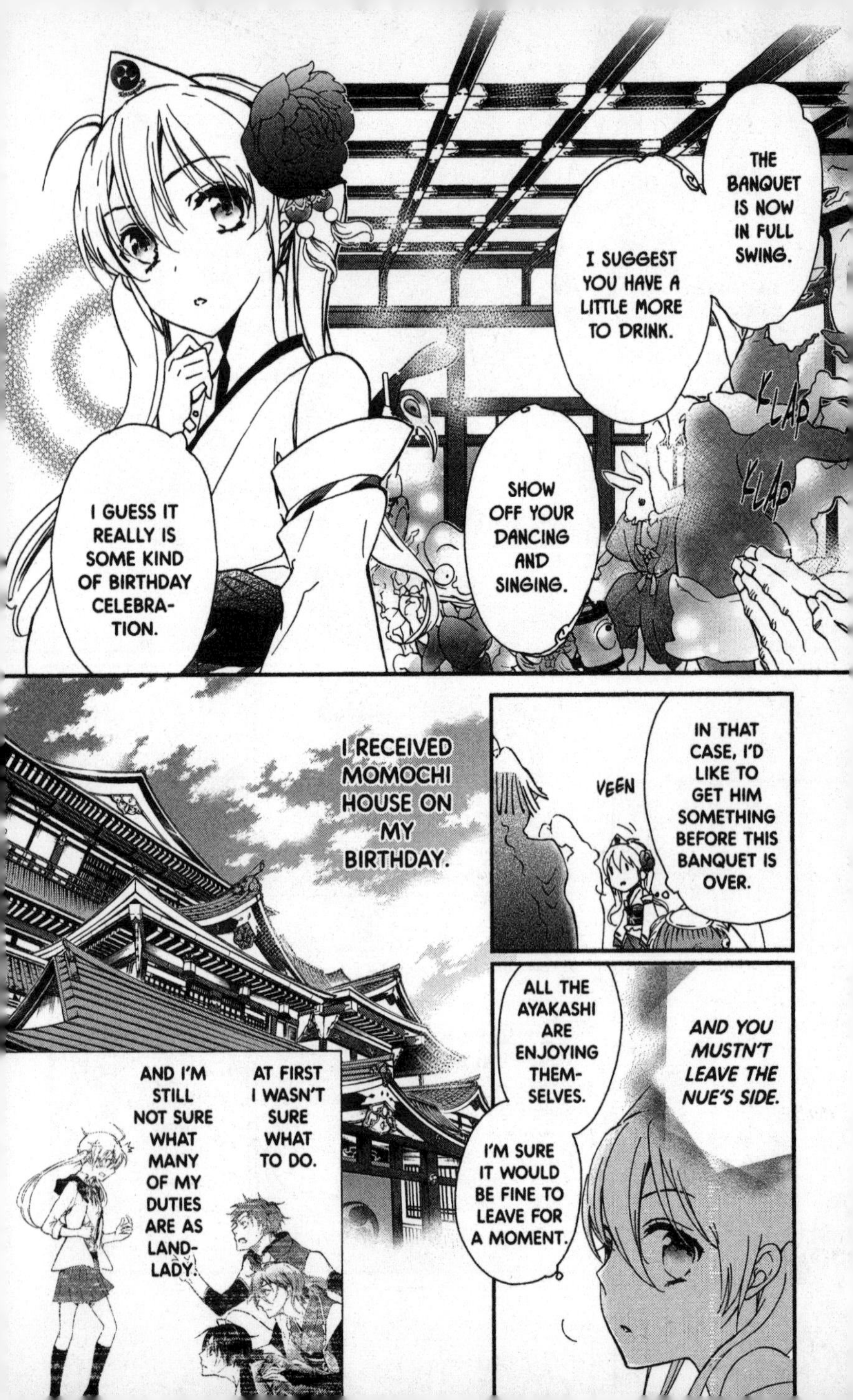
THE BANQUET IS NOW IN FULL SWING.
I SUGGEST YOU HAVE A LITTLE MORE TO DRINK.
KLAP
KLAP
SHOW OFF YOUR DANCING AND SINGING.
I GUESS IT REALLY IS SOME KIND OF BIRTHDAY CELEBRA-TION.
IN THAT CASE, I'D LIKE TO GET HIM SOMETHING BEFORE THIS BANQUET IS OVER.
VEEN
AND YOU MUSTN'T LEAVE THE NUE'S SIDE.
ALL THE AYAKASHI ARE ENJOYING THEM-SELVES.
I'M SURE IT WOULD BE FINE TO LEAVE FOR A MOMENT.
I RECEIVED MOMOCHI HOUSE ON MY BIRTHDAY.
AT FIRST I WASN'T SURE WHAT TO DO.
AND I'M STILL NOT SURE WHAT MANY OF MY DUTIES ARE AS LAND-LADY.

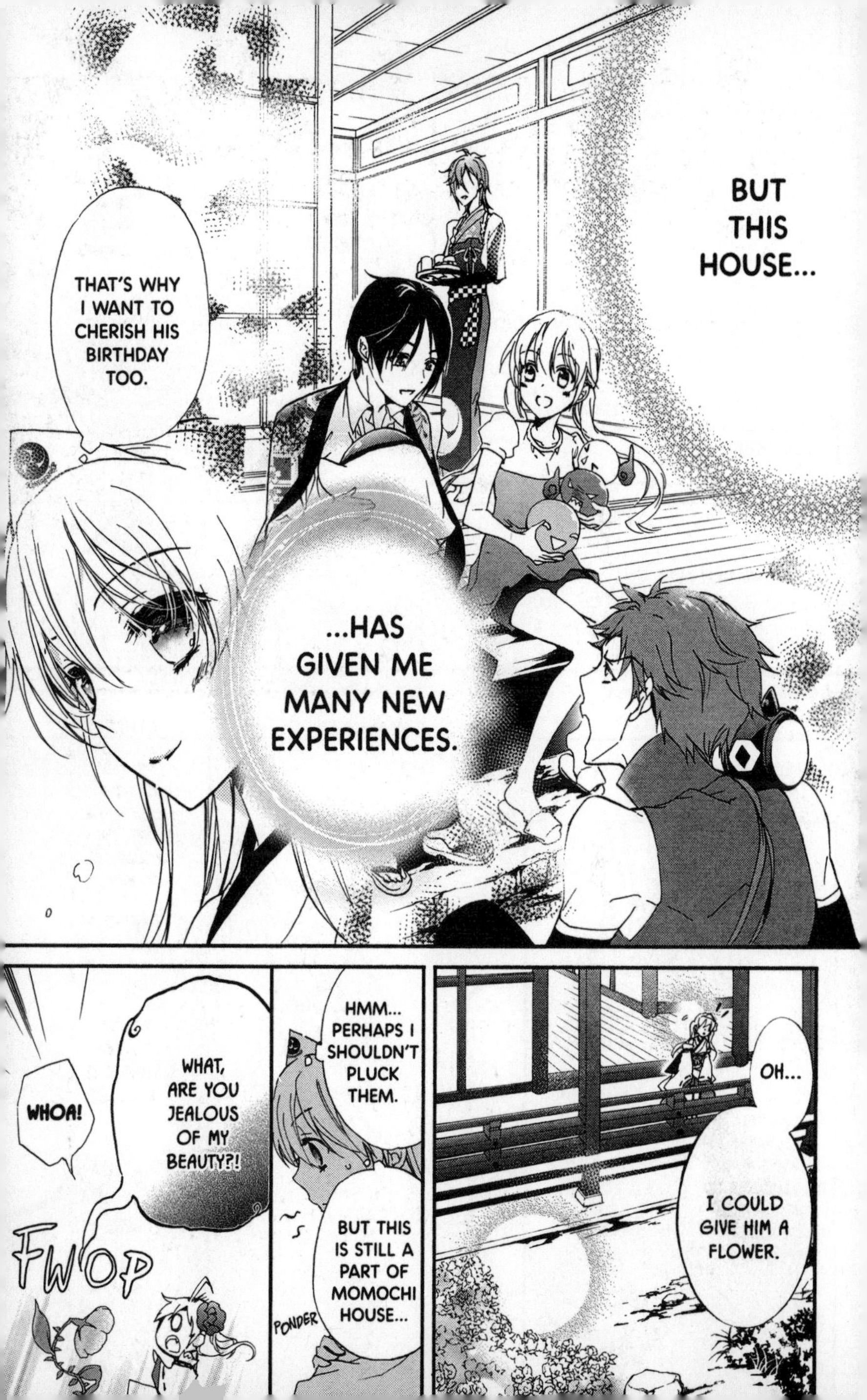
BUT THIS HOUSE...
...HAS GIVEN ME MANY NEW EXPERIENCES.
THAT'S WHY I WANT TO CHERISH HIS BIRTHDAY TOO.
OH...
I COULD GIVE HIM A FLOWER.
HMM... PERHAPS I SHOULDN'T PLUCK THEM.
BUT THIS IS STILL A PART OF MOMOCHI HOUSE...
PONDER
WHOA!
WHAT, ARE YOU JEALOUS OF MY BEAUTY?!
FWOP

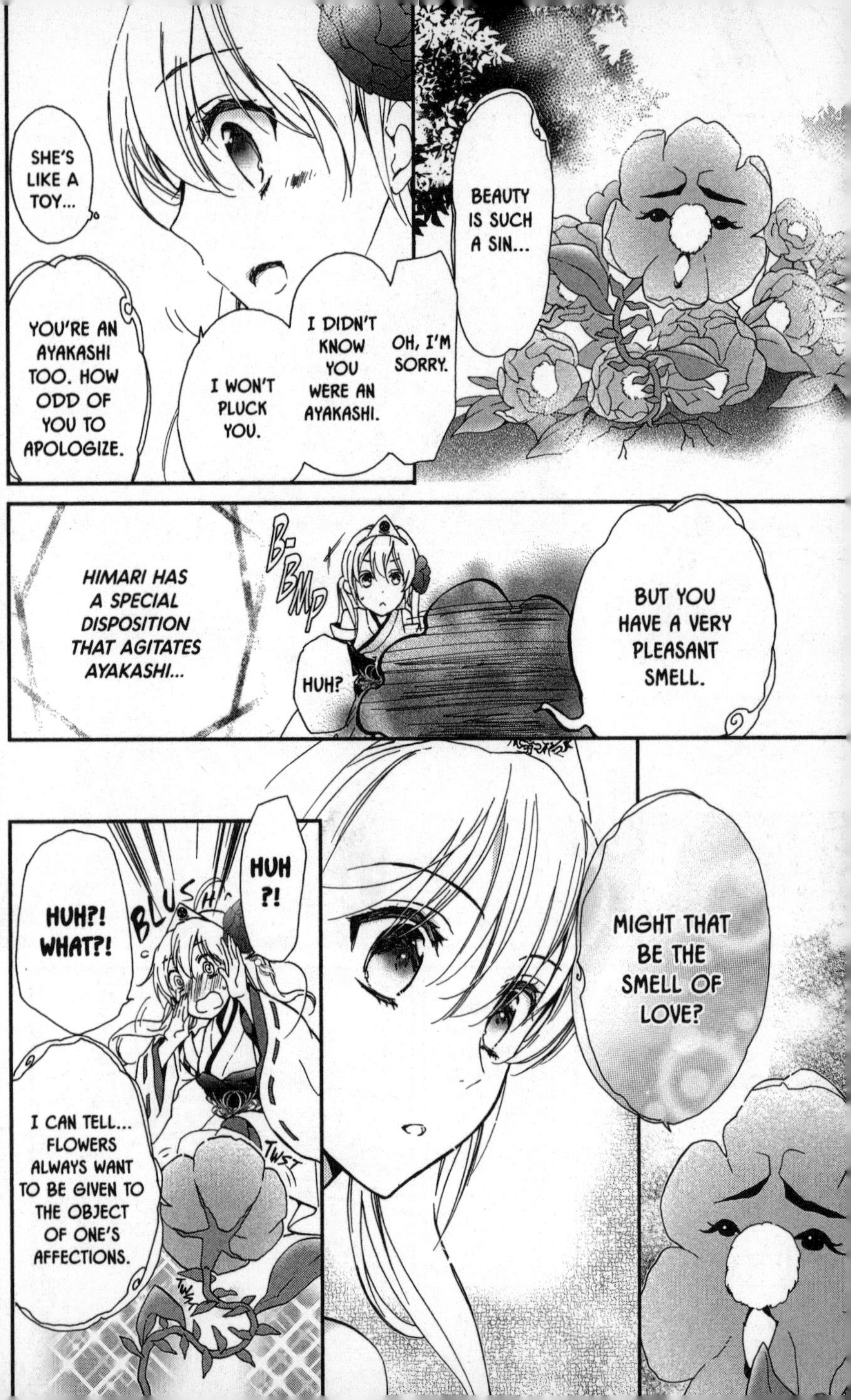
BEAUTY IS SUCH A SIN...
OH, I'M SORRY.
I DIDN'T KNOW YOU WERE AN AYAKASHI.
I WON'T PLUCK YOU.
SHE'S LIKE A TOY...
YOU'RE AN AYAKASHI TOO. HOW ODD OF YOU TO APOLOGIZE.
BUT YOU HAVE A VERY PLEASANT SMELL.
B-BMP
HUH?
HIMARI HAS A SPECIAL DISPOSITION THAT AGITATES AYAKASHI...
MIGHT THAT BE THE SMELL OF LOVE?
HUH ?!
BLUSH
HUH?! WHAT?!
TWIST
I CAN TELL... FLOWERS ALWAYS WANT TO BE GIVEN TO THE OBJECT OF ONE'S AFFECTIONS.

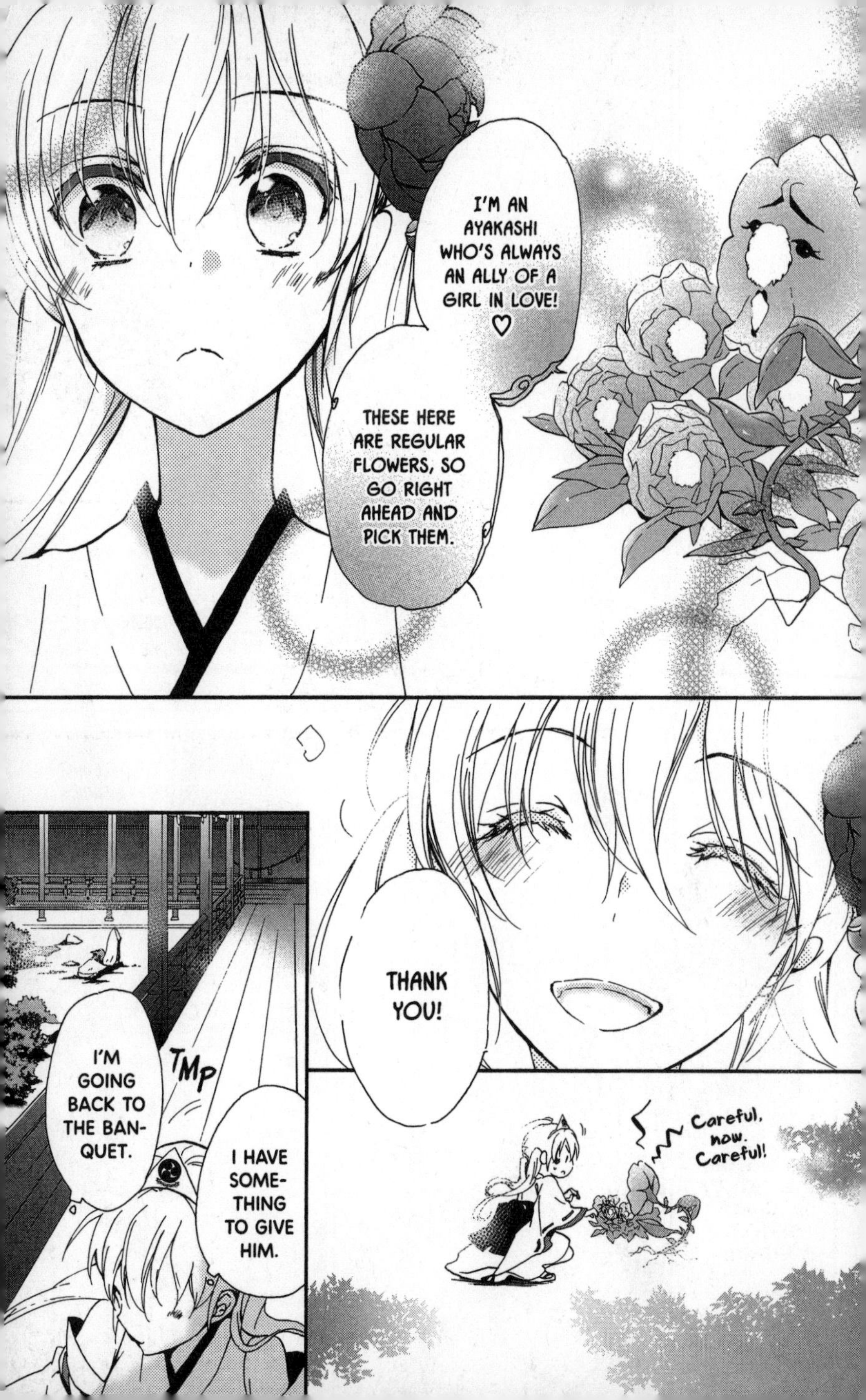
I'M AN AYAKASHI WHO'S ALWAYS AN ALLY OF A GIRL IN LOVE! ♡
THESE HERE ARE REGULAR FLOWERS, SO GO RIGHT AHEAD AND PICK THEM.
THANK YOU!
Careful, now. Careful!
TMP
I'M GOING BACK TO THE BAN-QUET.
I HAVE SOME-THING TO GIVE HIM.

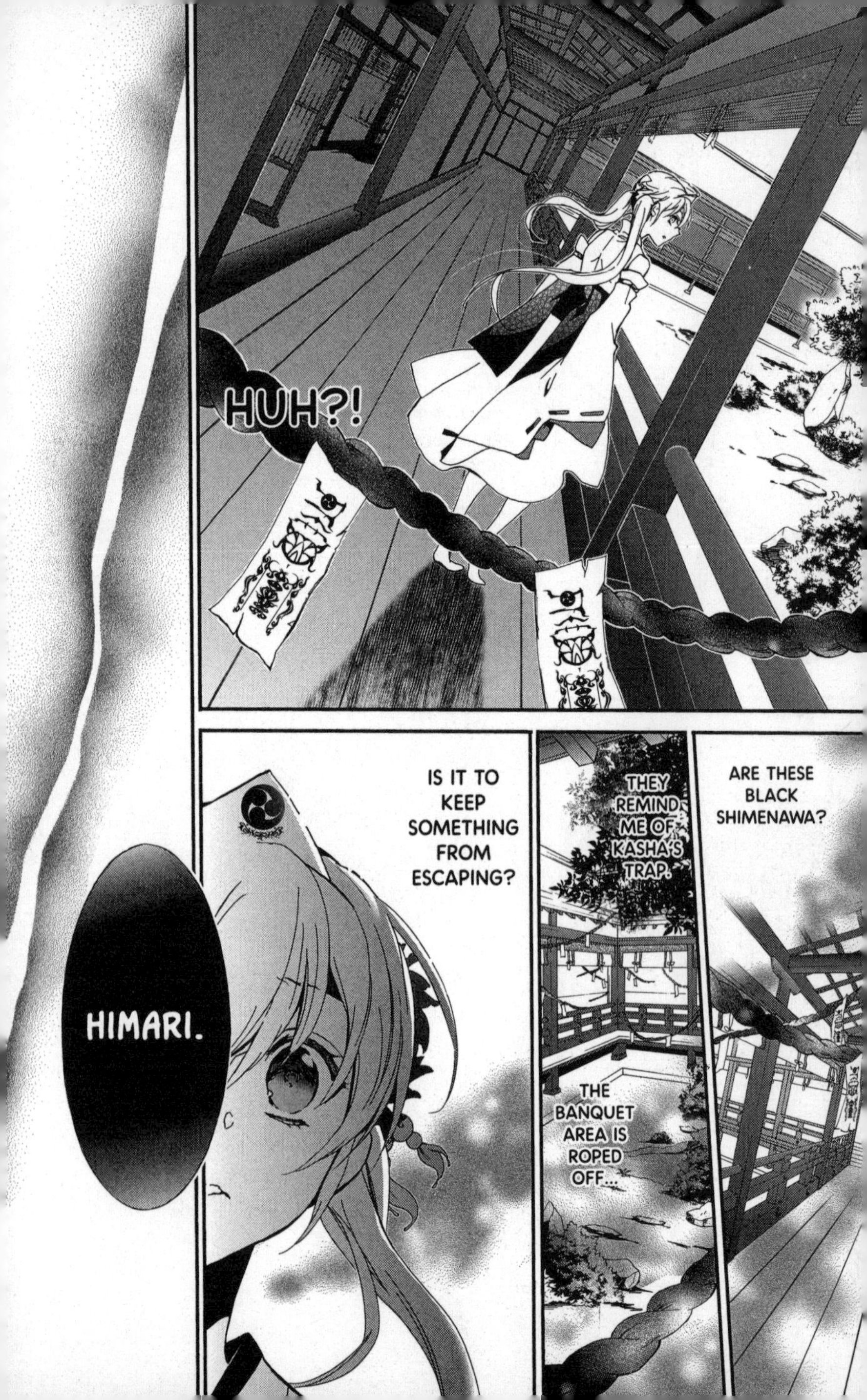
HUH?!
ARE THESE BLACK SHIMENAWA?
THEY REMIND ME OF KASHA'S TRAP.
THE BANQUET AREA IS ROPED OFF...
IS IT TO KEEP SOMETHING FROM ESCAPING?
HIMARI.

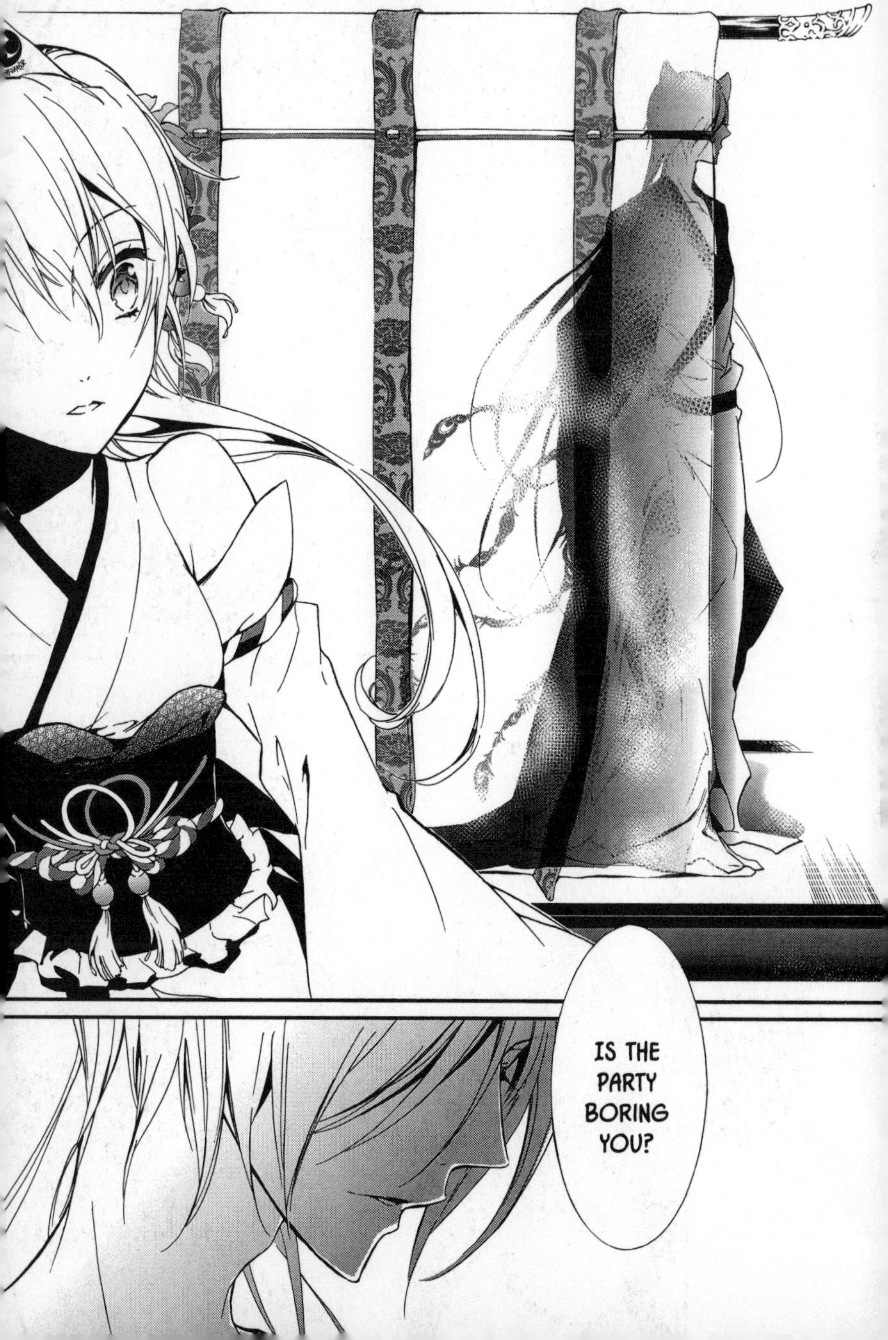
IS THE PARTY BORING YOU?

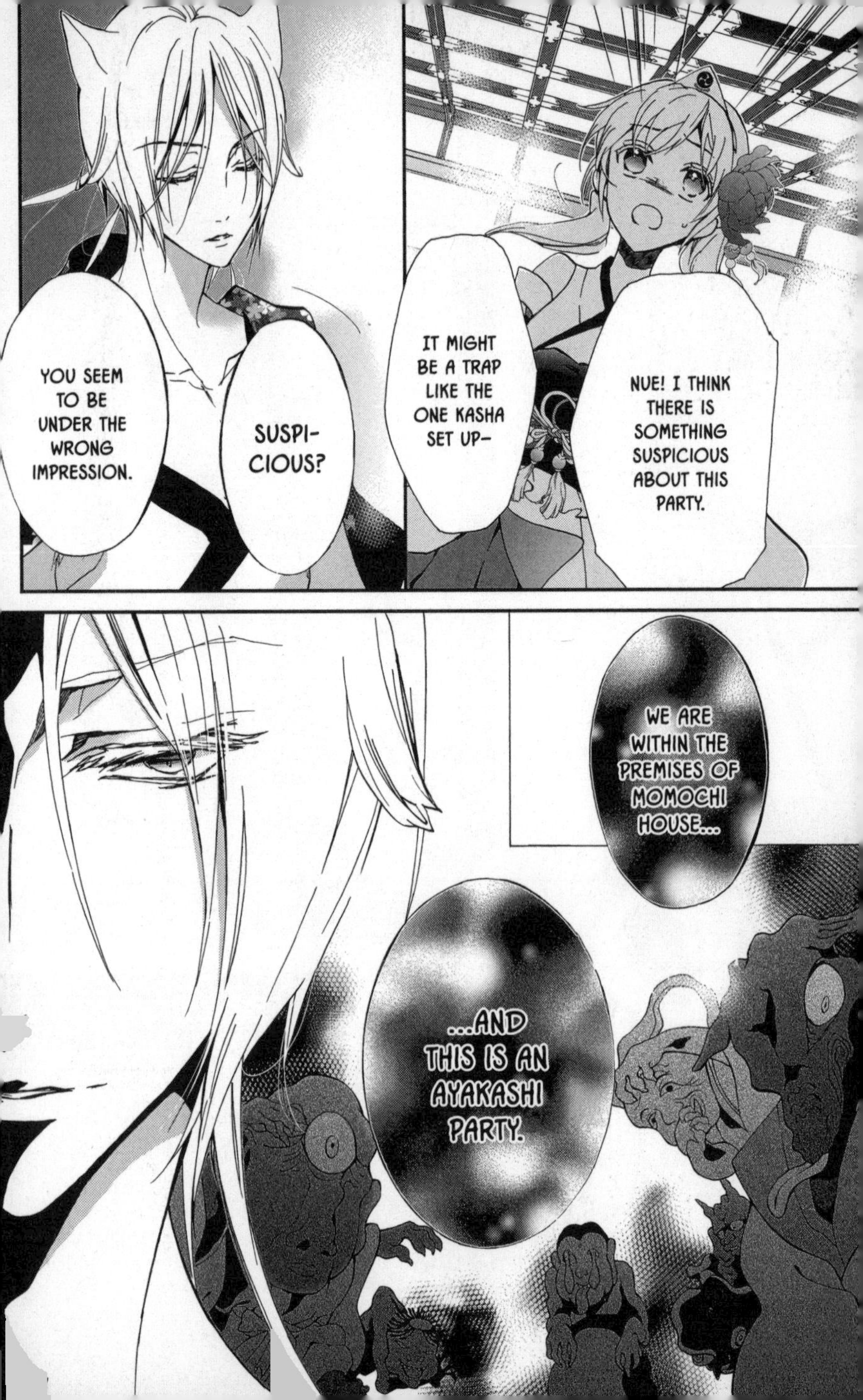
NUE! I THINK THERE IS SOMETHING SUSPICIOUS ABOUT THIS PARTY.
IT MIGHT BE A TRAP LIKE THE ONE KASHA SET UP–
SUSPI-CIOUS?
YOU SEEM TO BE UNDER THE WRONG IMPRESSION.
WE ARE WITHIN THE PREMISES OF MOMOCHI HOUSE...
...AND THIS IS AN AYAKASHI PARTY.

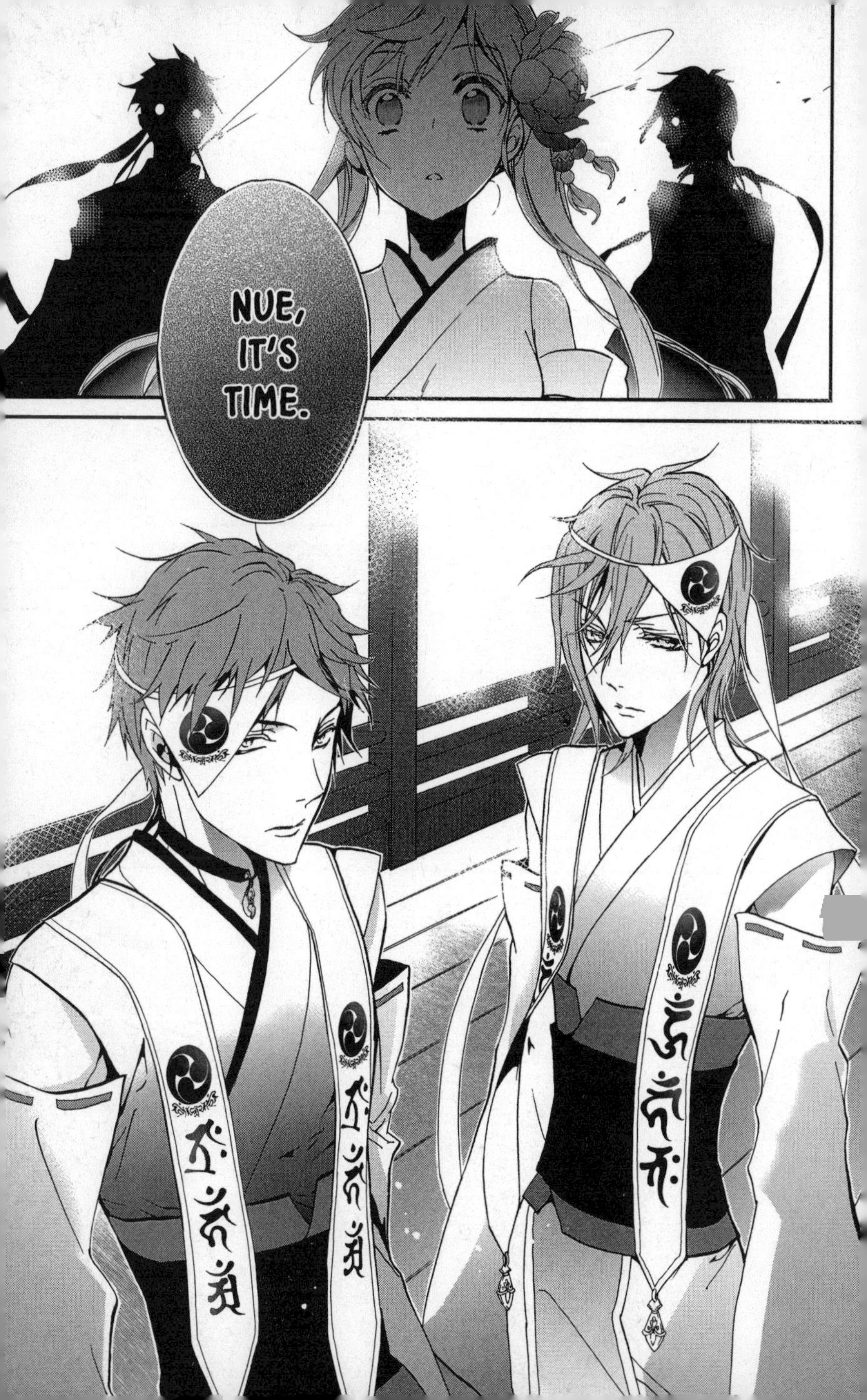
NUE, IT'S TIME.

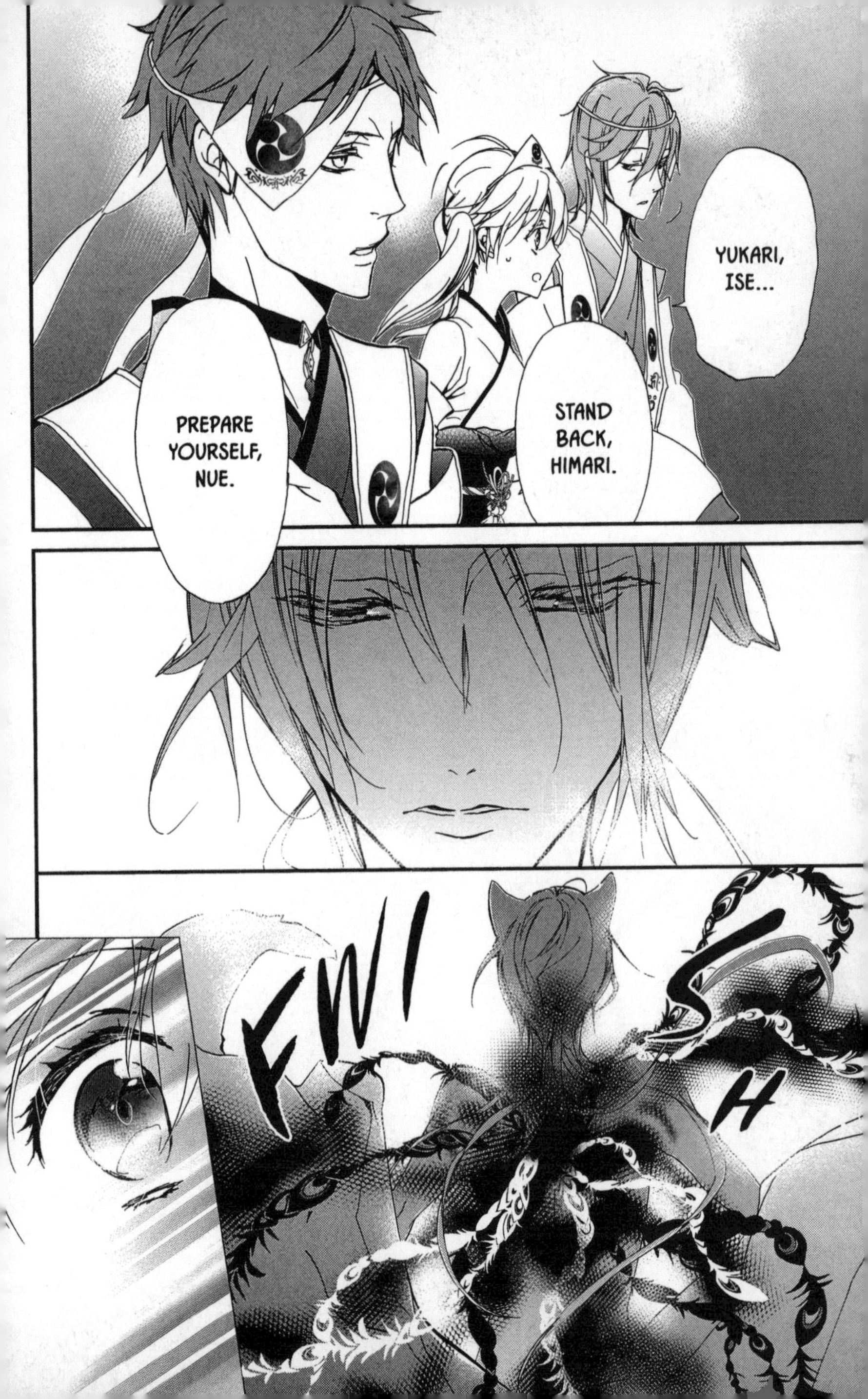
YUKARI, ISE...
STAND BACK, HIMARI.
PREPARE YOURSELF, NUE.
FWISH

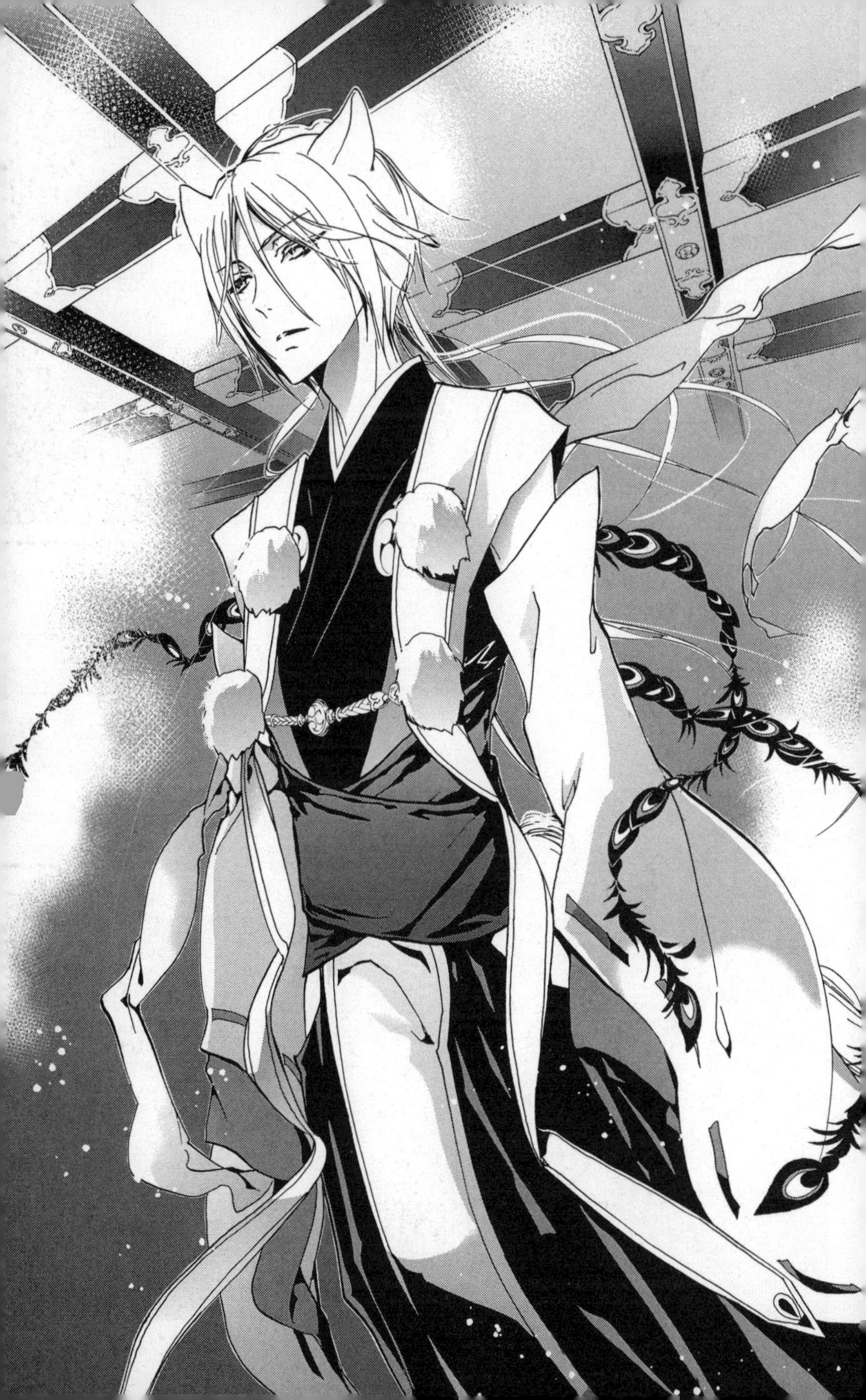

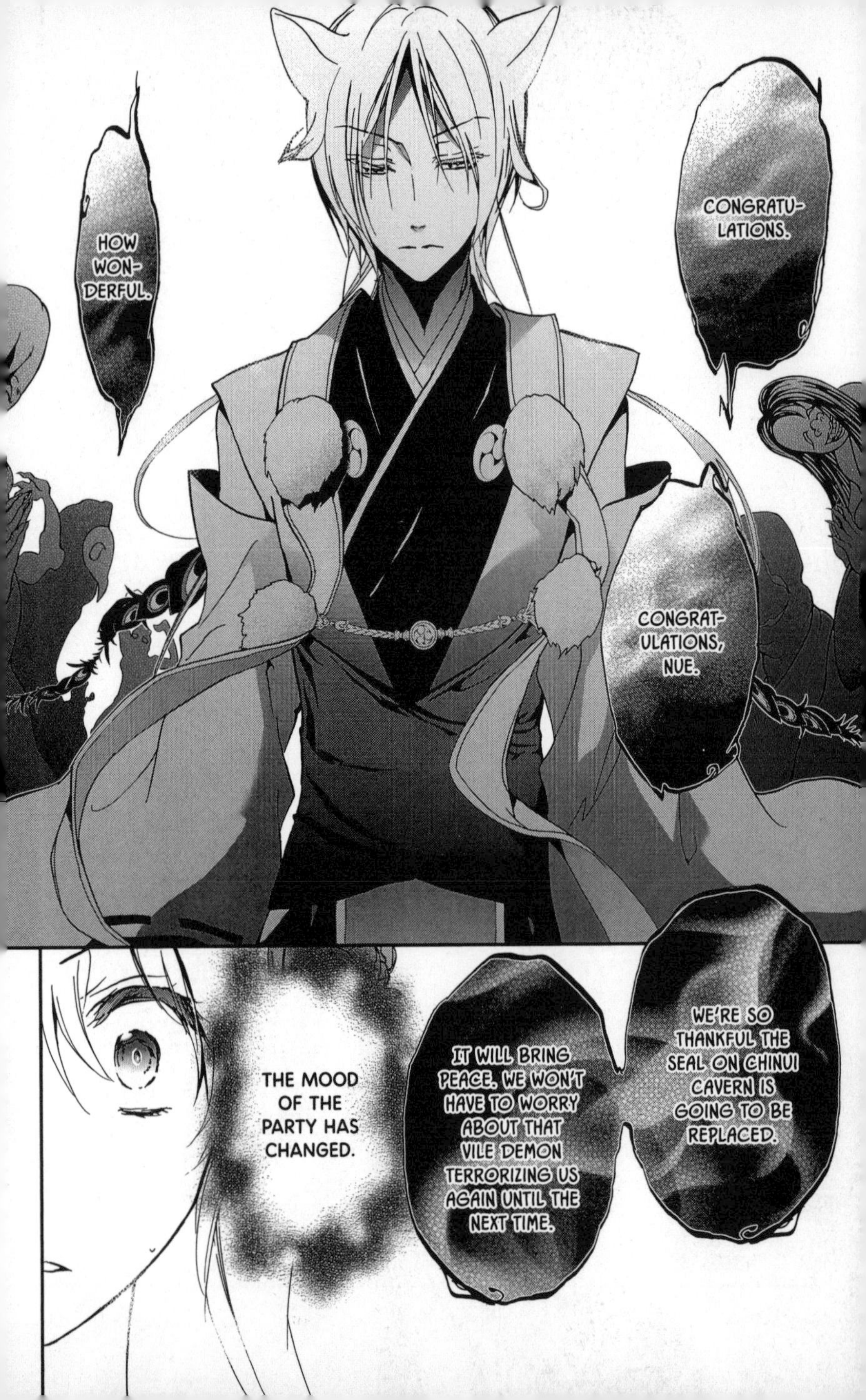
CONGRATULATIONS.
HOW WONDERFUL.
CONGRATULATIONS, NUE.
WE'RE SO THANKFUL THE SEAL ON CHINUI CAVERN IS GOING TO BE REPLACED.
IT WILL BRING PEACE. WE WON'T HAVE TO WORRY ABOUT THAT VILE DEMON TERRORIZING US AGAIN UNTIL THE NEXT TIME.
THE MOOD OF THE PARTY HAS CHANGED.

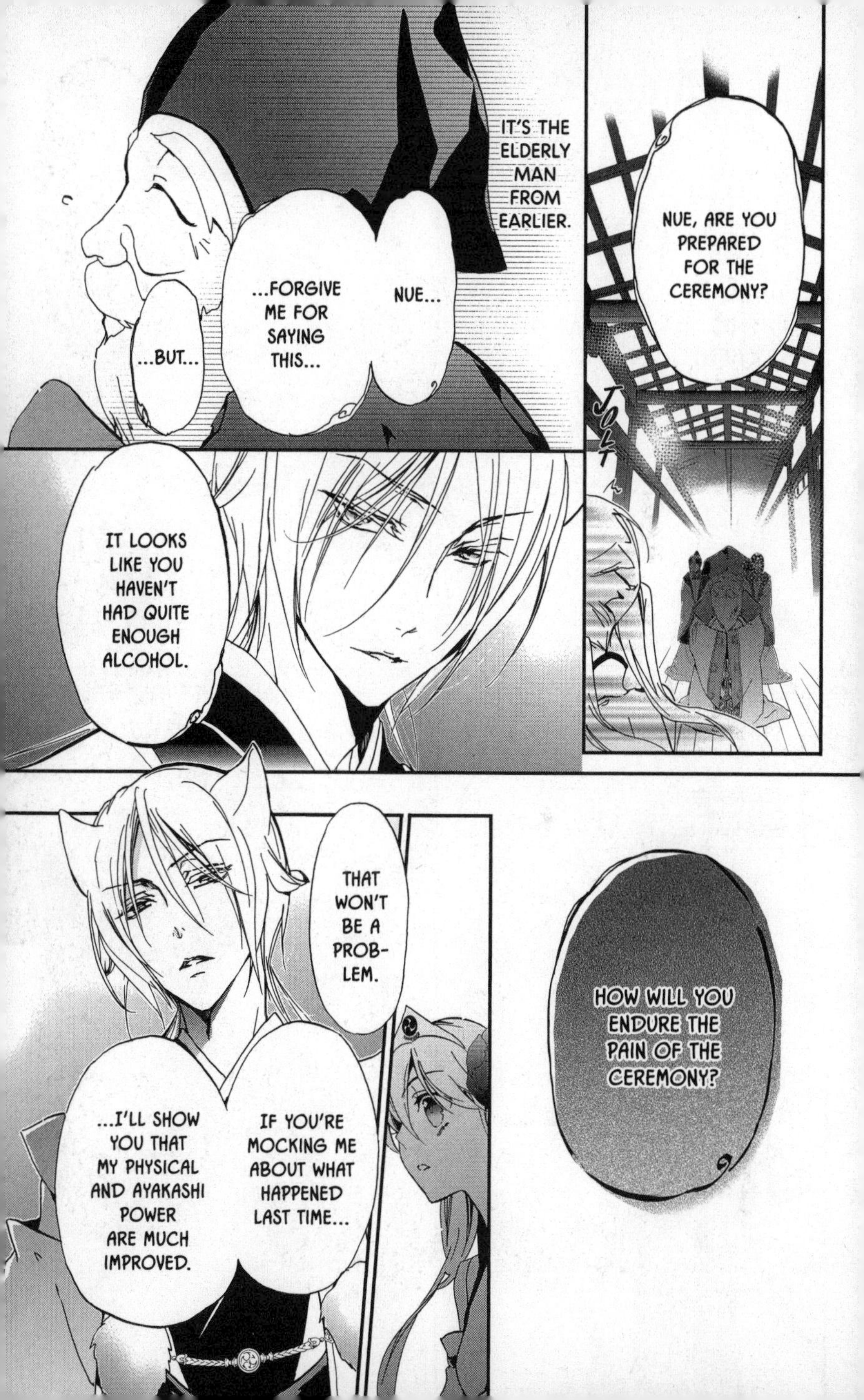
NUE, ARE YOU PREPARED FOR THE CEREMONY?
JOLT
IT'S THE ELDERLY MAN FROM EARLIER.
NUE...
...FORGIVE ME FOR SAYING THIS...
...BUT...
IT LOOKS LIKE YOU HAVEN'T HAD QUITE ENOUGH ALCOHOL.
HOW WILL YOU ENDURE THE PAIN OF THE CEREMONY?
THAT WON'T BE A PROB-LEM.
IF YOU'RE MOCKING ME ABOUT WHAT HAPPENED LAST TIME...
...I'LL SHOW YOU THAT MY PHYSICAL AND AYAKASHI POWER ARE MUCH IMPROVED.

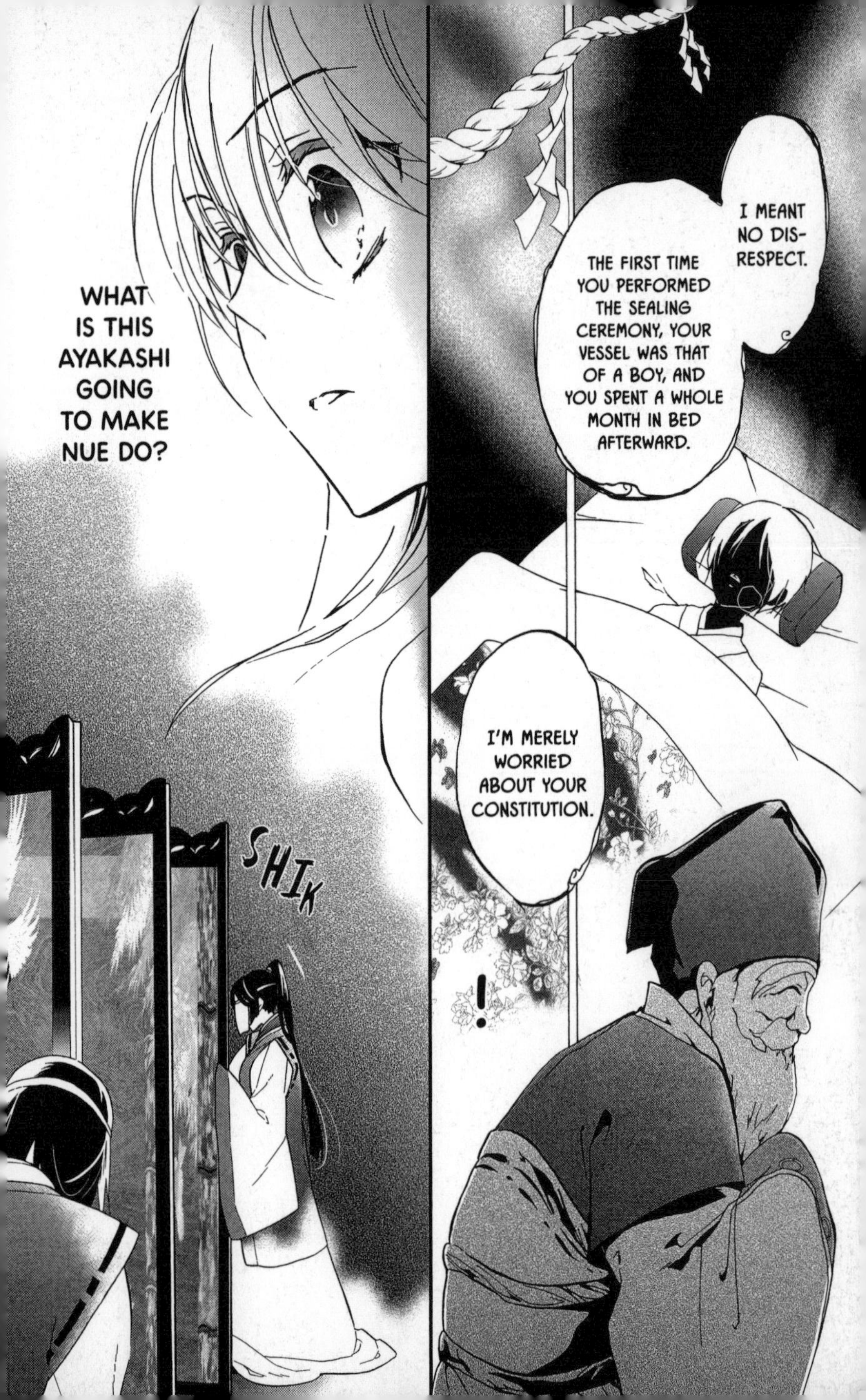
I MEANT NO DISRESPECT.
THE FIRST TIME YOU PERFORMED THE SEALING CEREMONY, YOUR VESSEL WAS THAT OF A BOY, AND YOU SPENT A WHOLE MONTH IN BED AFTERWARD.
I'M MERELY WORRIED ABOUT YOUR CONSTITUTION.
!
WHAT IS THIS AYAKASHI GOING TO MAKE NUE DO?
SHIK

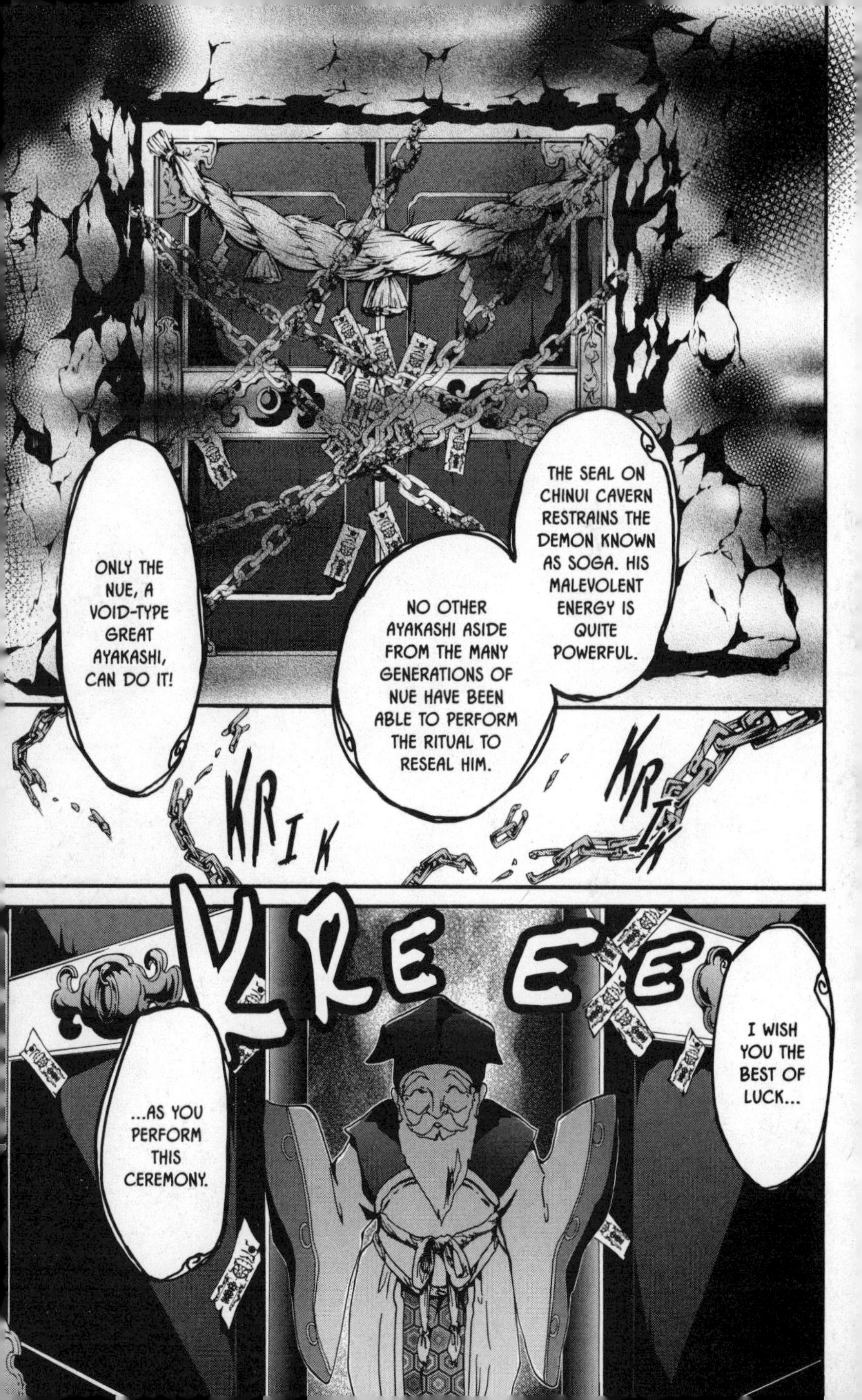
THE SEAL ON CHINUI CAVERN RESTRAINS THE DEMON KNOWN AS SOGA. HIS MALEVOLENT ENERGY IS QUITE POWERFUL.
NO OTHER AYAKASHI ASIDE FROM THE MANY GENERATIONS OF NUE HAVE BEEN ABLE TO PERFORM THE RITUAL TO RESEAL HIM.
ONLY THE NUE, A VOID-TYPE GREAT AYAKASHI, CAN DO IT!
KRIK
KRIK
VREEE
I WISH YOU THE BEST OF LUCK...
...AS YOU PERFORM THIS CEREMONY.

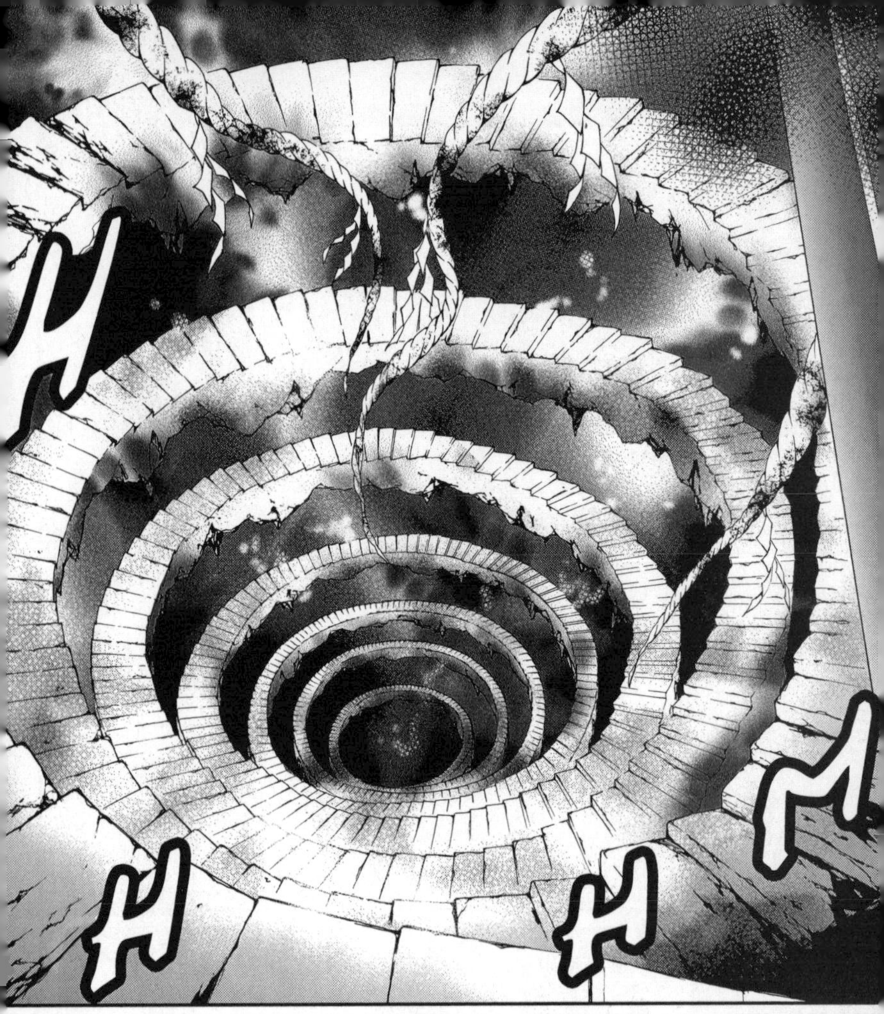

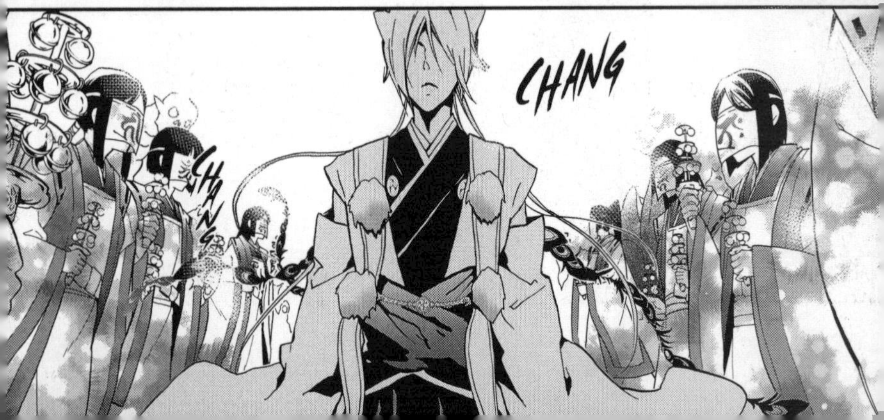
CHANG
CHANG

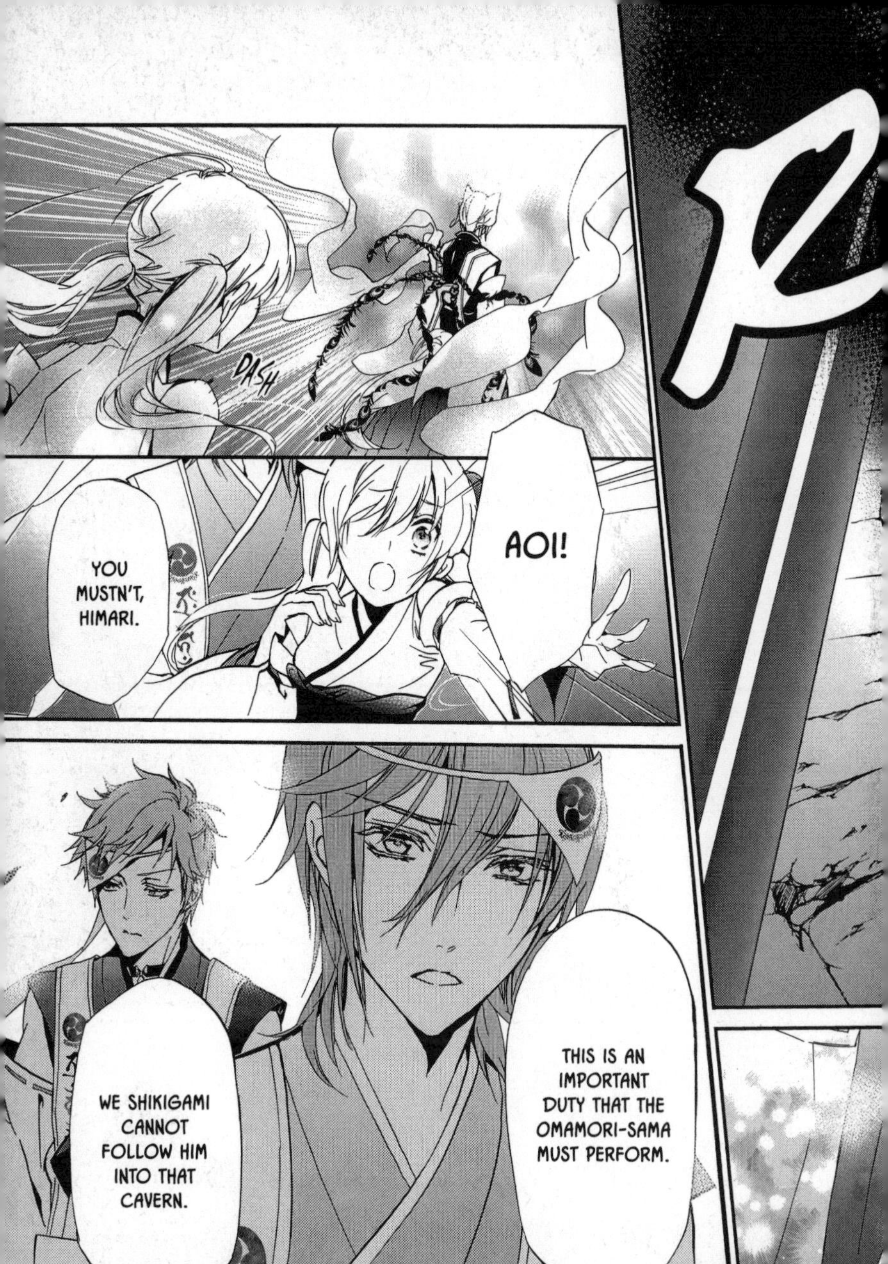
DASH
AOI!
YOU MUSTN'T, HIMARI.
THIS IS AN IMPORTANT DUTY THAT THE OMAMORI-SAMA MUST PERFORM.
WE SHIKIGAMI CANNOT FOLLOW HIM INTO THAT CAVERN.

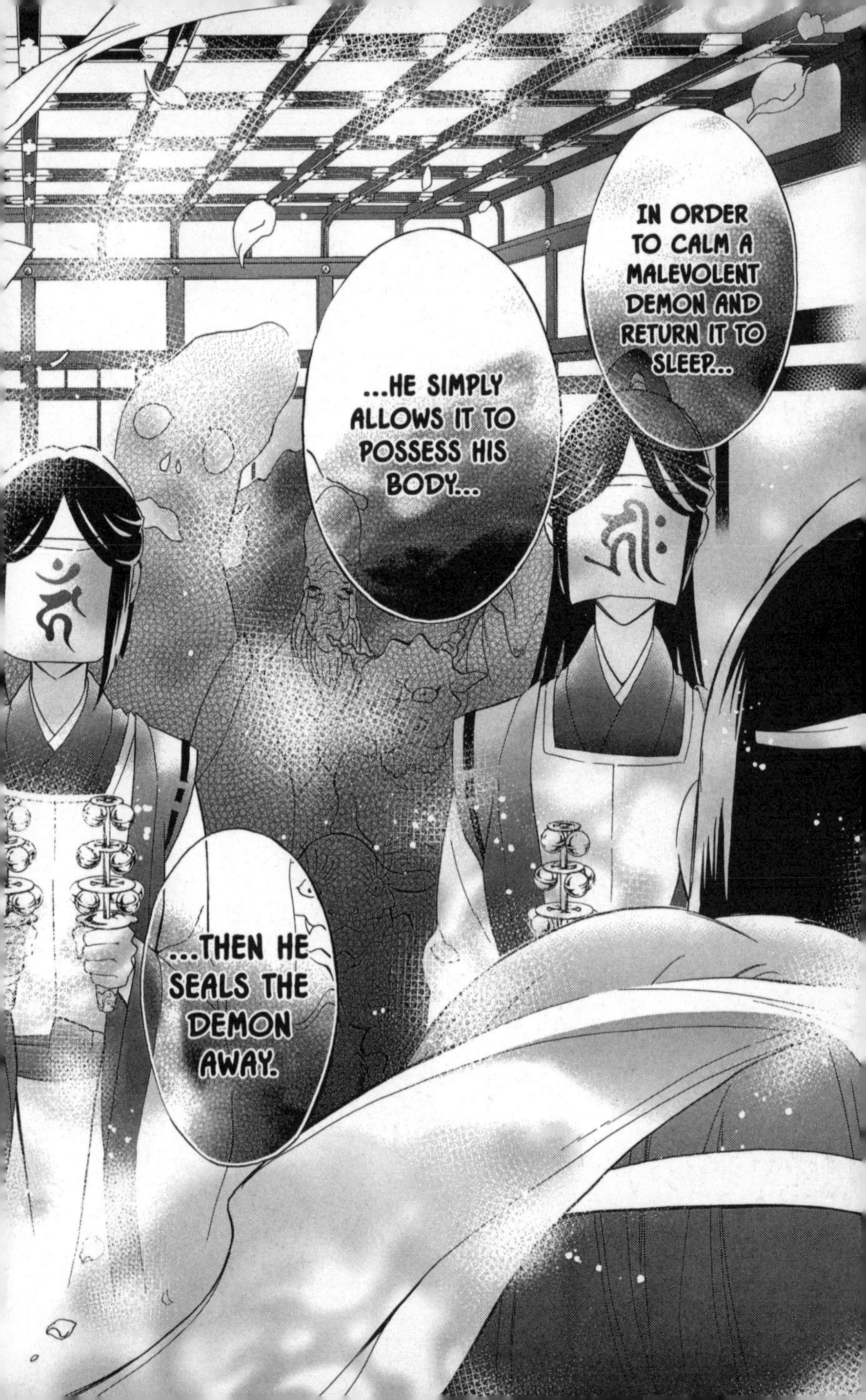
IN ORDER TO CALM A MALEVOLENT DEMON AND RETURN IT TO SLEEP...
...HE SIMPLY ALLOWS IT TO POSSESS HIS BODY...
...THEN HE SEALS THE DEMON AWAY.

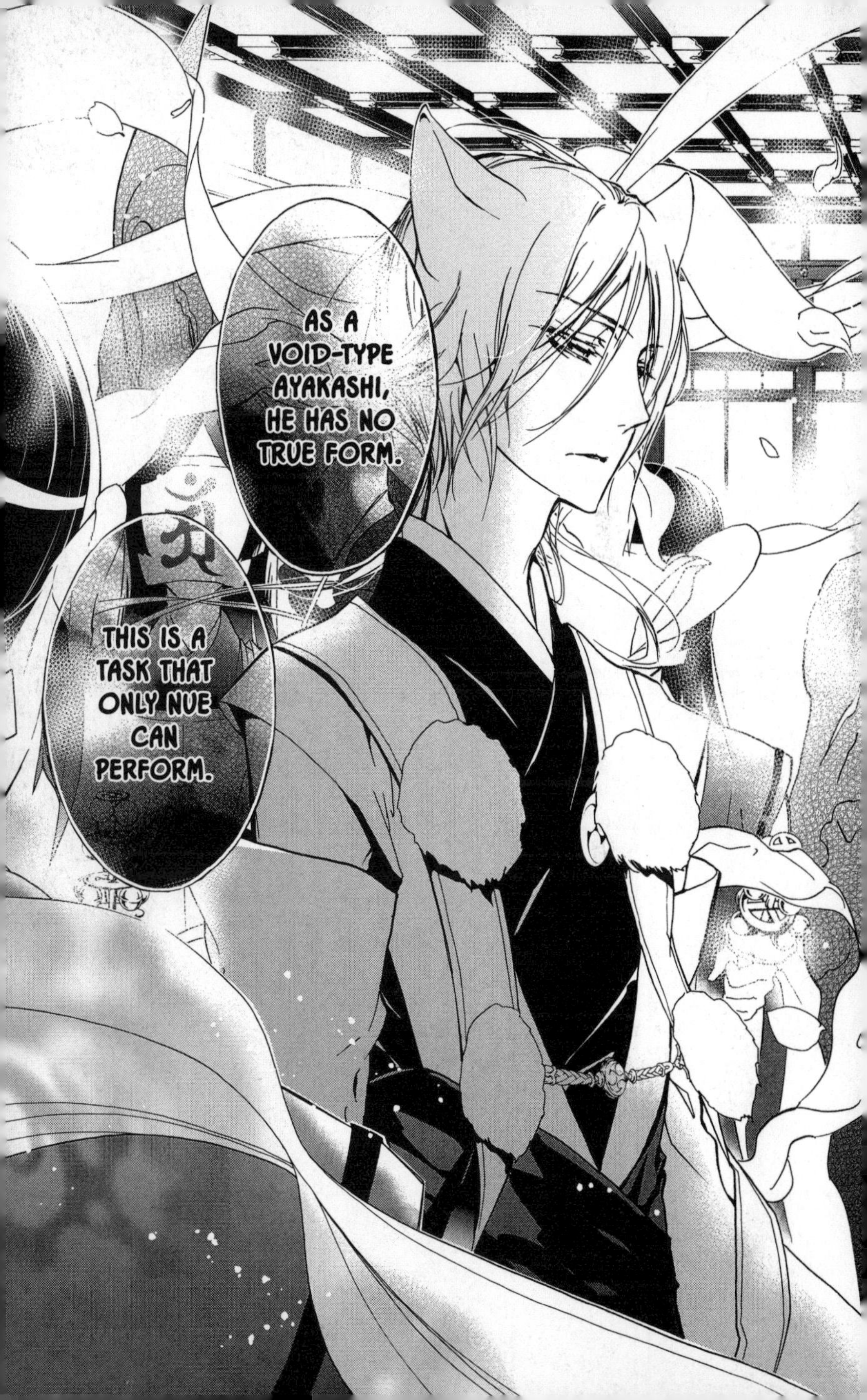
AS A VOID-TYPE AYAKASHI, HE HAS NO TRUE FORM.
THIS IS A TASK THAT ONLY NUE CAN PERFORM.

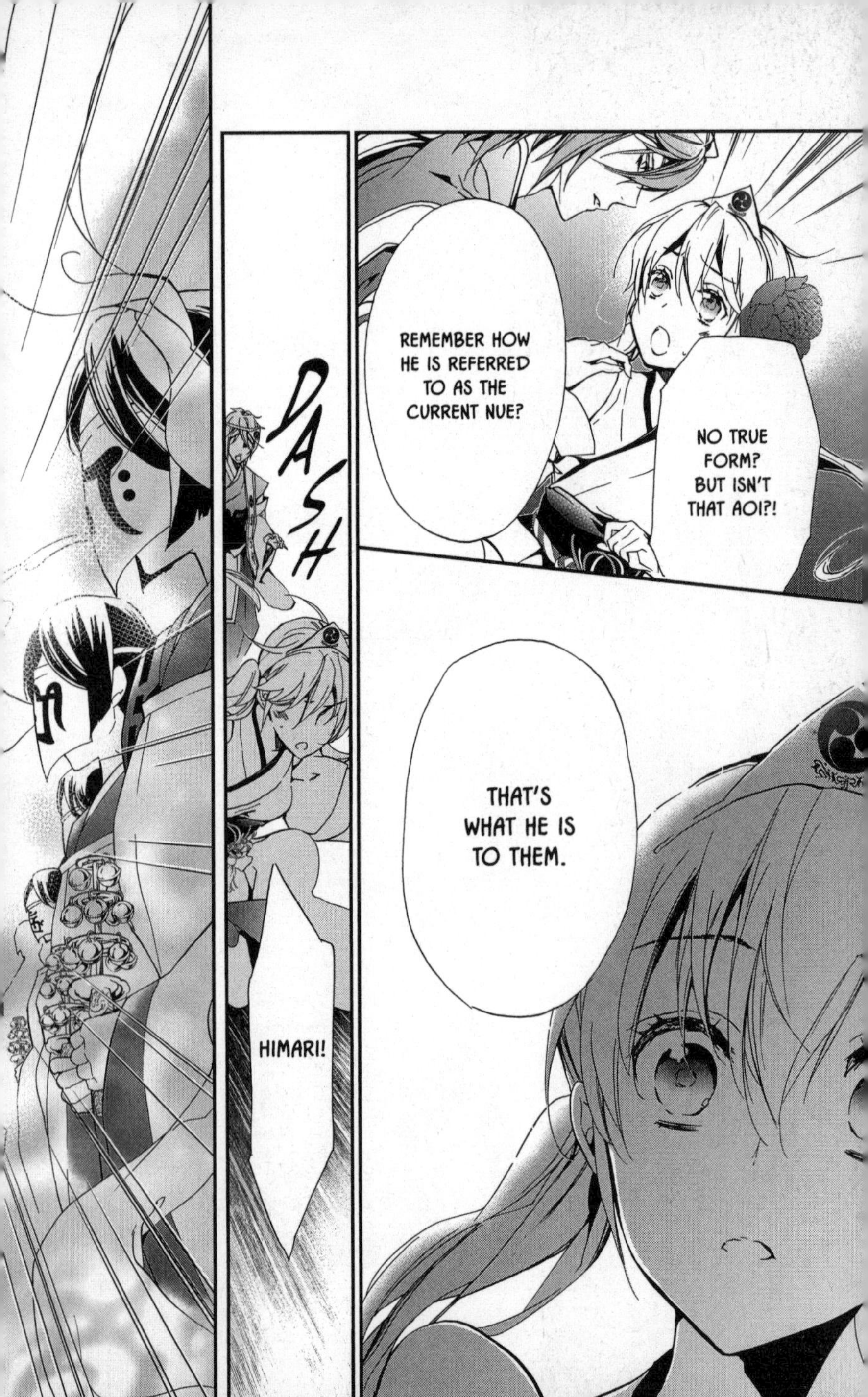
NO TRUE FORM? BUT ISN'T THAT AOI?!
REMEMBER HOW HE IS REFERRED TO AS THE CURRENT NUE?
THAT'S WHAT HE IS TO THEM.
DASH
HIMARI!

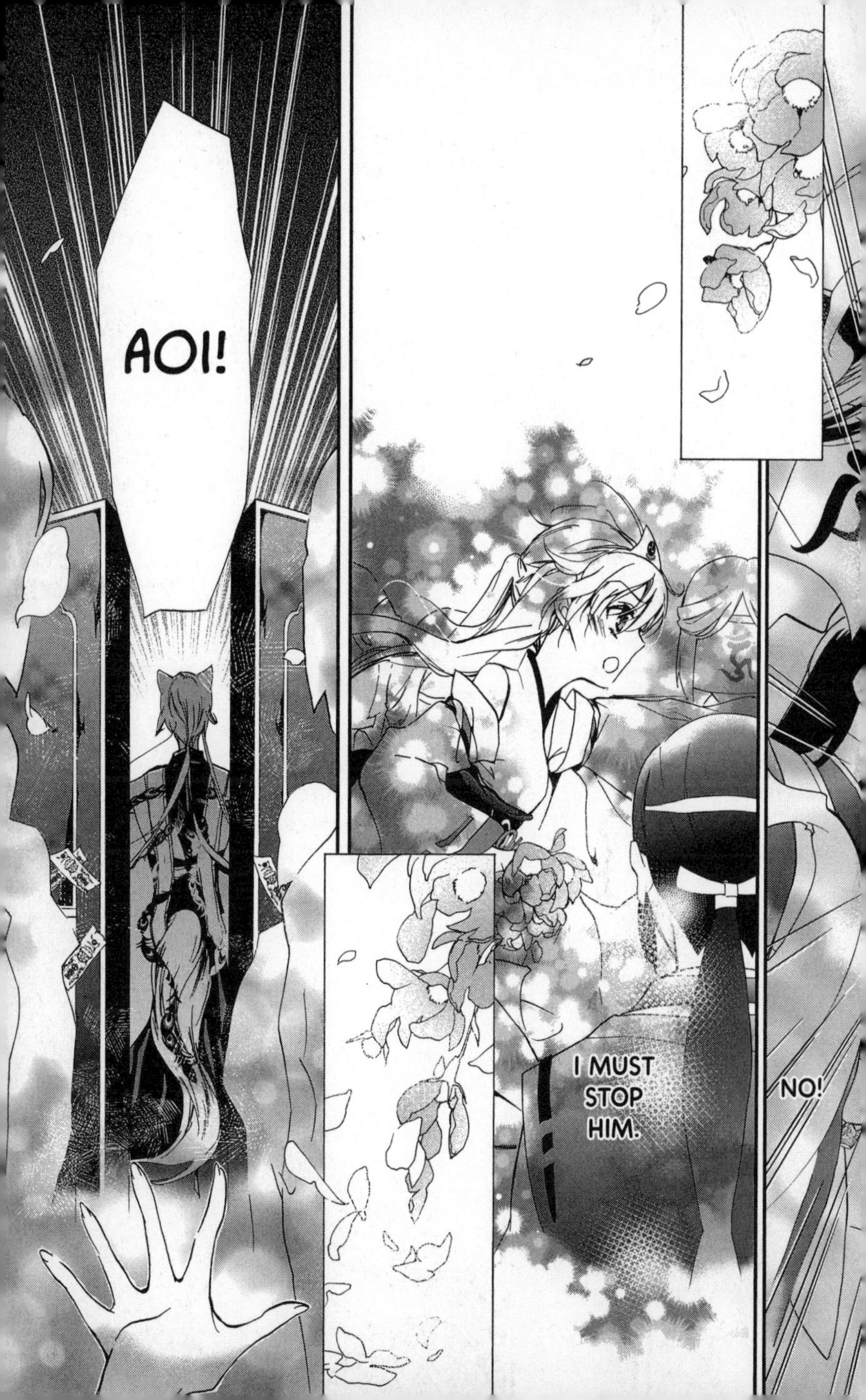
NO!
I MUST STOP HIM.
AOI!

KA-
CHAK

CONGRATULATIONS.

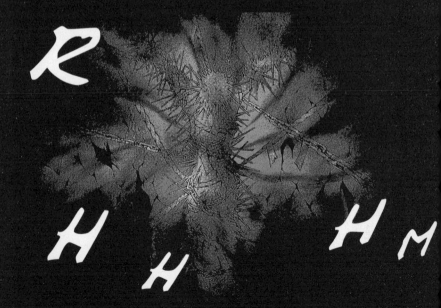

R

H

H

H M

Chapter 10/End

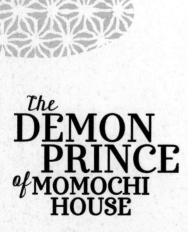

The
DEMON
PRINCE
of MOMOCHI
HOUSE

The
DEMON
PRINCE
of MOMOCHI
HOUSE

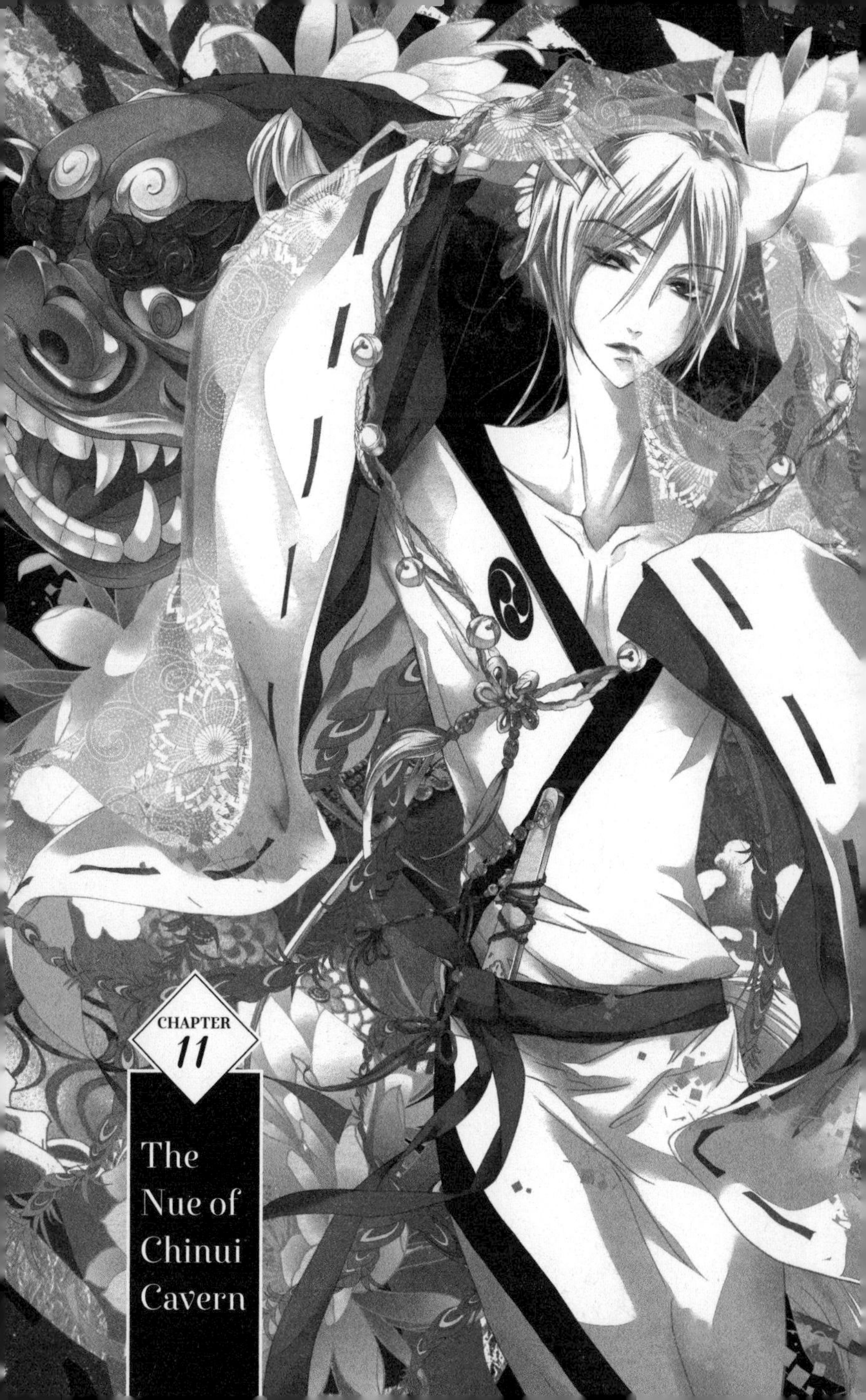
CHAPTER 11
The Nue of Chinui Cavern

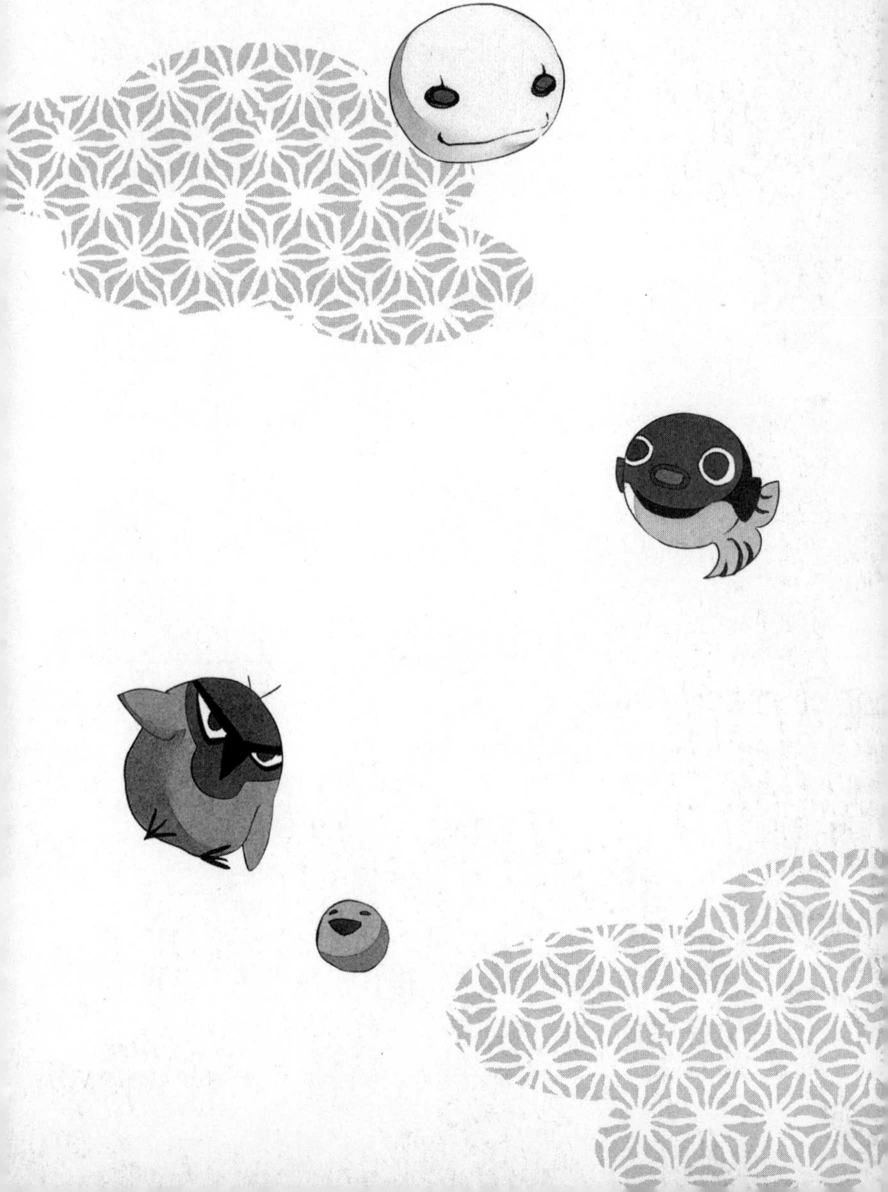

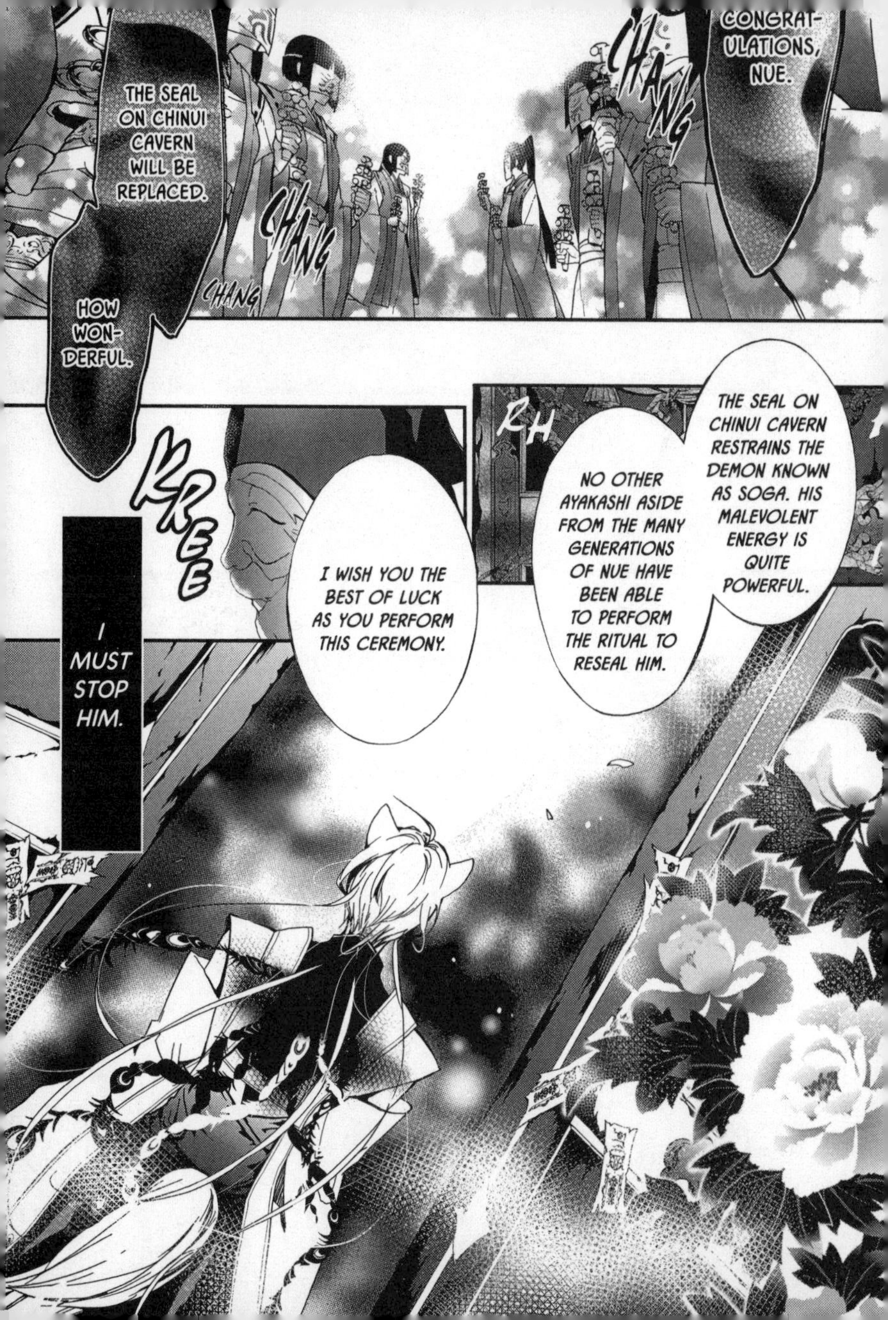
CONGRAT-ULATIONS, NUE.
CHANG
CHANG
THE SEAL ON CHINUI CAVERN WILL BE REPLACED.
CHANG
CHANG
HOW WON-DERFUL.
THE SEAL ON CHINUI CAVERN RESTRAINS THE DEMON KNOWN AS SOGA. HIS MALEVOLENT ENERGY IS QUITE POWERFUL.
NO OTHER AYAKASHI ASIDE FROM THE MANY GENERATIONS OF NUE HAVE BEEN ABLE TO PERFORM THE RITUAL TO RESEAL HIM.
RH
KREE
I WISH YOU THE BEST OF LUCK AS YOU PERFORM THIS CEREMONY.
I MUST STOP HIM.

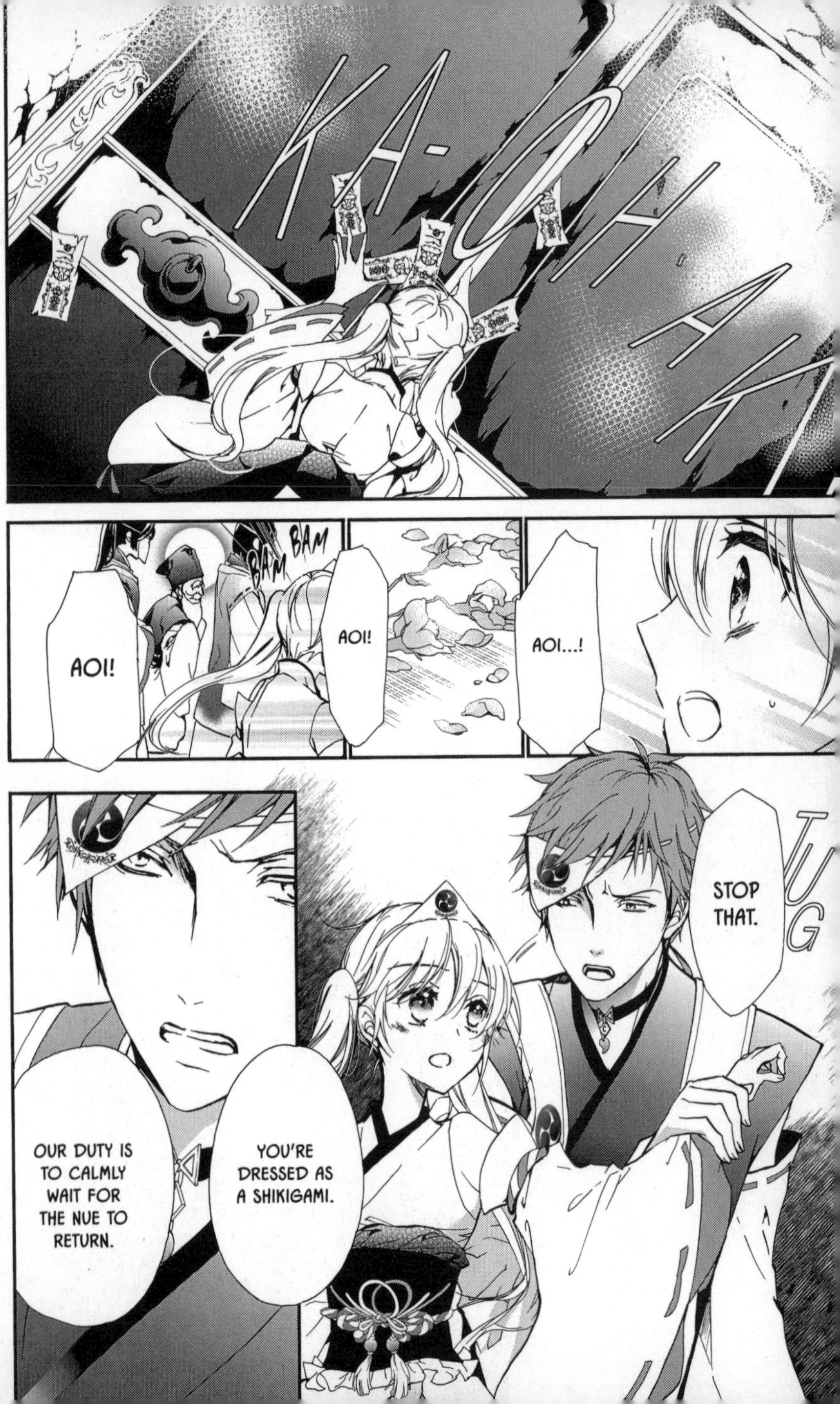
KA-CHAAK
AOI...!
AOI!
BAM BAM BAM
AOI!
TUG
STOP THAT.
YOU'RE DRESSED AS A SHIKIGAMI.
OUR DUTY IS TO CALMLY WAIT FOR THE NUE TO RETURN.

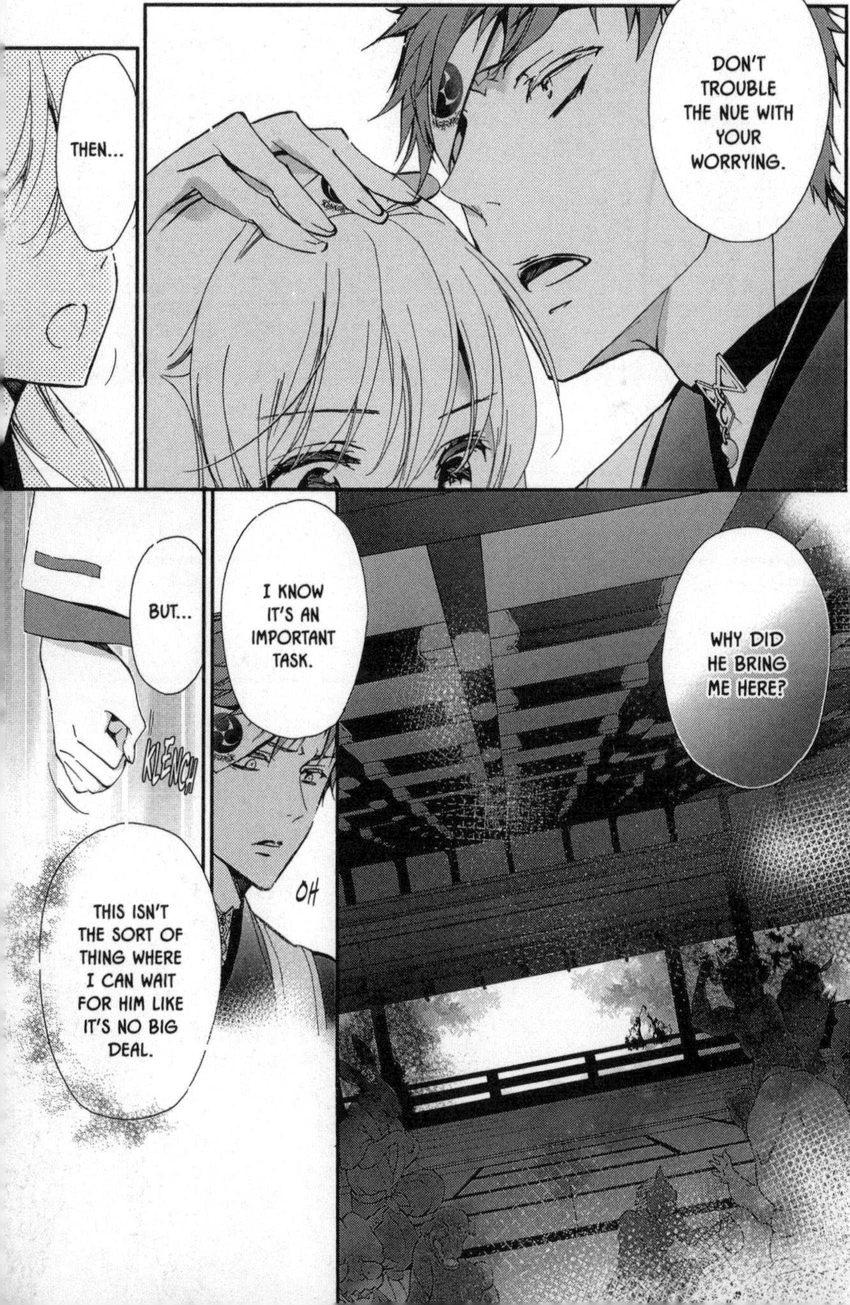
DON'T TROUBLE THE NUE WITH YOUR WORRYING.
THEN...
WHY DID HE BRING ME HERE?
I KNOW IT'S AN IMPORTANT TASK.
OH
BUT...
KLENCH
THIS ISN'T THE SORT OF THING WHERE I CAN WAIT FOR HIM LIKE IT'S NO BIG DEAL.

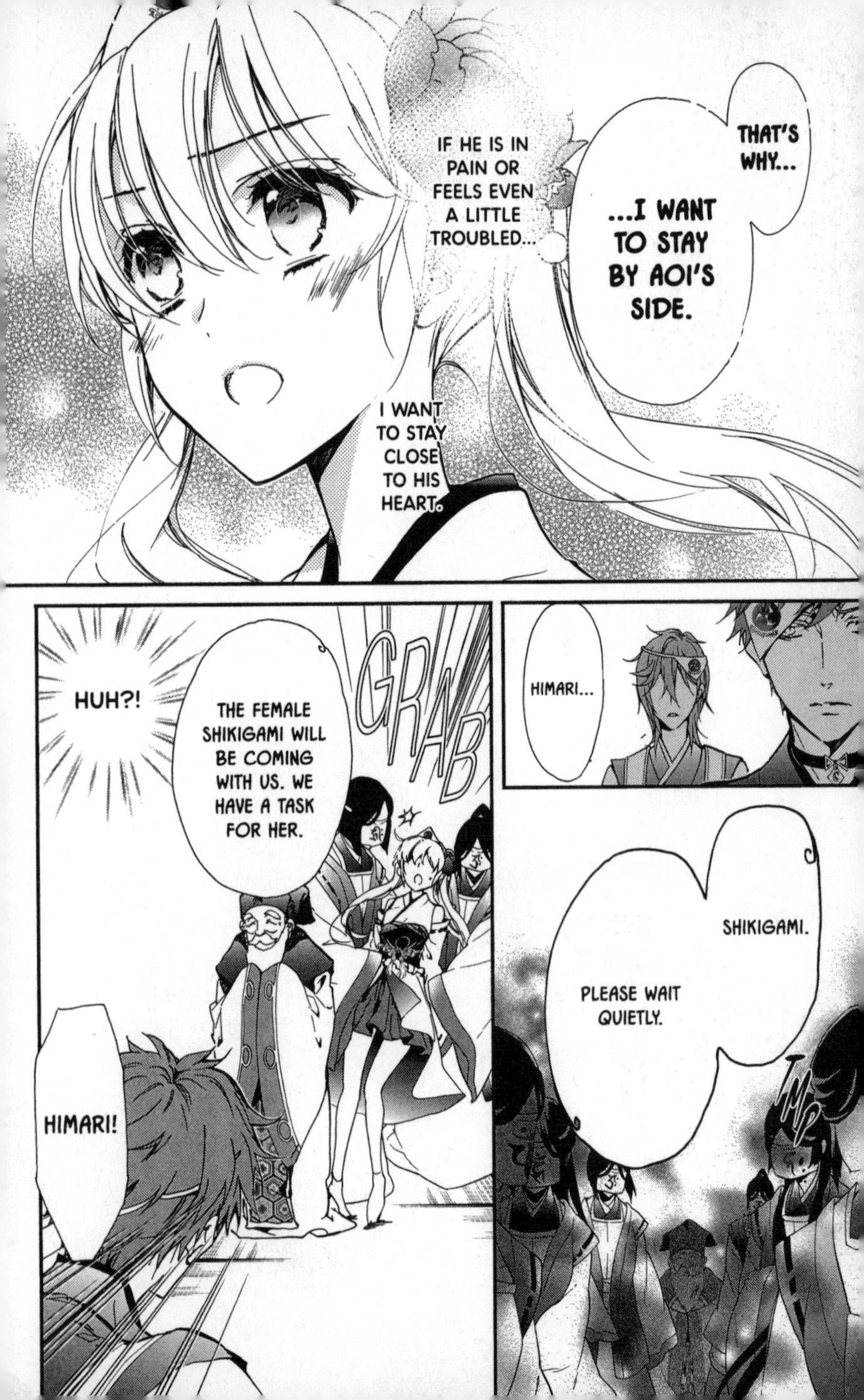
THAT'S WHY...
...I WANT TO STAY BY AOI'S SIDE.
IF HE IS IN PAIN OR FEELS EVEN A LITTLE TROUBLED...
I WANT TO STAY CLOSE TO HIS HEART.
HIMARI...
SHIKIGAMI.
PLEASE WAIT QUIETLY.
GRAB
THE FEMALE SHIKIGAMI WILL BE COMING WITH US. WE HAVE A TASK FOR HER.
HUH?!
HIMARI!

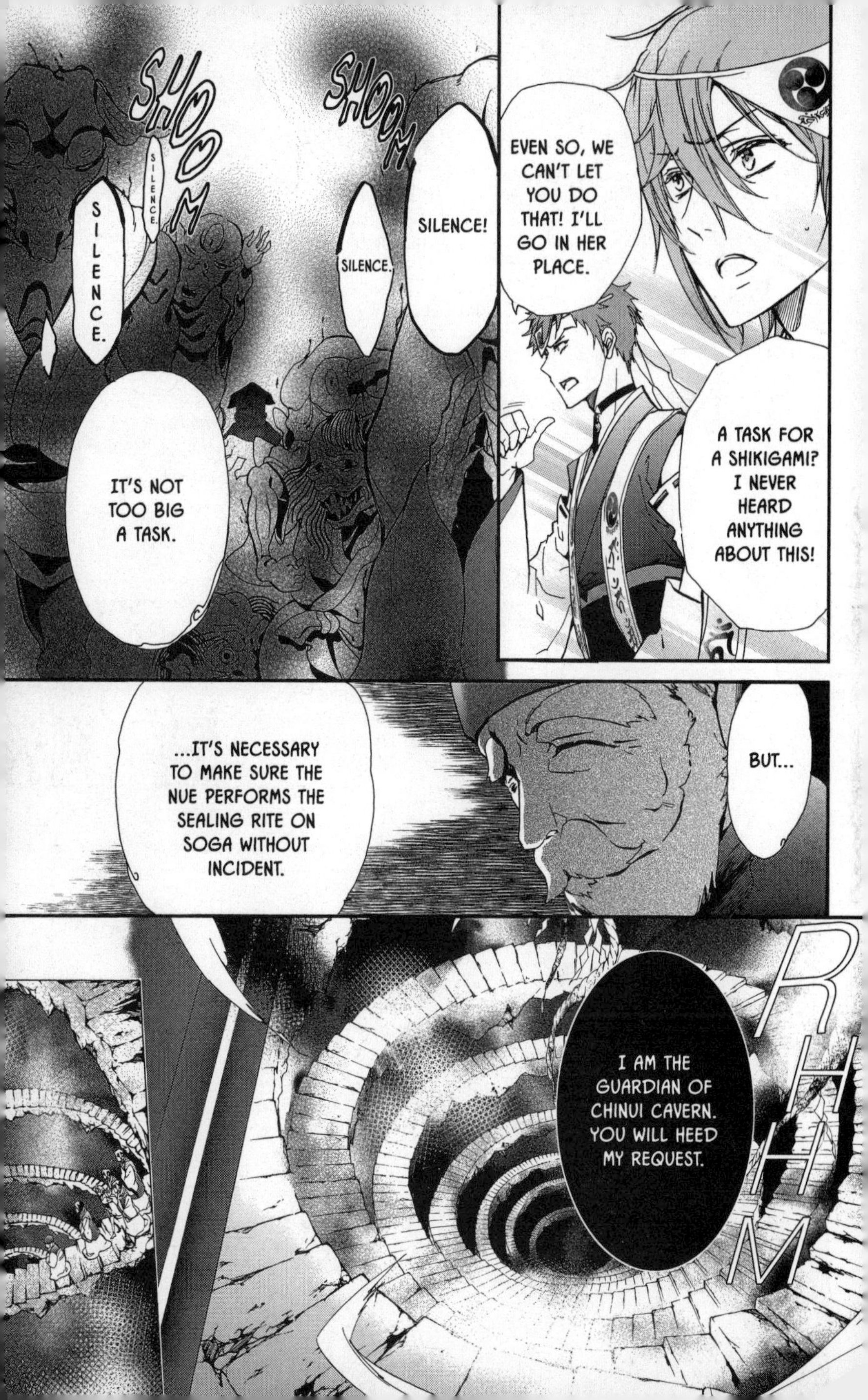
EVEN SO, WE CAN'T LET YOU DO THAT! I'LL GO IN HER PLACE.
A TASK FOR A SHIKIGAMI? I NEVER HEARD ANYTHING ABOUT THIS!
SHOOM
SILENCE!
SILENCE.
SHOOM
SILENCE.
SILENCE.
IT'S NOT TOO BIG A TASK.
BUT...
...IT'S NECESSARY TO MAKE SURE THE NUE PERFORMS THE SEALING RITE ON SOGA WITHOUT INCIDENT.
RHHM
I AM THE GUARDIAN OF CHINUI CAVERN. YOU WILL HEED MY REQUEST.

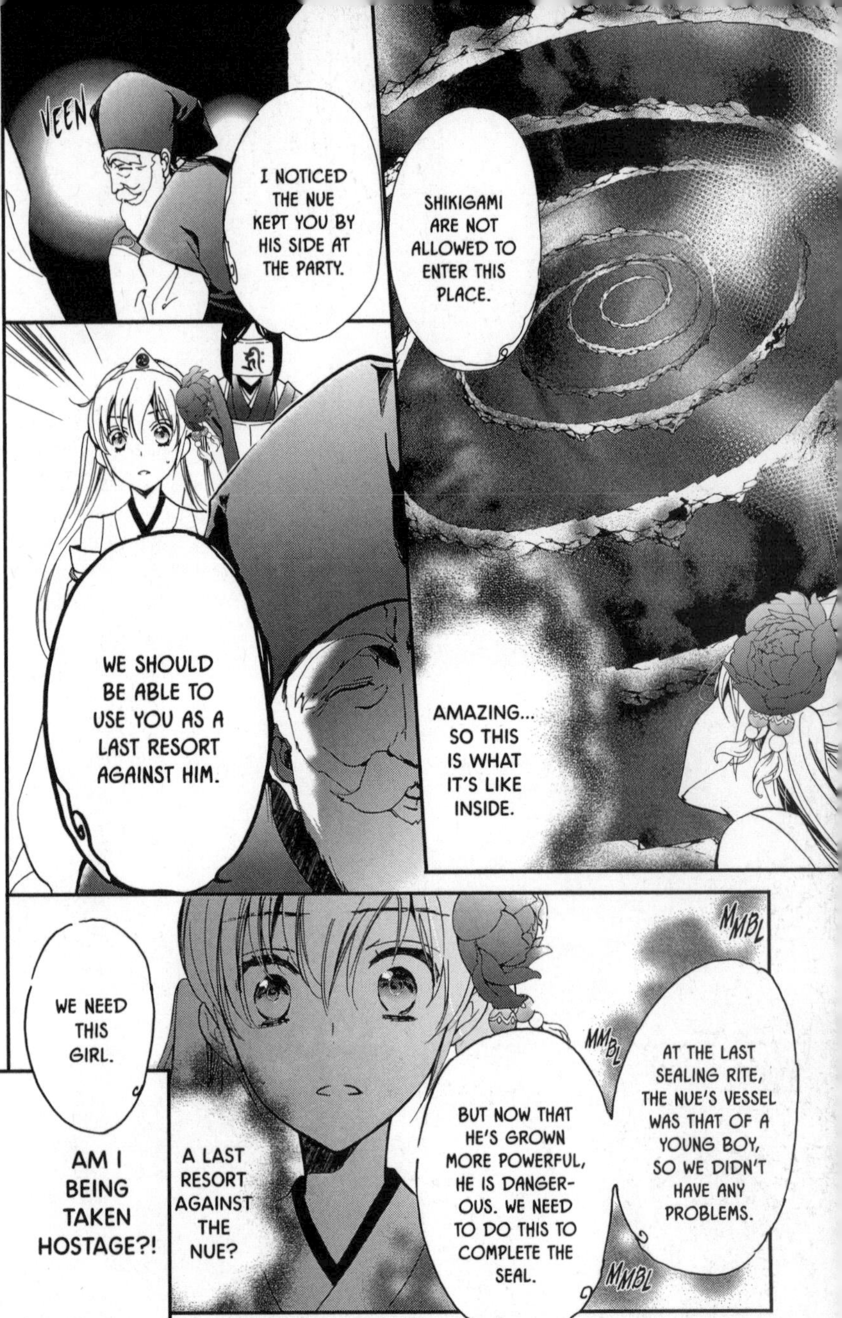
SHIKIGAMI ARE NOT ALLOWED TO ENTER THIS PLACE.
AMAZING... SO THIS IS WHAT IT'S LIKE INSIDE.
VEEN
I NOTICED THE NUE KEPT YOU BY HIS SIDE AT THE PARTY.
WE SHOULD BE ABLE TO USE YOU AS A LAST RESORT AGAINST HIM.
MMBL
AT THE LAST SEALING RITE, THE NUE'S VESSEL WAS THAT OF A YOUNG BOY, SO WE DIDN'T HAVE ANY PROBLEMS.
MMBL
BUT NOW THAT HE'S GROWN MORE POWERFUL, HE IS DANGER-OUS. WE NEED TO DO THIS TO COMPLETE THE SEAL.
MMBL
WE NEED THIS GIRL.
A LAST RESORT AGAINST THE NUE?
AM I BEING TAKEN HOSTAGE?!

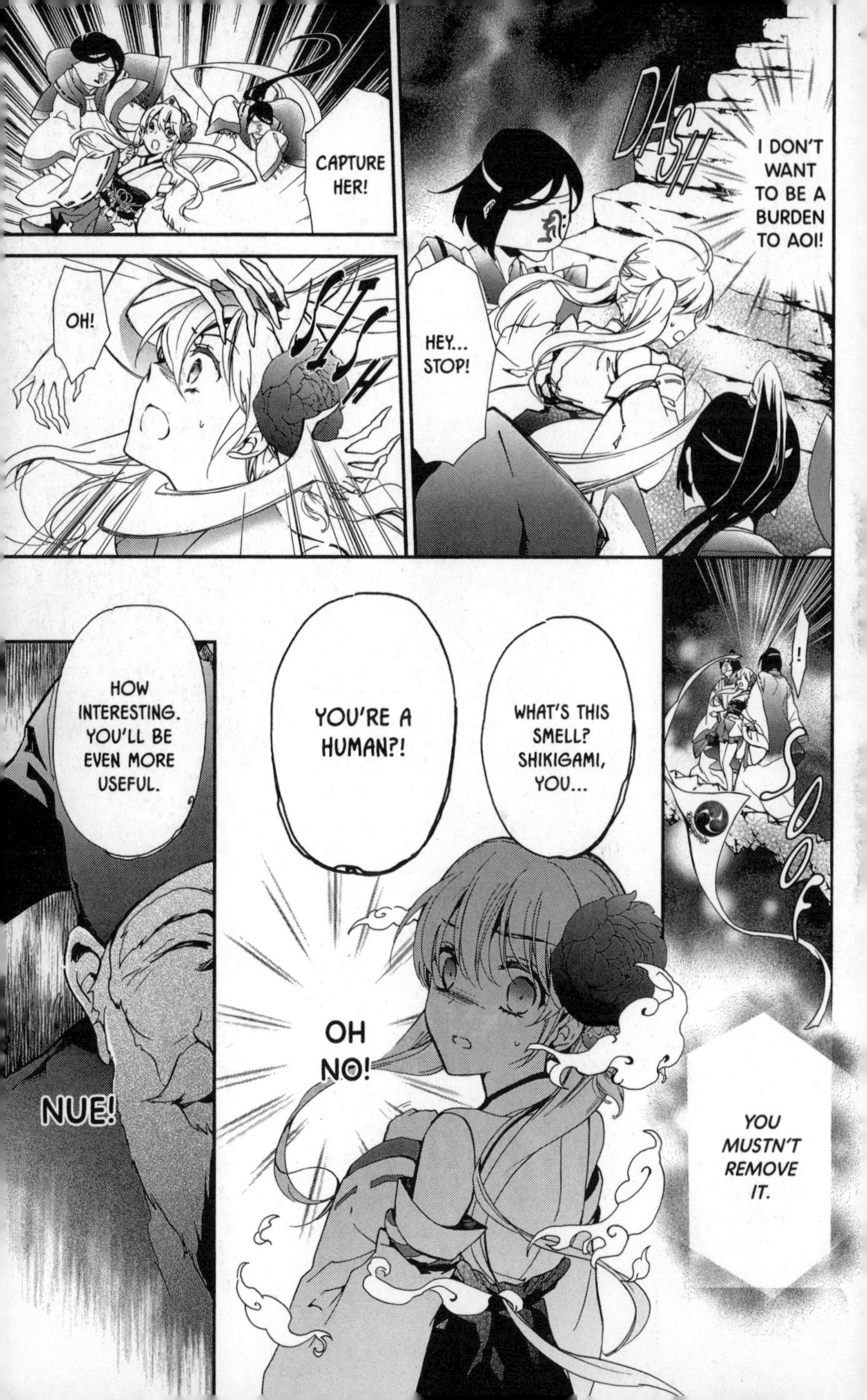
I DON'T WANT TO BE A BURDEN TO AOI!
DASH
HEY... STOP!
CAPTURE HER!
OH!
SISH
!
WHAT'S THIS SMELL? SHIKIGAMI, YOU...
YOU'RE A HUMAN?!
OH NO!
YOU MUSTN'T REMOVE IT.
HOW INTERESTING. YOU'LL BE EVEN MORE USEFUL.
NUE!

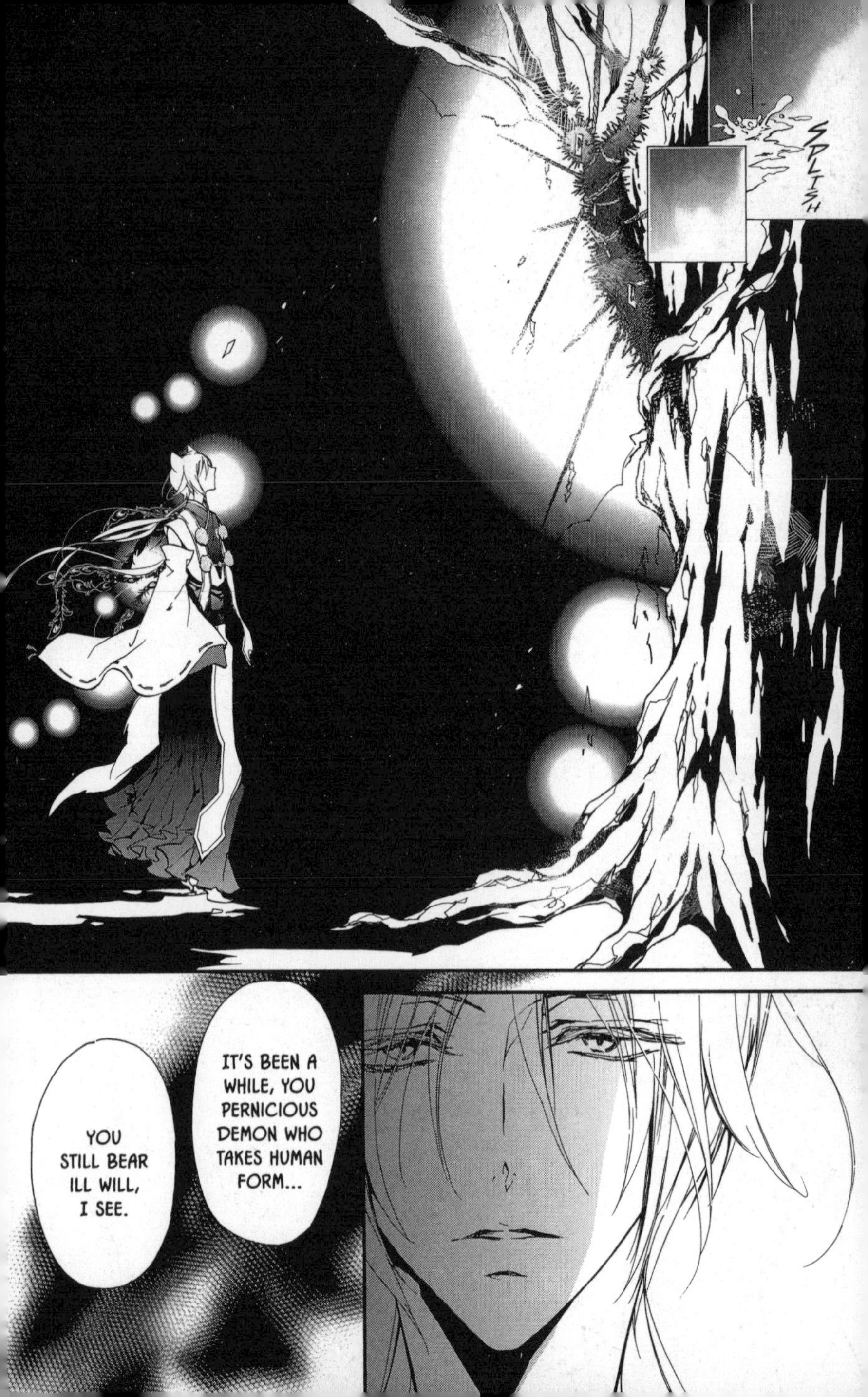
SPLISH
IT'S BEEN A WHILE, YOU PERNICIOUS DEMON WHO TAKES HUMAN FORM...
YOU STILL BEAR ILL WILL, I SEE.

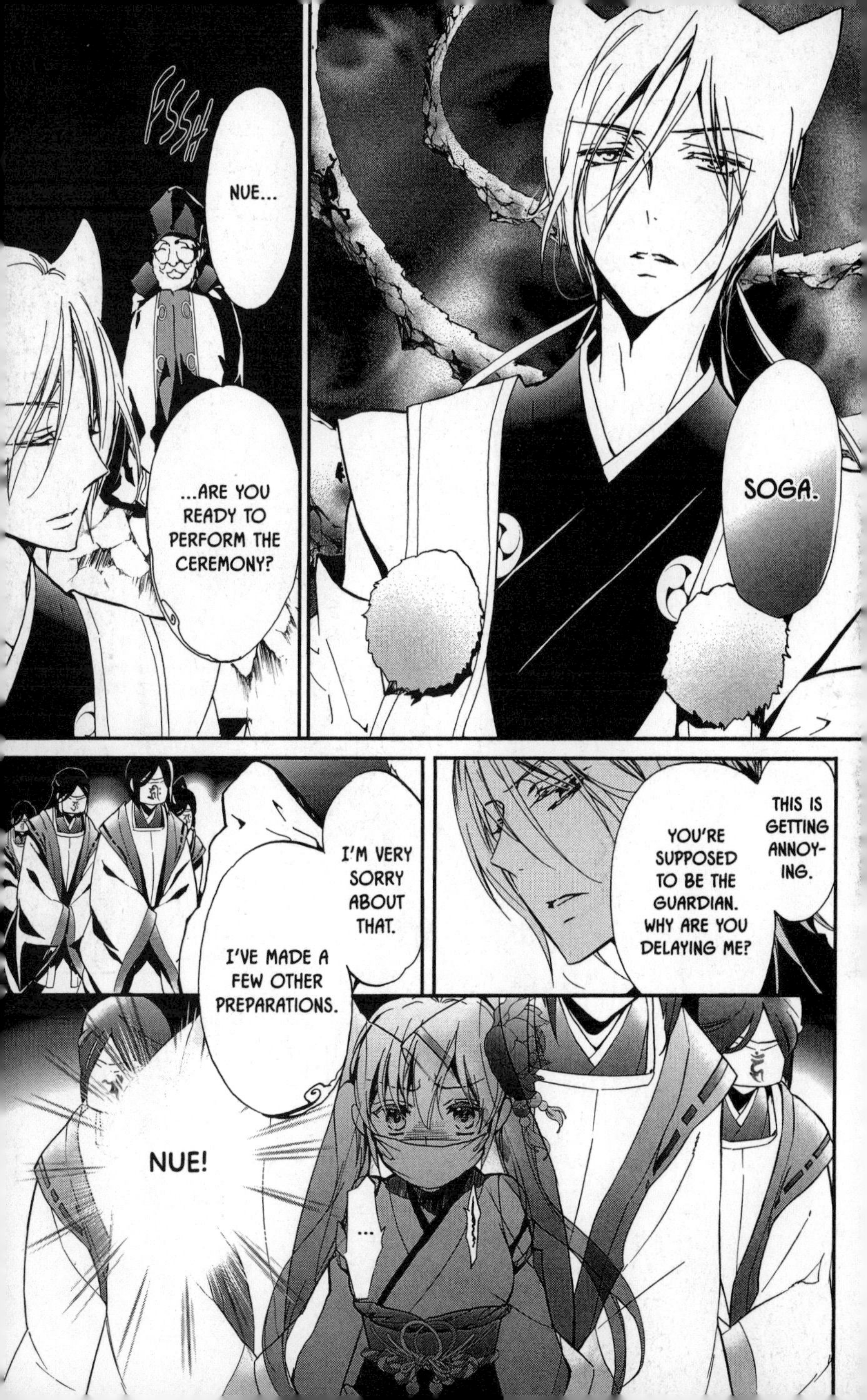
SOGA.
FSSH
NUE...
...ARE YOU READY TO PERFORM THE CEREMONY?
THIS IS GETTING ANNOY-ING.
YOU'RE SUPPOSED TO BE THE GUARDIAN. WHY ARE YOU DELAYING ME?
I'M VERY SORRY ABOUT THAT.
I'VE MADE A FEW OTHER PREPARATIONS.
NUE!
...

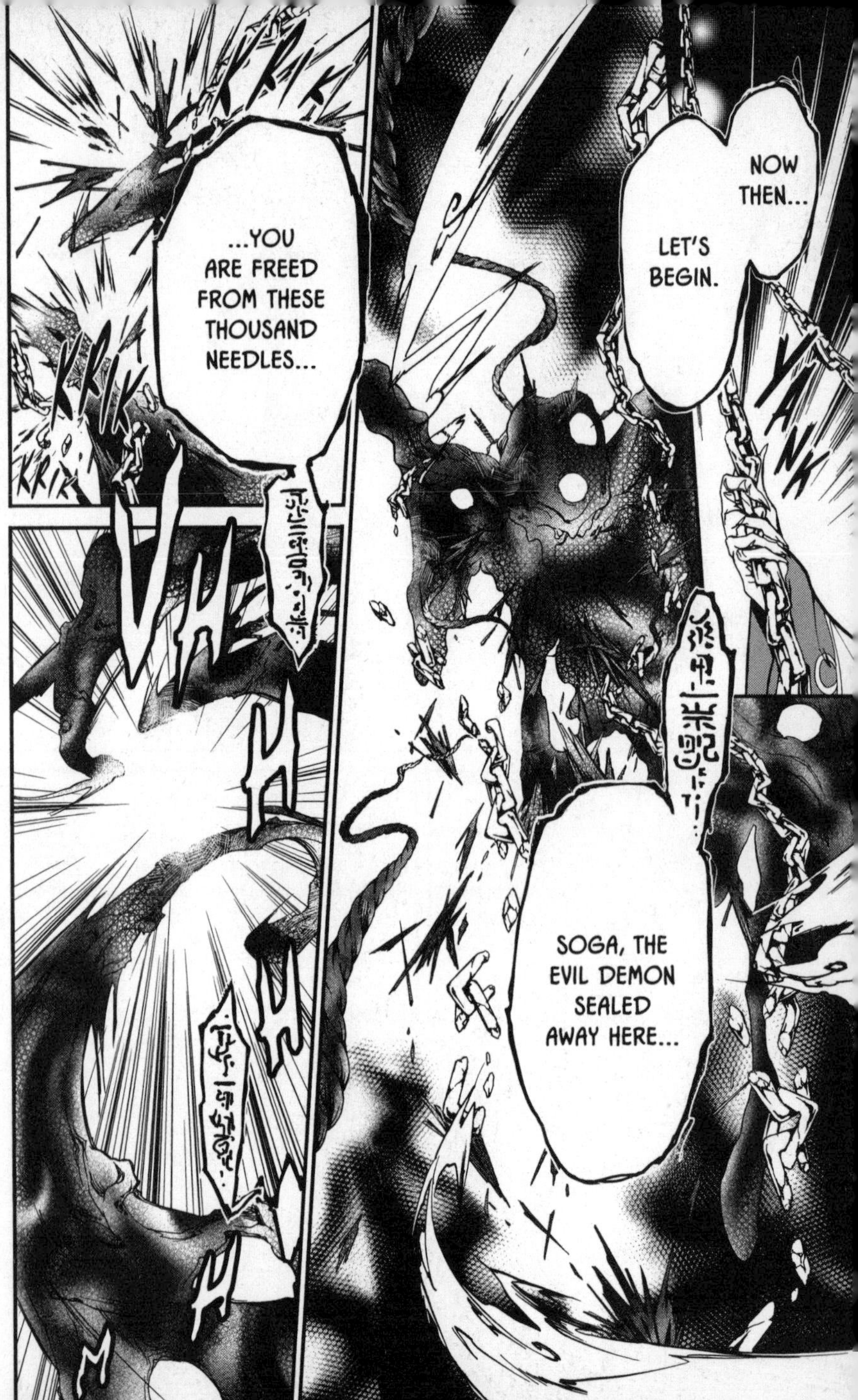
NOW THEN...
LET'S BEGIN.
YANK
SOGA, THE EVIL DEMON SEALED AWAY HERE...
KRIK KRIK
...YOU ARE FREED FROM THESE THOUSAND NEEDLES...
KRIK KRIK

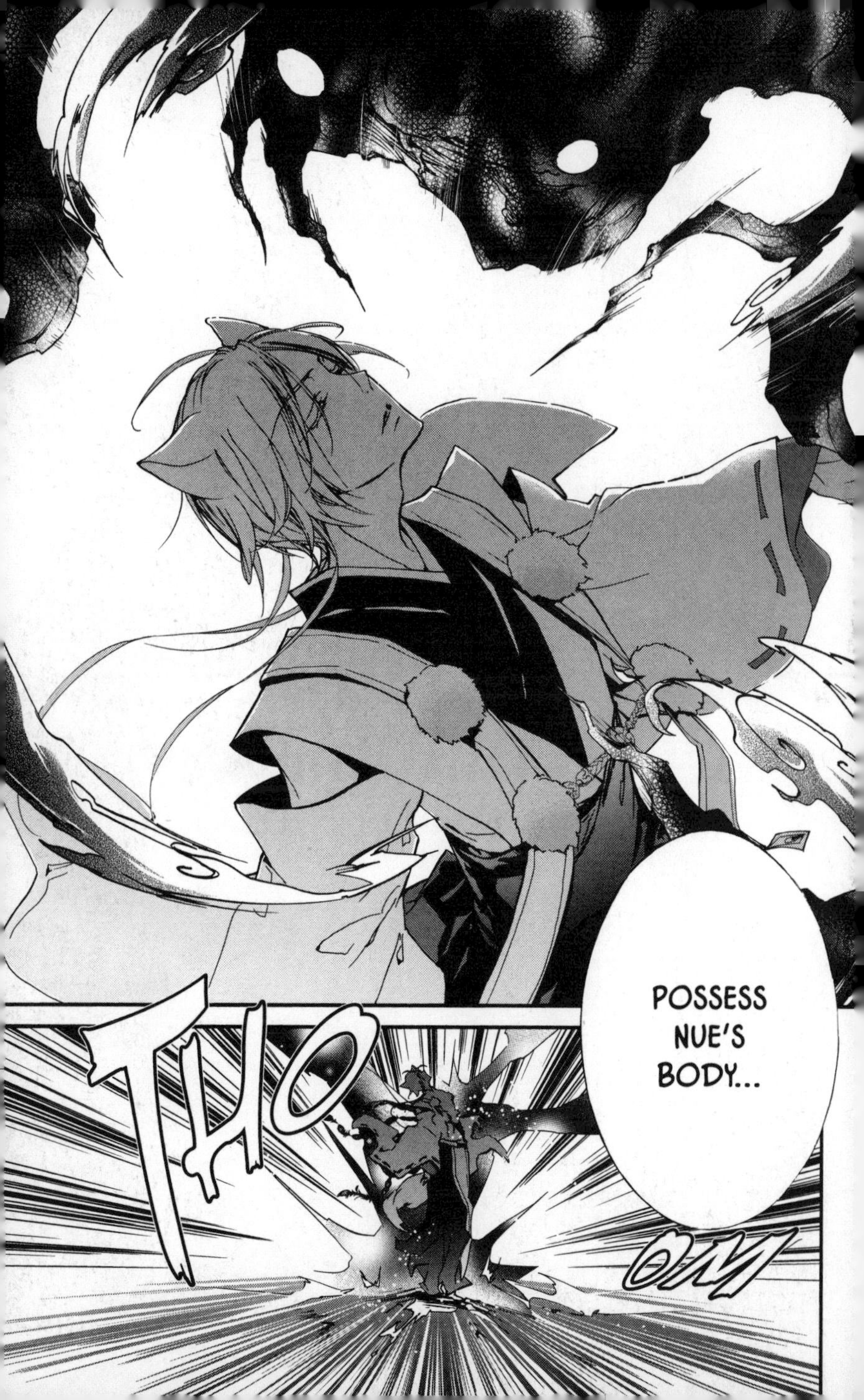
POSSESS NUE'S BODY...
THO
OM

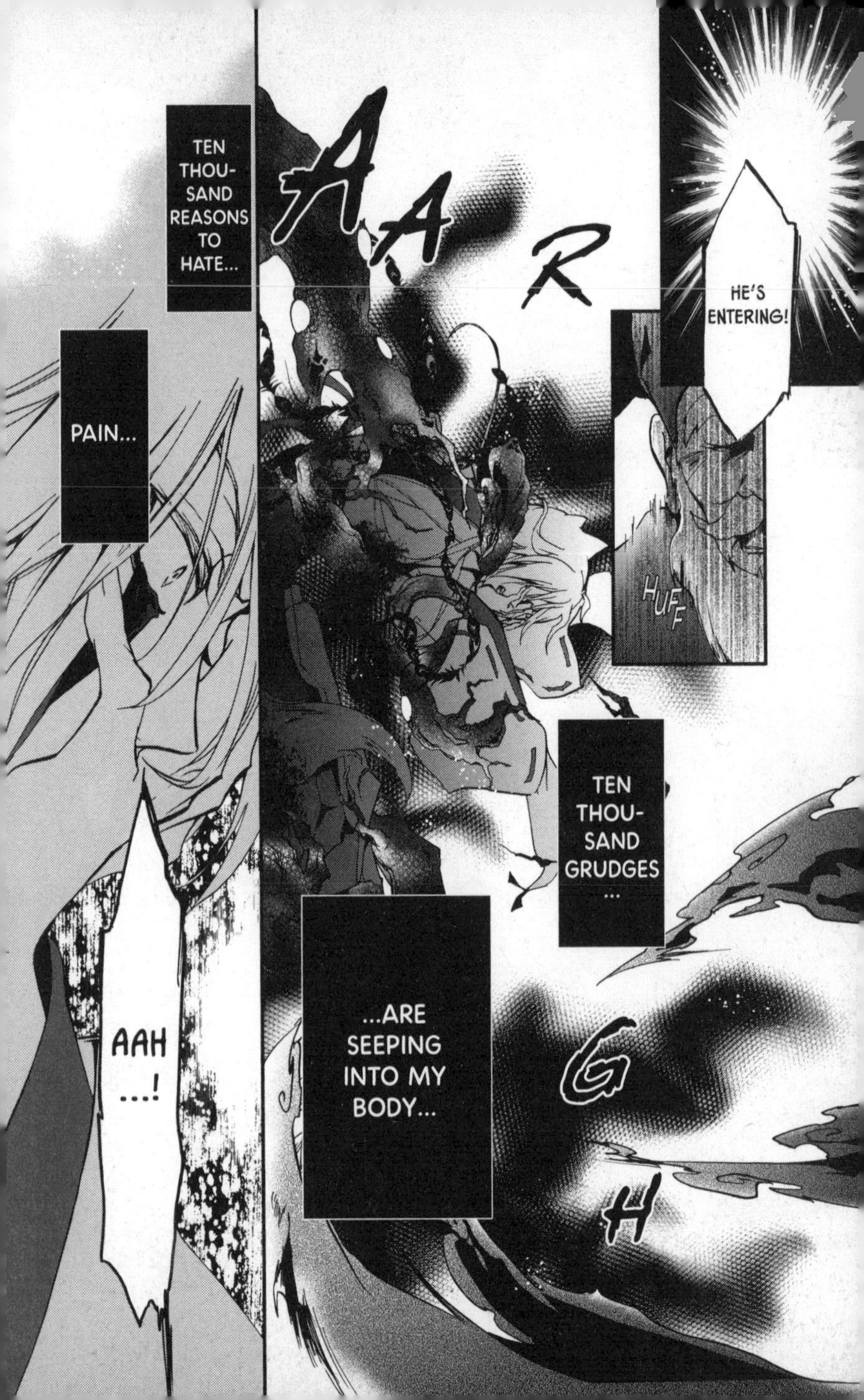
HE'S ENTERING!
HUFF
AAR
TEN THOUSAND GRUDGES...
...ARE SEEPING INTO MY BODY...
GH
TEN THOUSAND REASONS TO HATE...
PAIN...
AAH...!

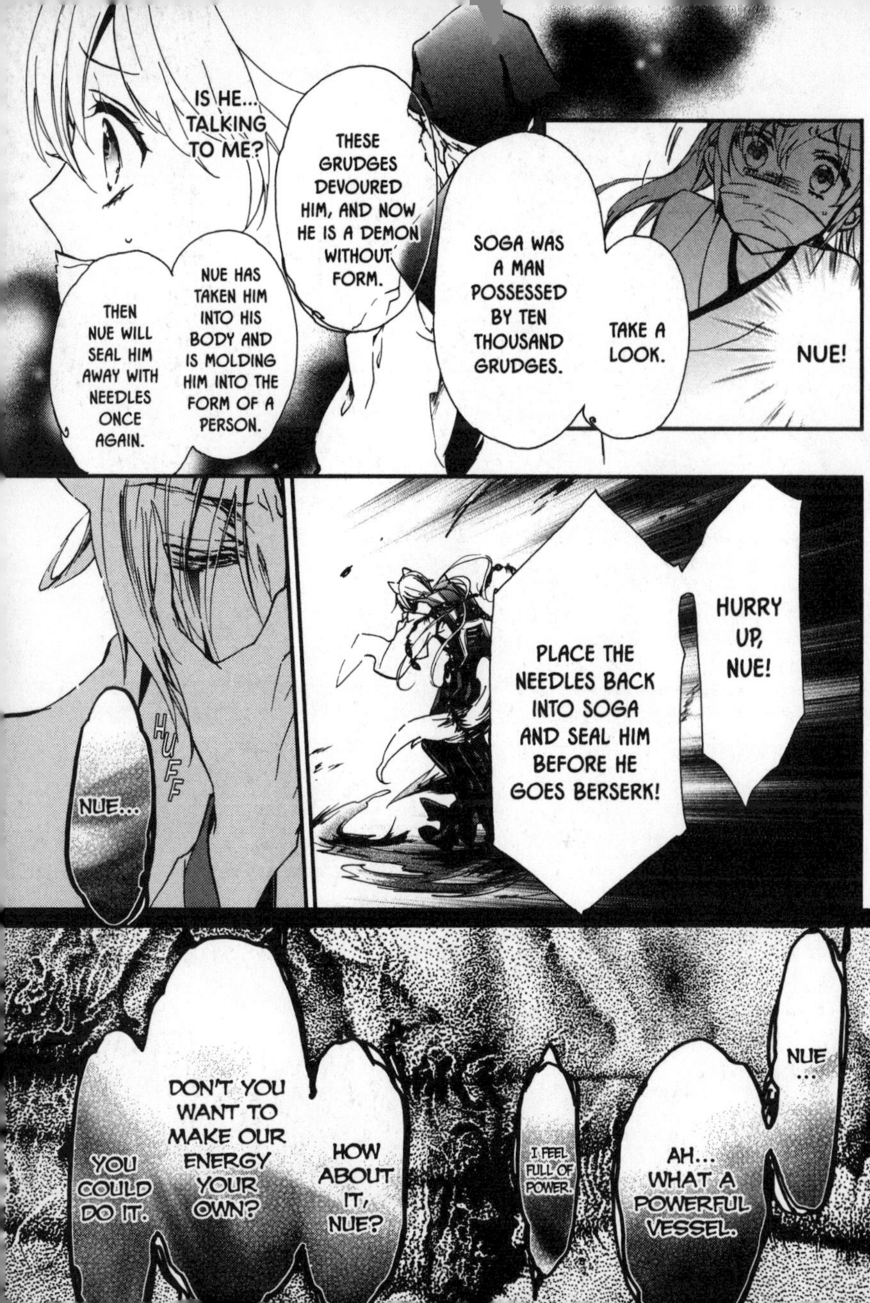
NUE!
TAKE A LOOK.
SOGA WAS A MAN POSSESSED BY TEN THOUSAND GRUDGES.
THESE GRUDGES DEVOURED HIM, AND NOW HE IS A DEMON WITHOUT FORM.
IS HE... TALKING TO ME?
NUE HAS TAKEN HIM INTO HIS BODY AND IS MOLDING HIM INTO THE FORM OF A PERSON.
THEN NUE WILL SEAL HIM AWAY WITH NEEDLES ONCE AGAIN.
HURRY UP, NUE!
PLACE THE NEEDLES BACK INTO SOGA AND SEAL HIM BEFORE HE GOES BERSERK!
HUFF
NUE...
NUE...
AH... WHAT A POWERFUL VESSEL.
I FEEL FULL OF POWER.
HOW ABOUT IT, NUE?
DON'T YOU WANT TO MAKE OUR ENERGY YOUR OWN?
YOU COULD DO IT.

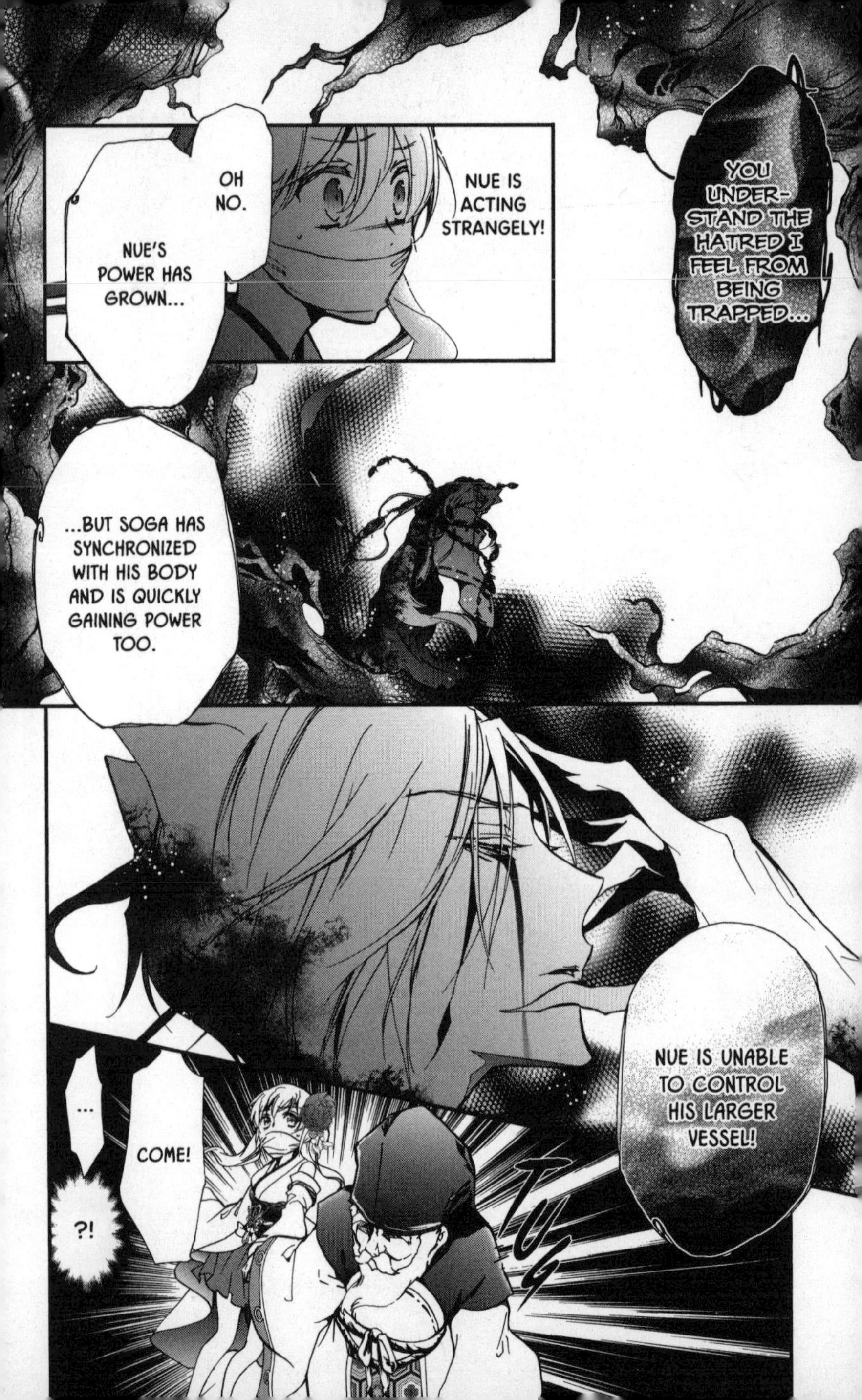
YOU UNDER-STAND THE HATRED I FEEL FROM BEING TRAPPED...
NUE IS ACTING STRANGELY!
OH NO.
NUE'S POWER HAS GROWN...
...BUT SOGA HAS SYNCHRONIZED WITH HIS BODY AND IS QUICKLY GAINING POWER TOO.
NUE IS UNABLE TO CONTROL HIS LARGER VESSEL!
TUG
COME!
...
?!

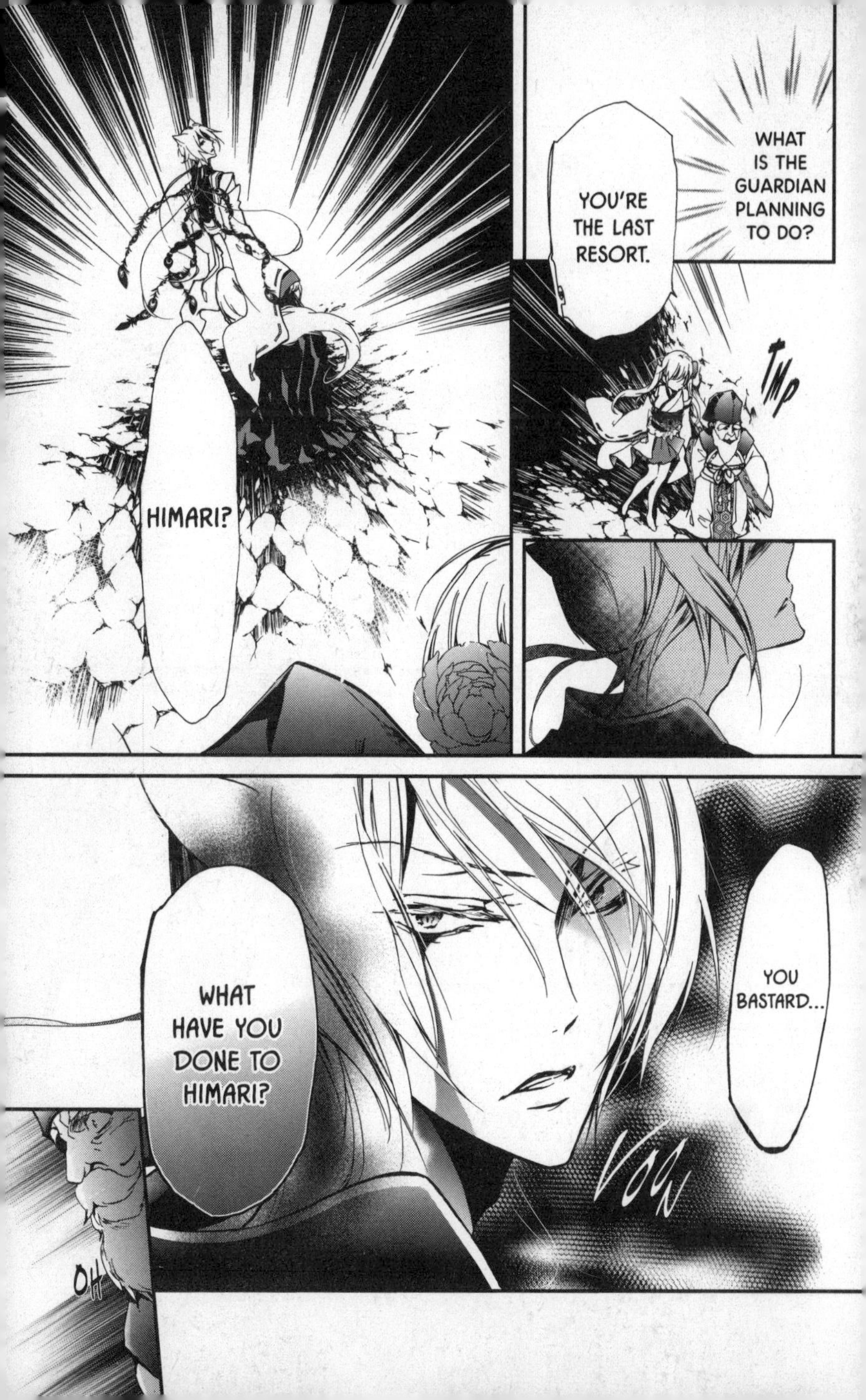
WHAT IS THE GUARDIAN PLANNING TO DO?
YOU'RE THE LAST RESORT.
TMP
HIMARI?
YOU BASTARD...
VOON
WHAT HAVE YOU DONE TO HIMARI?
OH

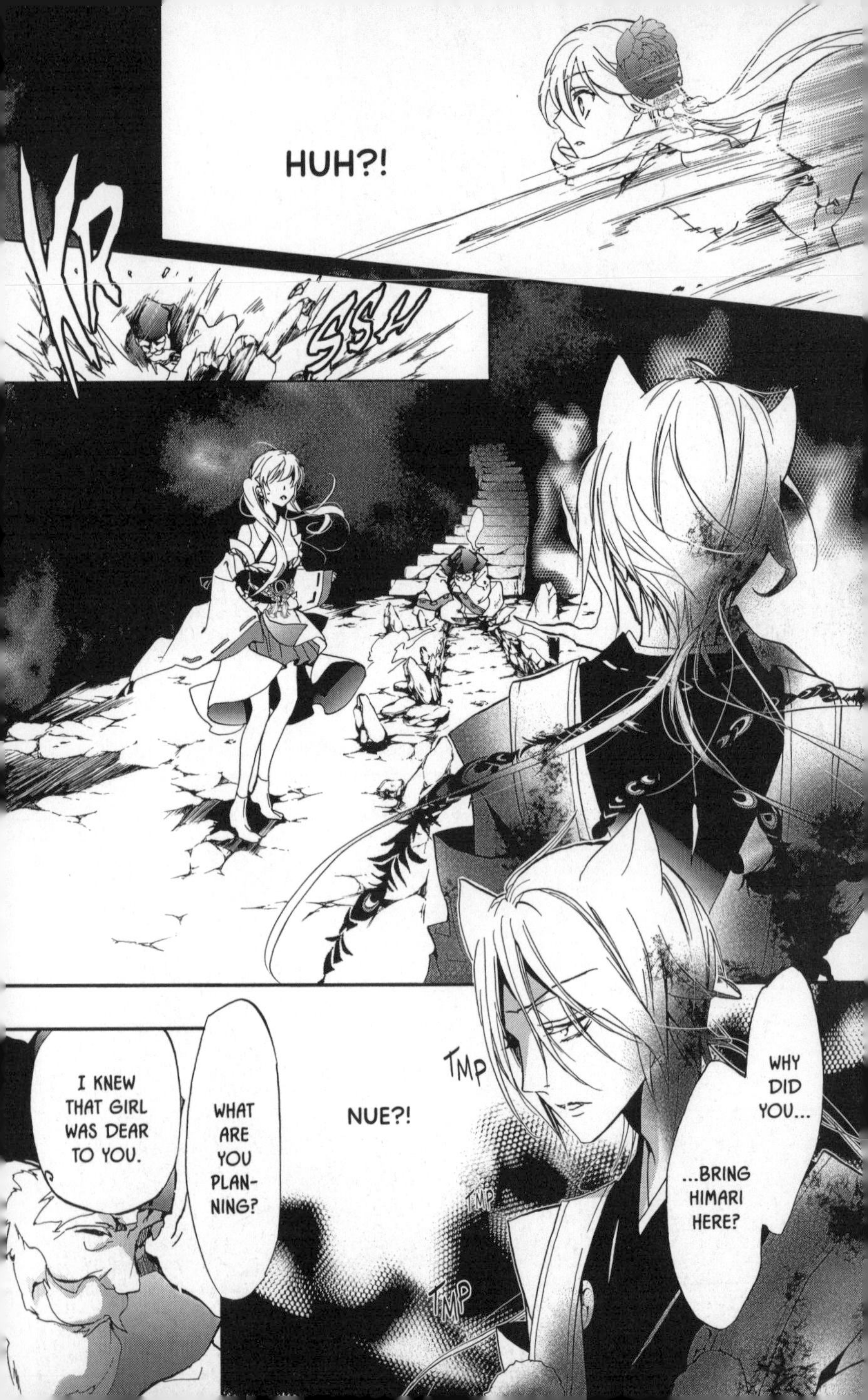
HUH?!
KR
SSH
WHY DID YOU...
...BRING HIMARI HERE?
TMP
TMP
TMP
NUE?!
WHAT ARE YOU PLAN-NING?
I KNEW THAT GIRL WAS DEAR TO YOU.

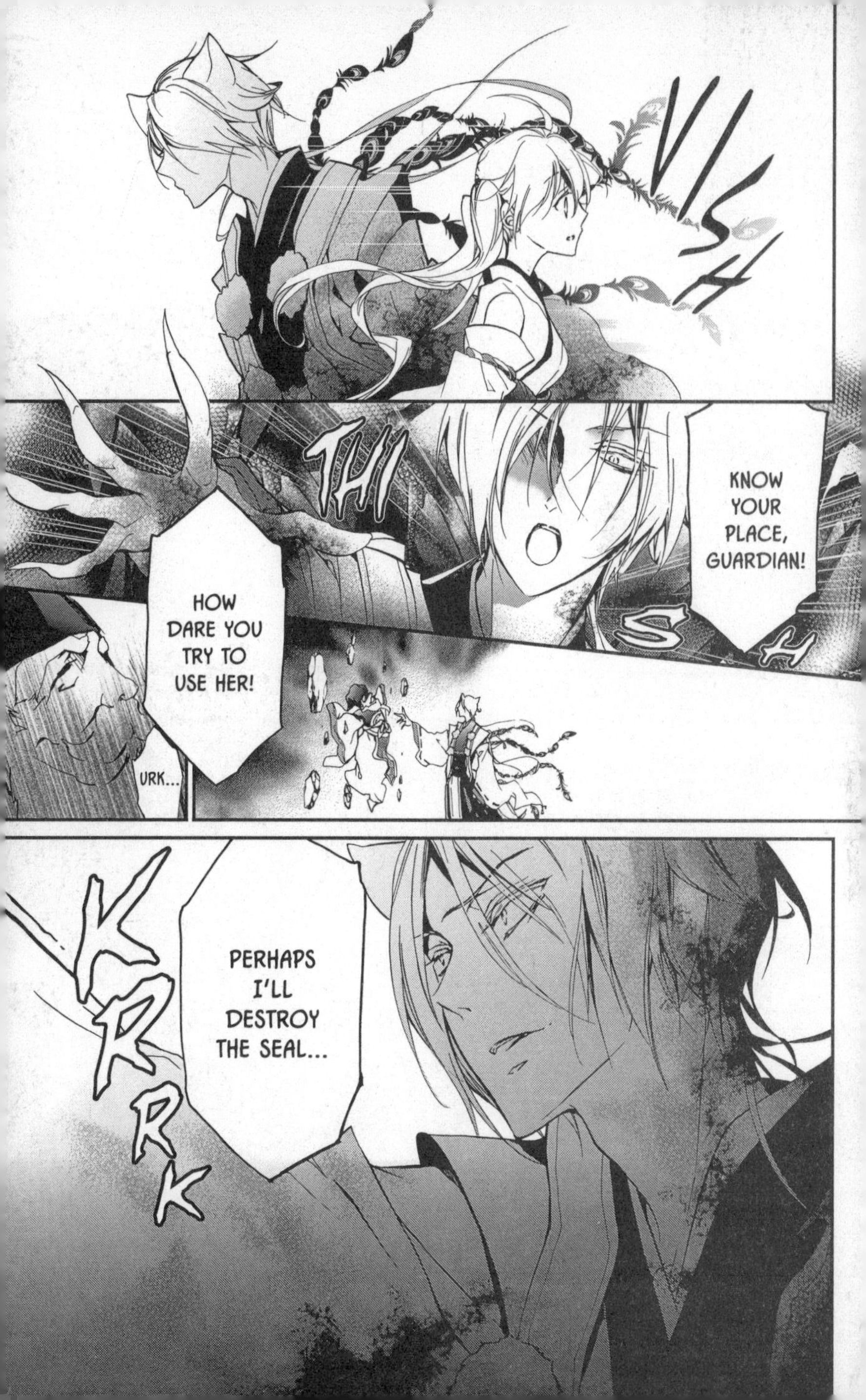
VISH
KNOW YOUR PLACE, GUARDIAN!
THI
SH
HOW DARE YOU TRY TO USE HER!
URK...
PERHAPS I'LL DESTROY THE SEAL...
KRRK

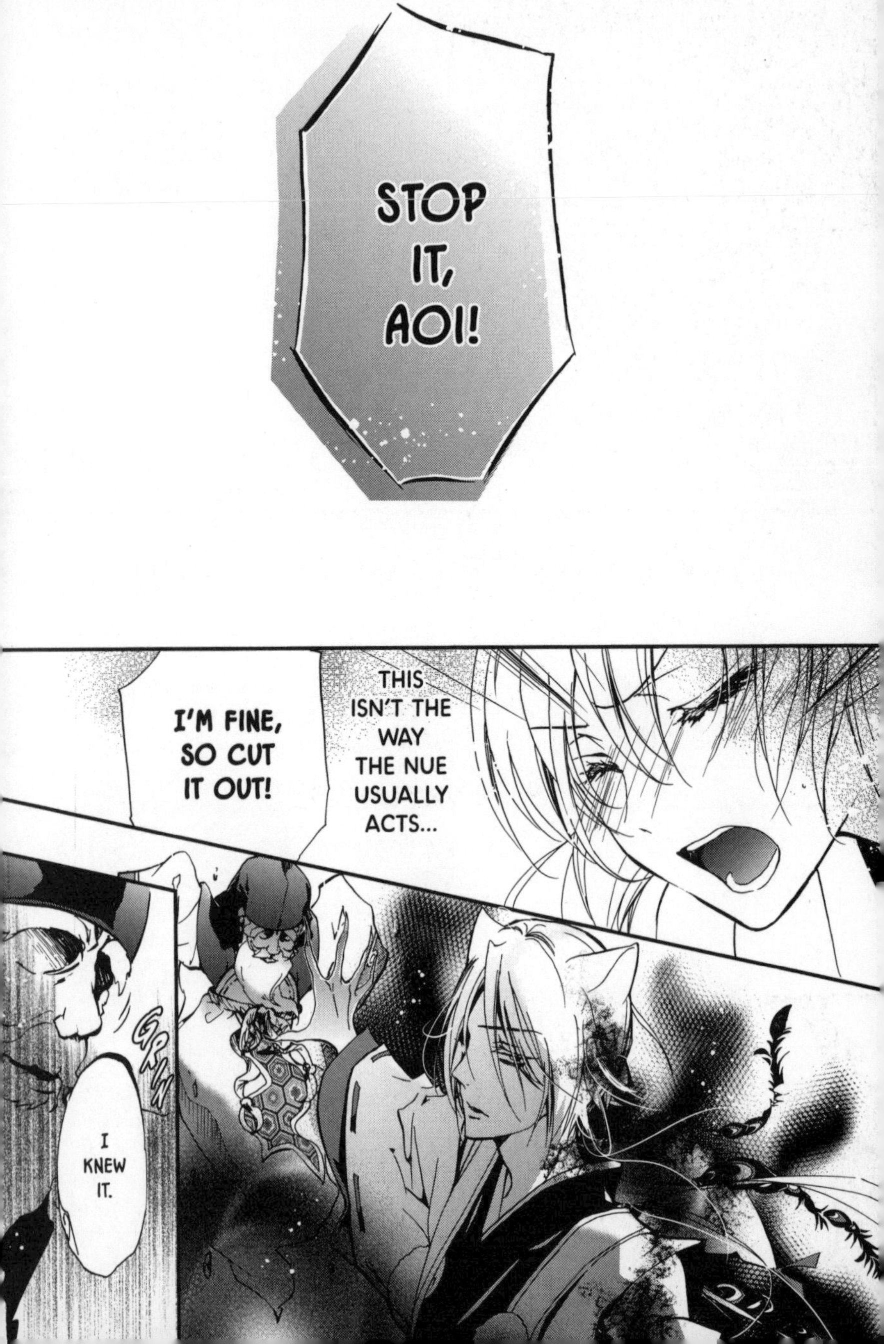
STOP IT, AOI!
THIS ISN'T THE WAY THE NUE USUALLY ACTS...
I'M FINE, SO CUT IT OUT!
GRIN
I KNEW IT.

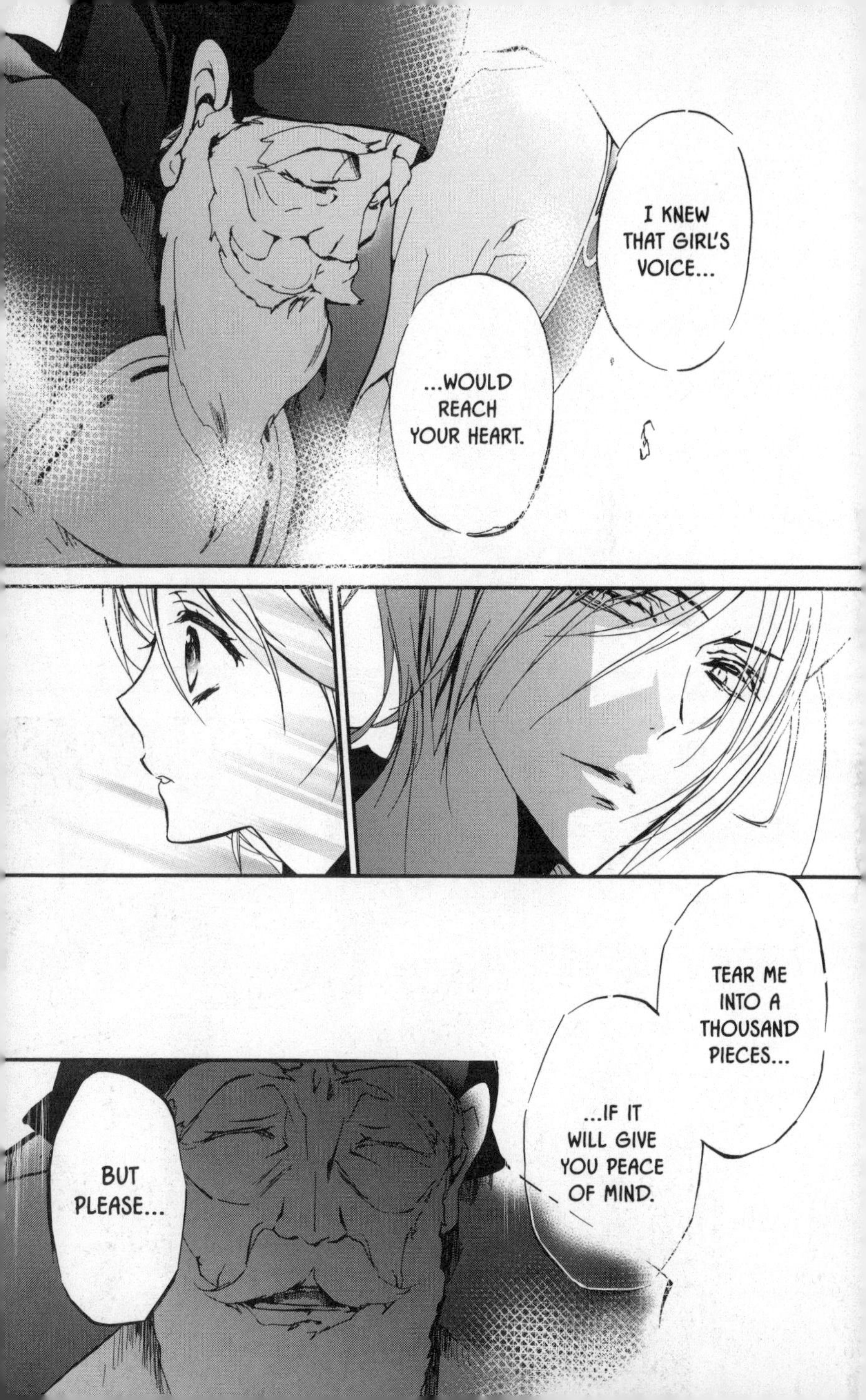
I KNEW THAT GIRL'S VOICE...
...WOULD REACH YOUR HEART.
TEAR ME INTO A THOUSAND PIECES...
...IF IT WILL GIVE YOU PEACE OF MIND.
BUT PLEASE...

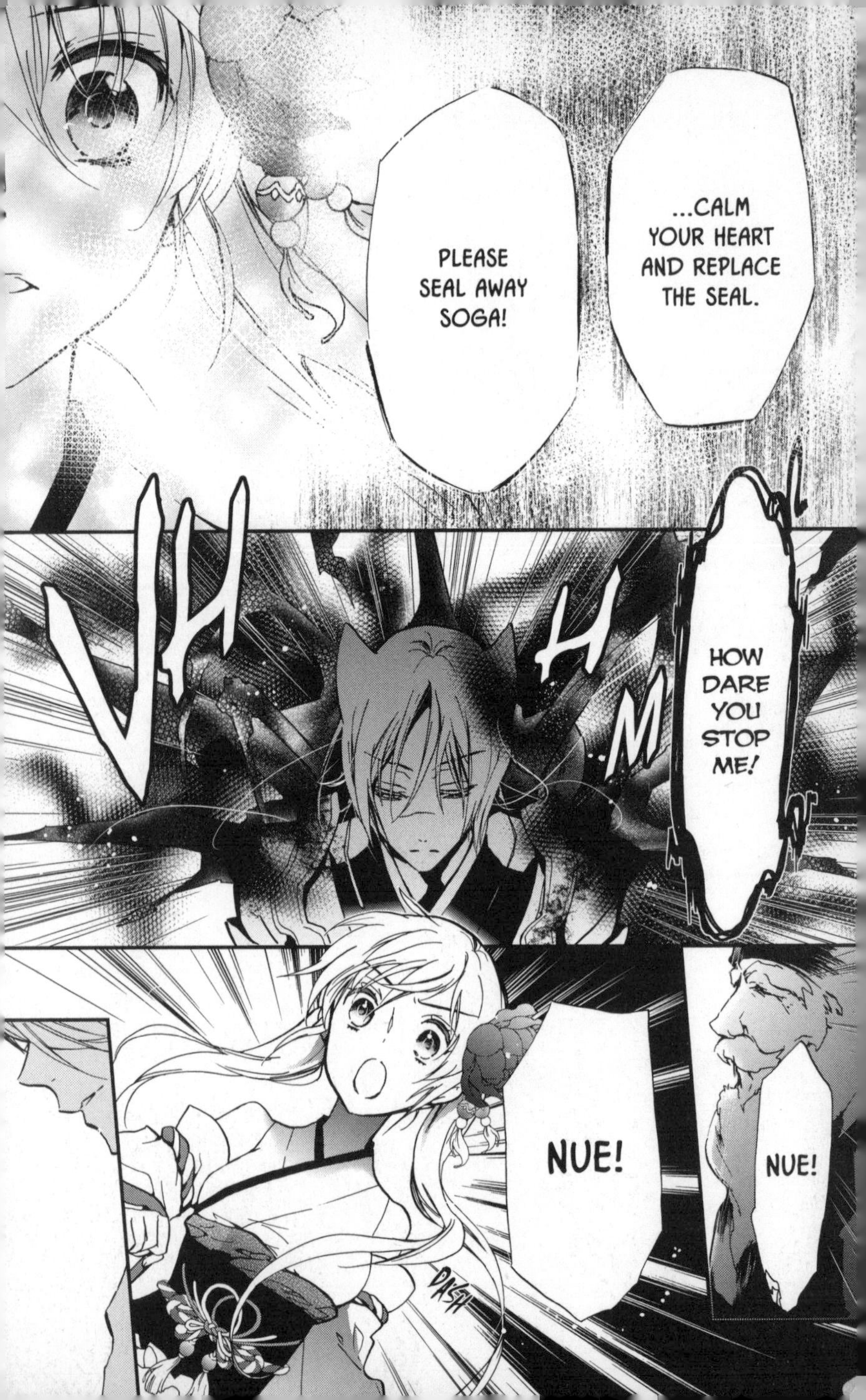
...CALM YOUR HEART AND REPLACE THE SEAL.
PLEASE SEAL AWAY SOGA!
HOW DARE YOU STOP ME!
VHHM
NUE!
NUE!
DASH

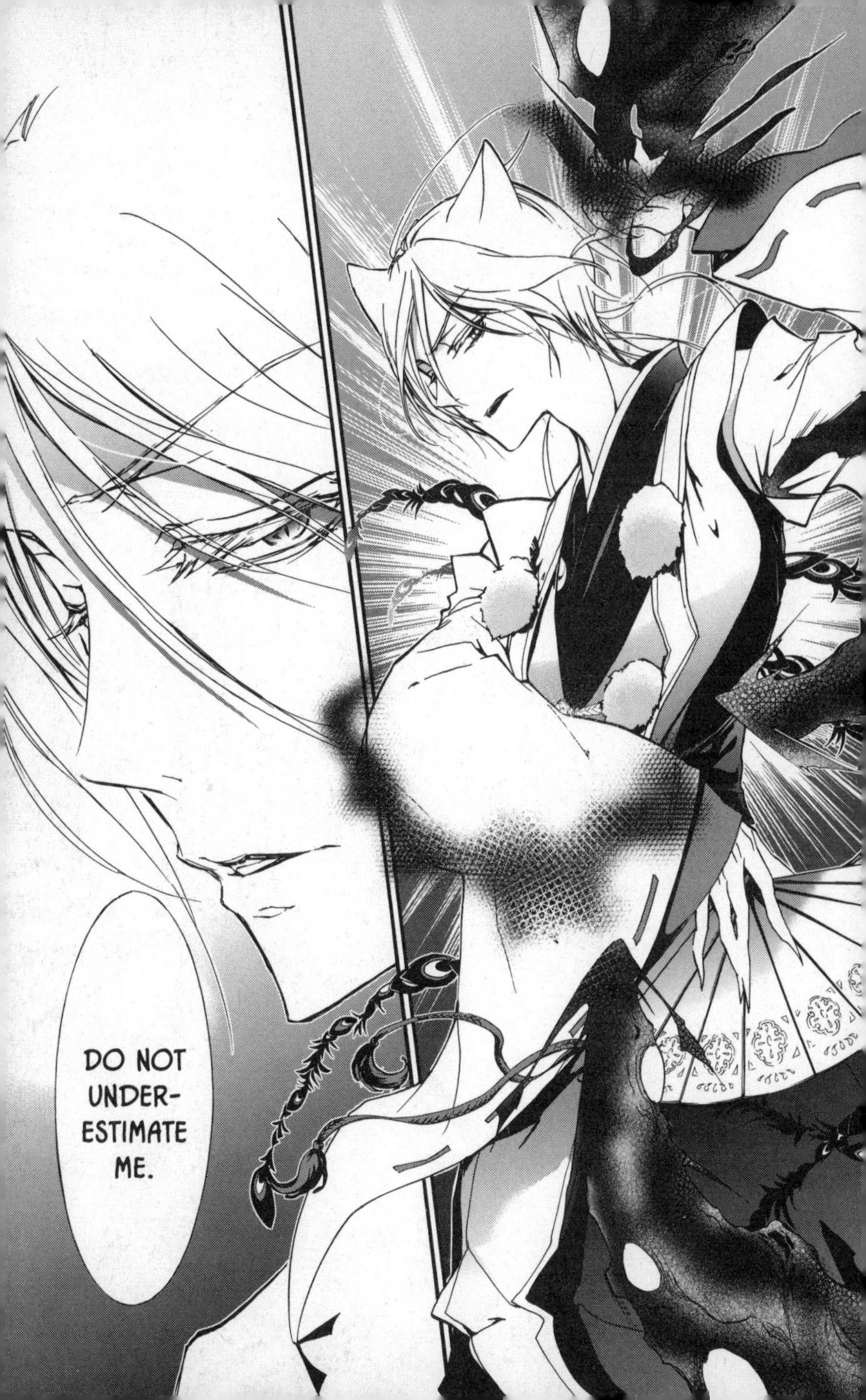
DO NOT UNDER-ESTIMATE ME.

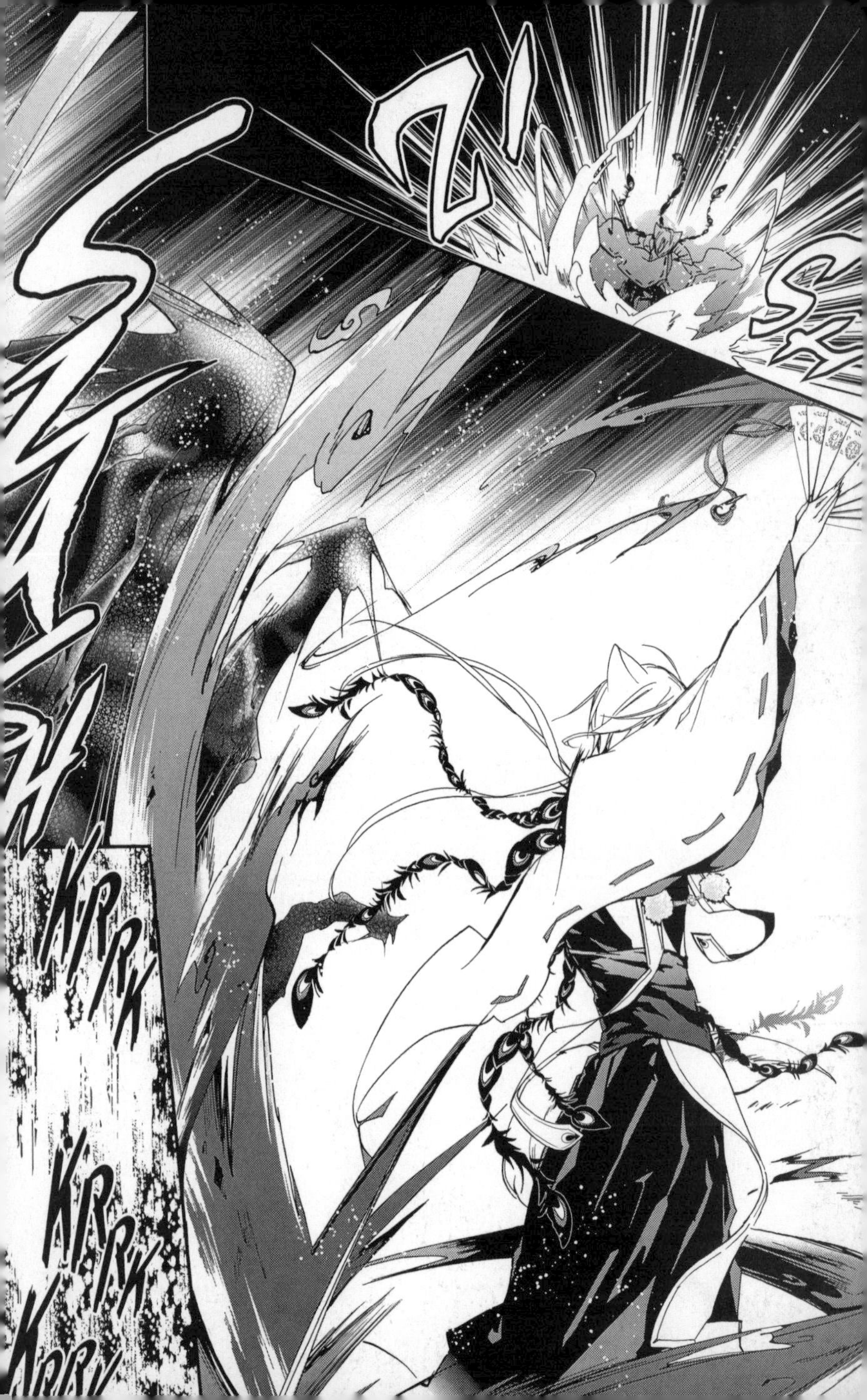
KRRK
KRRK

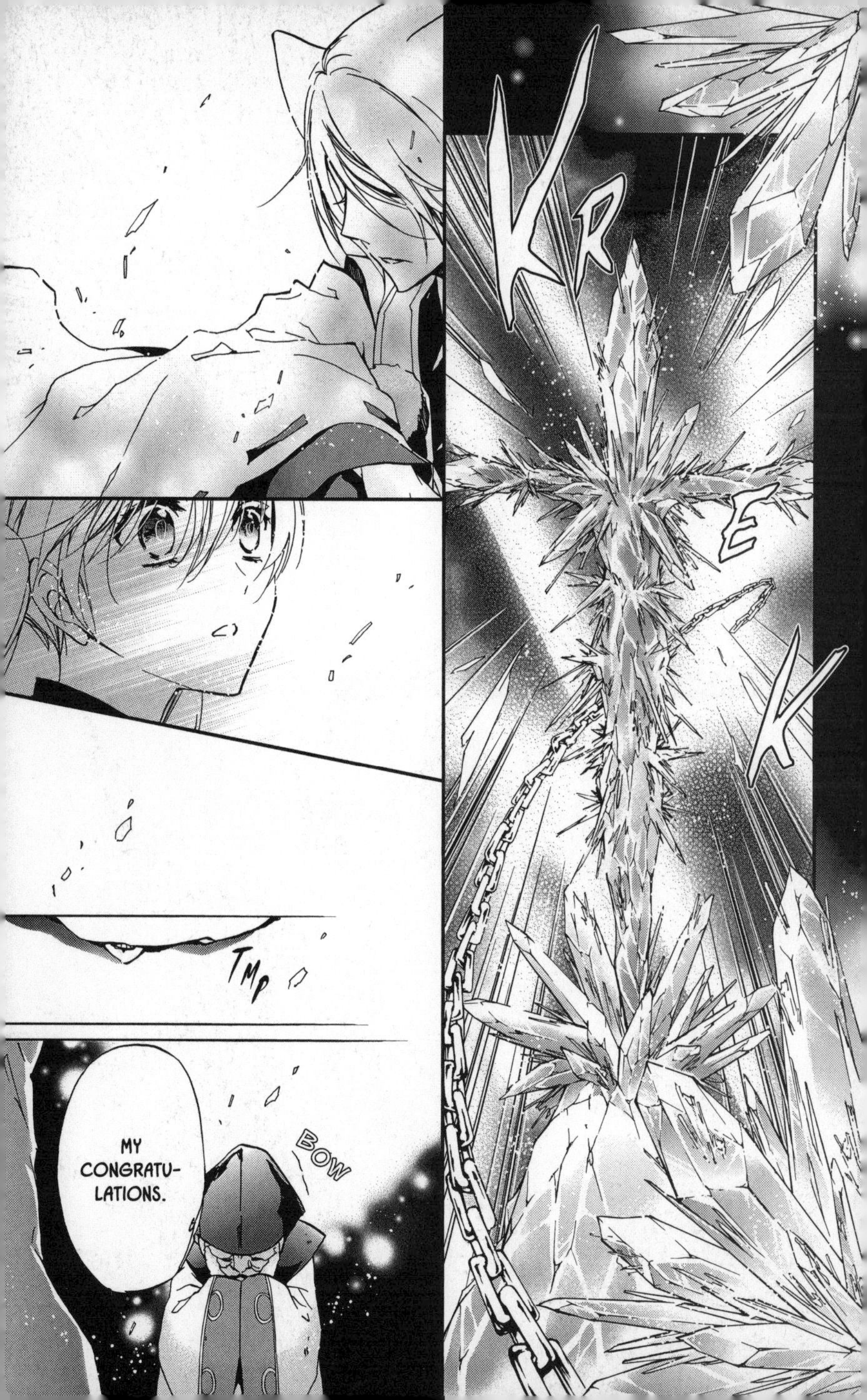
KREK
TMP
BOW
MY CONGRATU-LATIONS.

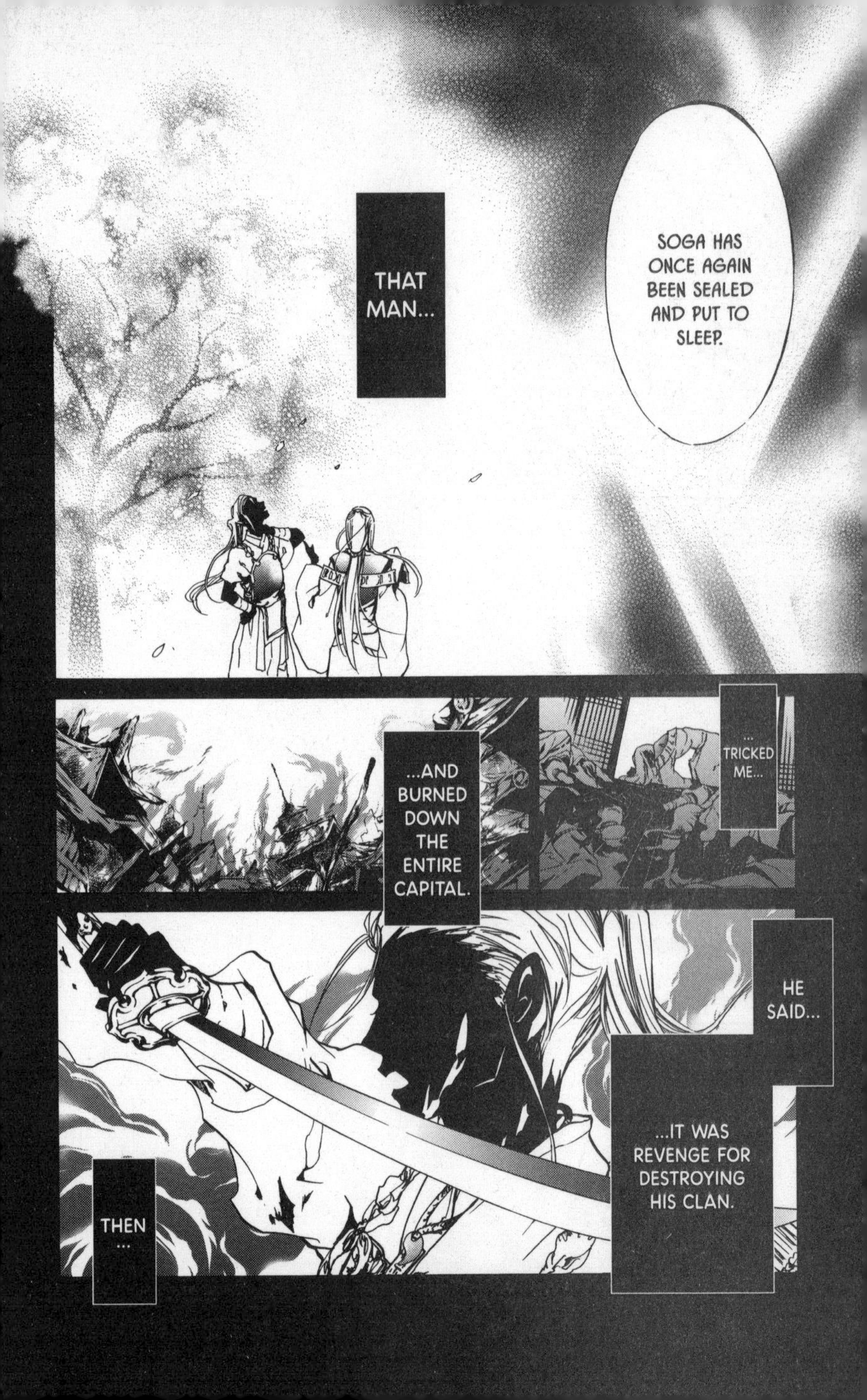
SOGA HAS ONCE AGAIN BEEN SEALED AND PUT TO SLEEP.
THAT MAN...
...TRICKED ME...
...AND BURNED DOWN THE ENTIRE CAPITAL.
HE SAID...
...IT WAS REVENGE FOR DESTROYING HIS CLAN.
THEN ...

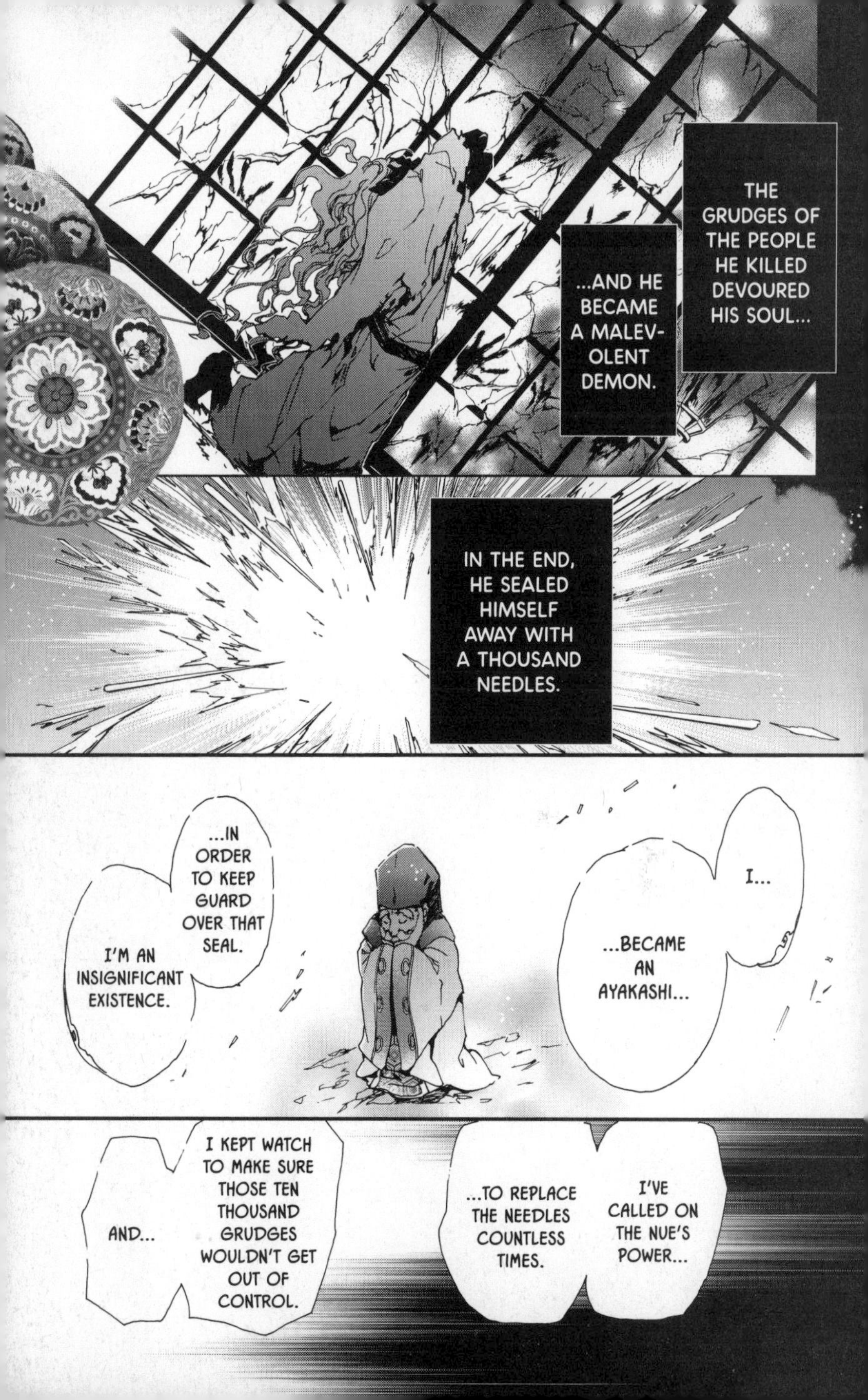
THE GRUDGES OF THE PEOPLE HE KILLED DEVOURED HIS SOUL...
...AND HE BECAME A MALEV-OLENT DEMON.
IN THE END, HE SEALED HIMSELF AWAY WITH A THOUSAND NEEDLES.
I...
...BECAME AN AYAKASHI...
...IN ORDER TO KEEP GUARD OVER THAT SEAL.
I'M AN INSIGNIFICANT EXISTENCE.
I'VE CALLED ON THE NUE'S POWER...
...TO REPLACE THE NEEDLES COUNTLESS TIMES.
I KEPT WATCH TO MAKE SURE THOSE TEN THOUSAND GRUDGES WOULDN'T GET OUT OF CONTROL.
AND...

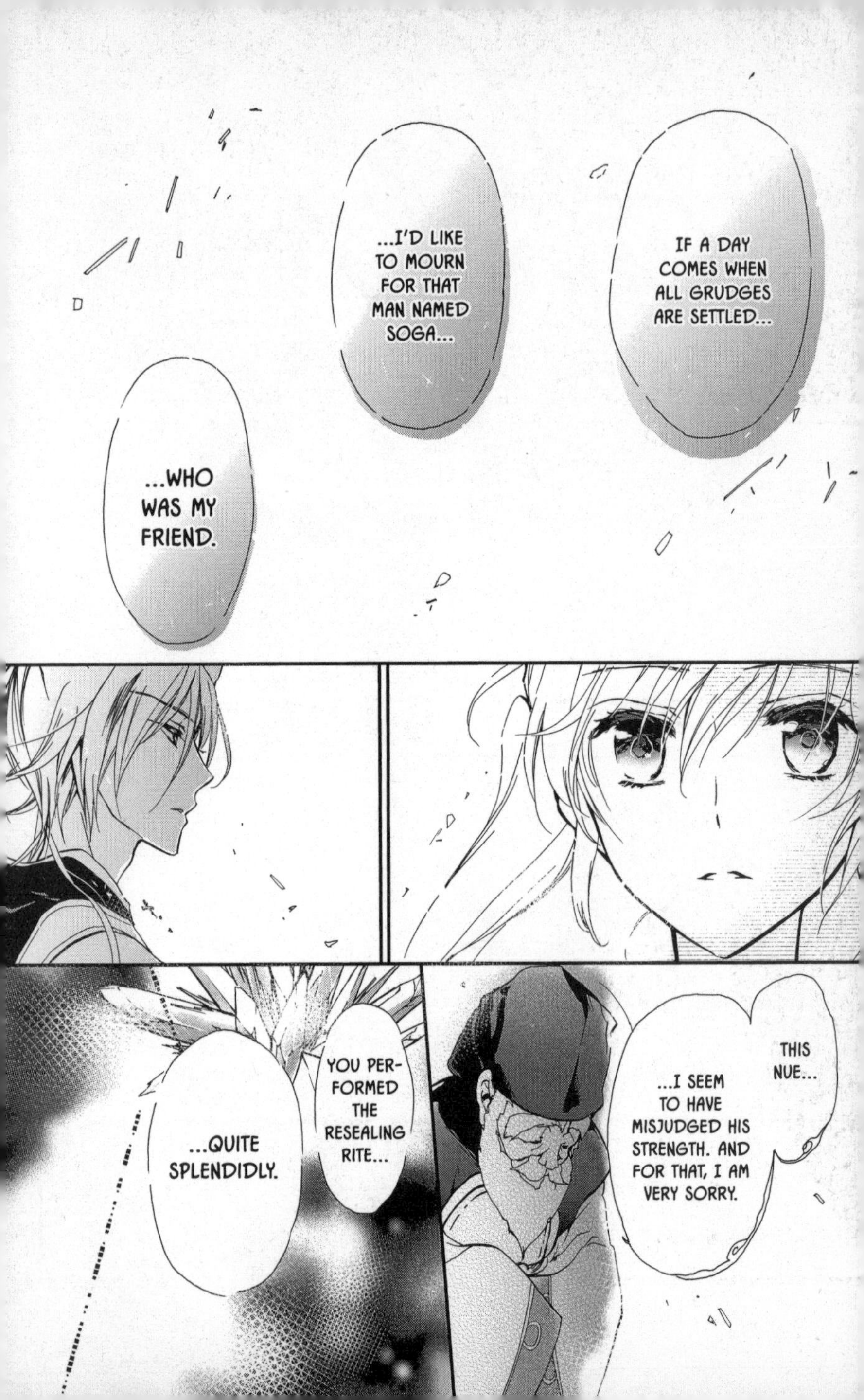
IF A DAY COMES WHEN ALL GRUDGES ARE SETTLED...
...I'D LIKE TO MOURN FOR THAT MAN NAMED SOGA...
...WHO WAS MY FRIEND.
THIS NUE...
...I SEEM TO HAVE MISJUDGED HIS STRENGTH. AND FOR THAT, I AM VERY SORRY.
YOU PER-FORMED THE RESEALING RITE...
...QUITE SPLENDIDLY.

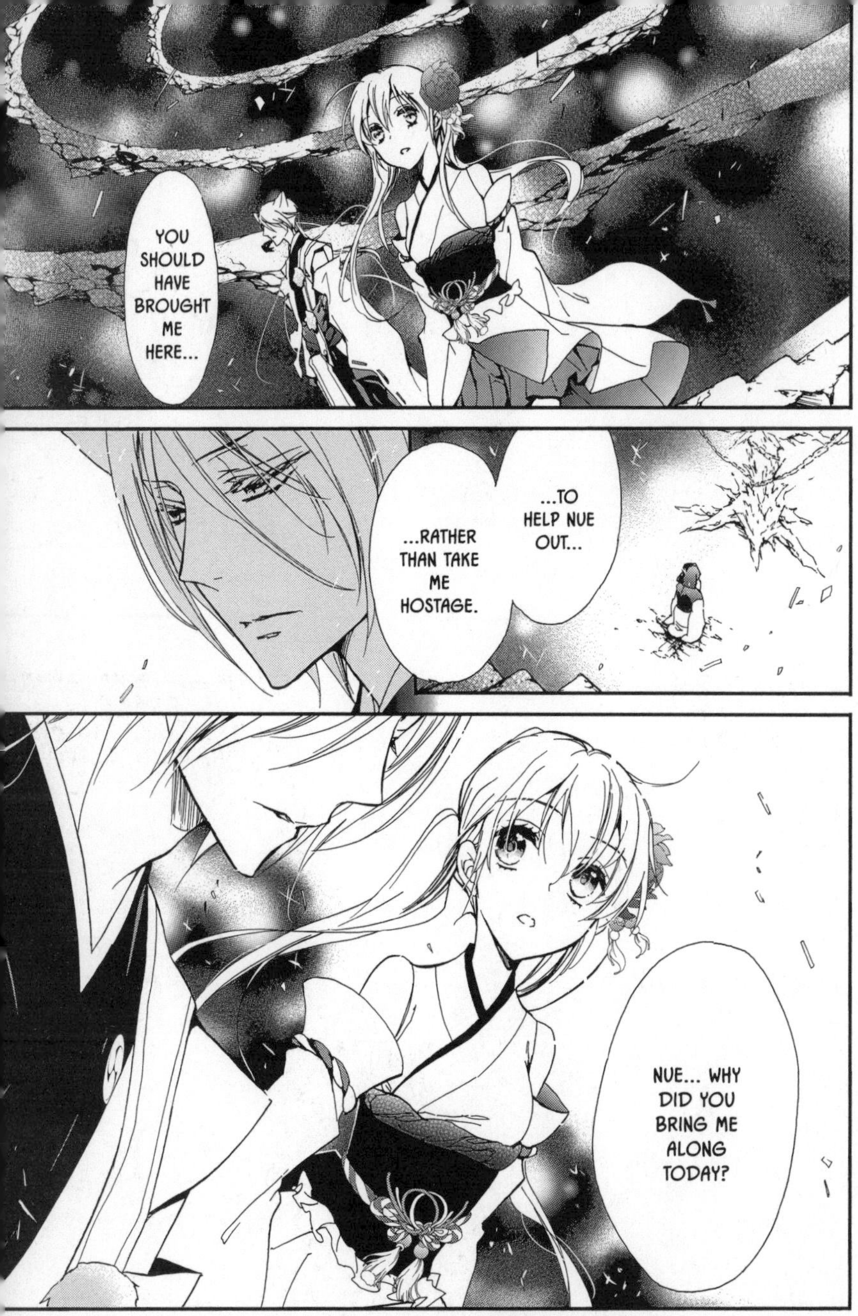
YOU SHOULD HAVE BROUGHT ME HERE...
...TO HELP NUE OUT...
...RATHER THAN TAKE ME HOSTAGE.
NUE... WHY DID YOU BRING ME ALONG TODAY?

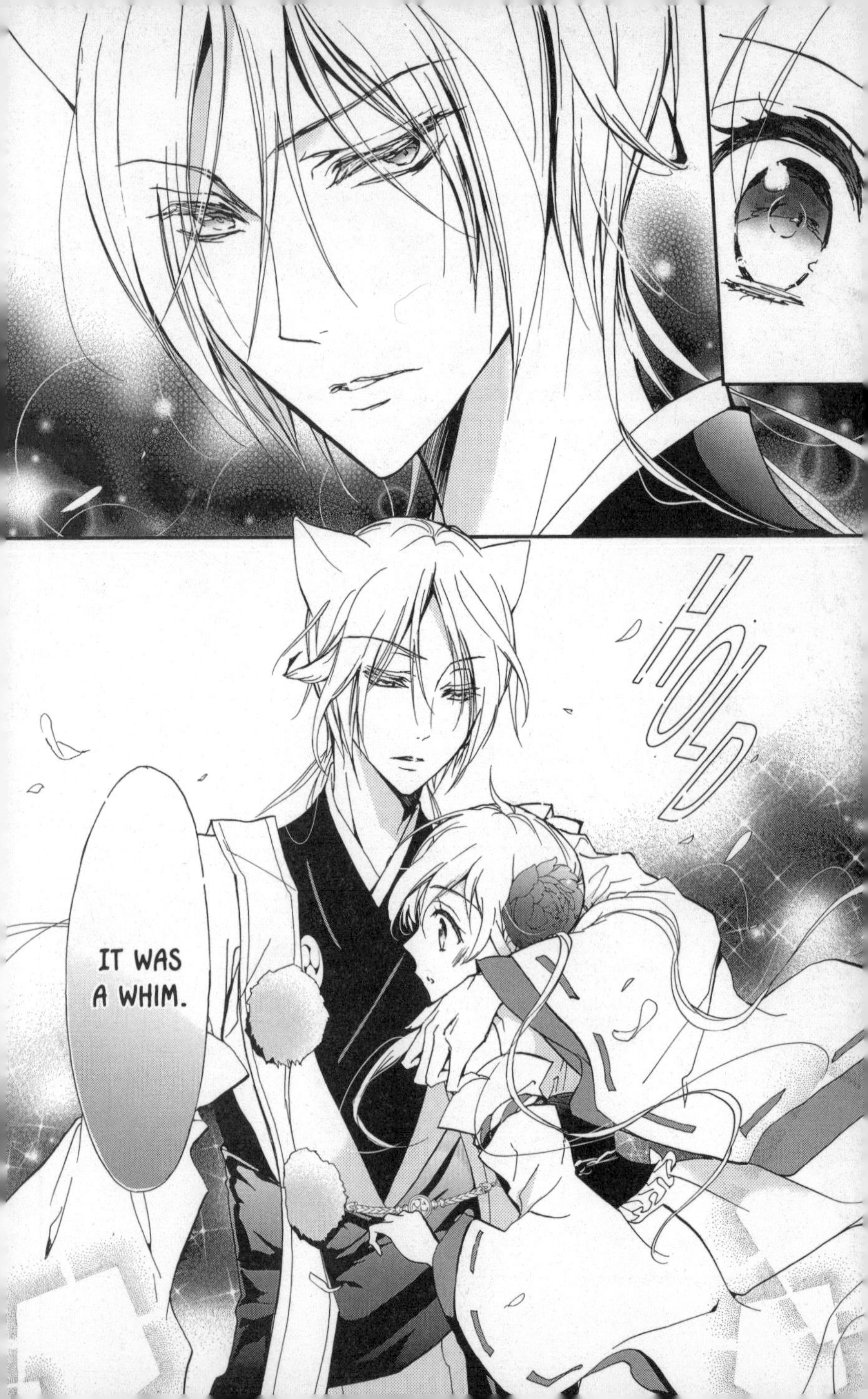
HOLD
IT WAS A WHIM.

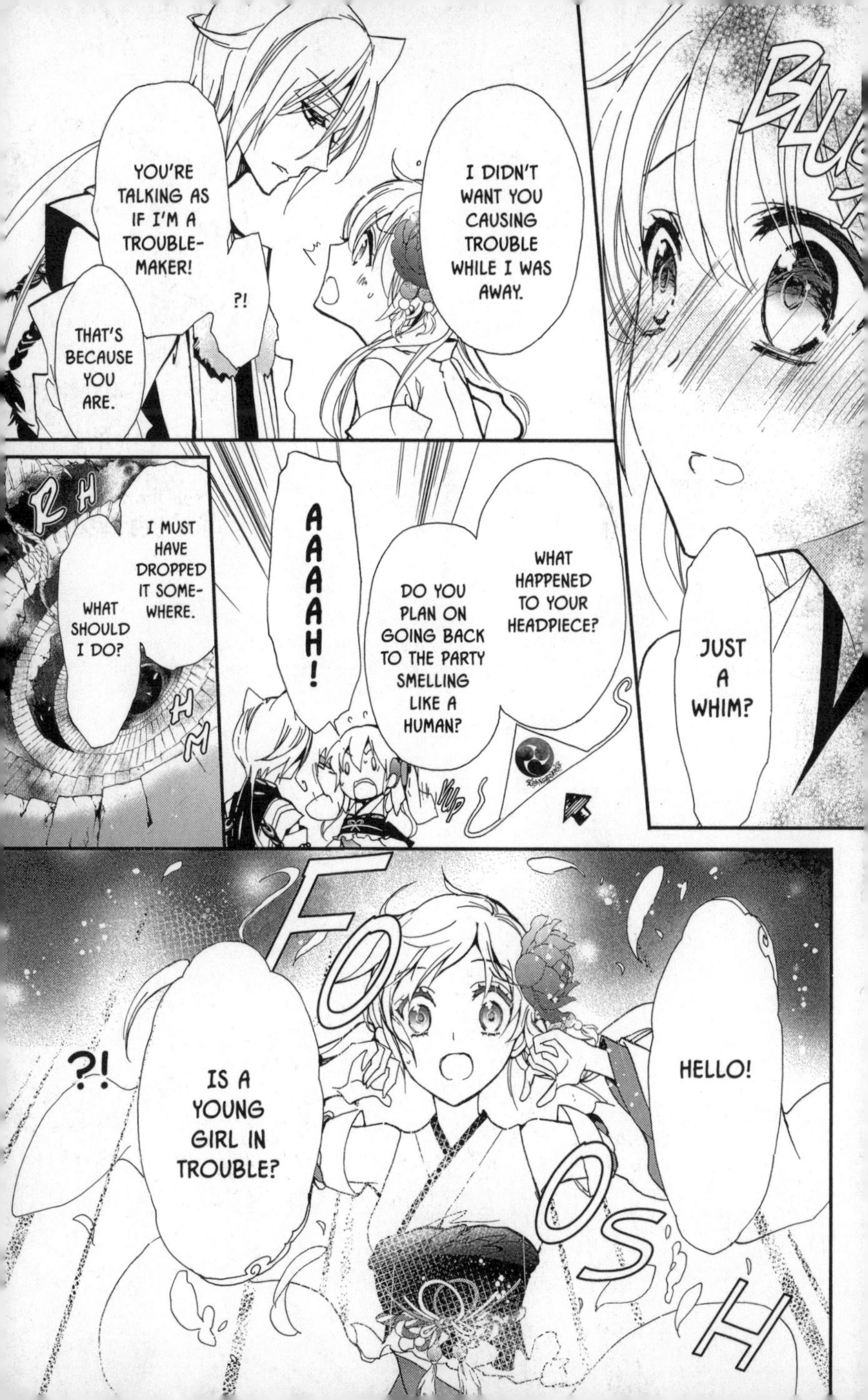
JUST A WHIM?
I DIDN'T WANT YOU CAUSING TROUBLE WHILE I WAS AWAY.
YOU'RE TALKING AS IF I'M A TROUBLE-MAKER!
?!
THAT'S BECAUSE YOU ARE.
WHAT HAPPENED TO YOUR HEADPIECE?
DO YOU PLAN ON GOING BACK TO THE PARTY SMELLING LIKE A HUMAN?
YUP
AAAAAH!
I MUST HAVE DROPPED IT SOME-WHERE.
WHAT SHOULD I DO?
HELLO!
FOOOSH
IS A YOUNG GIRL IN TROUBLE?
?!

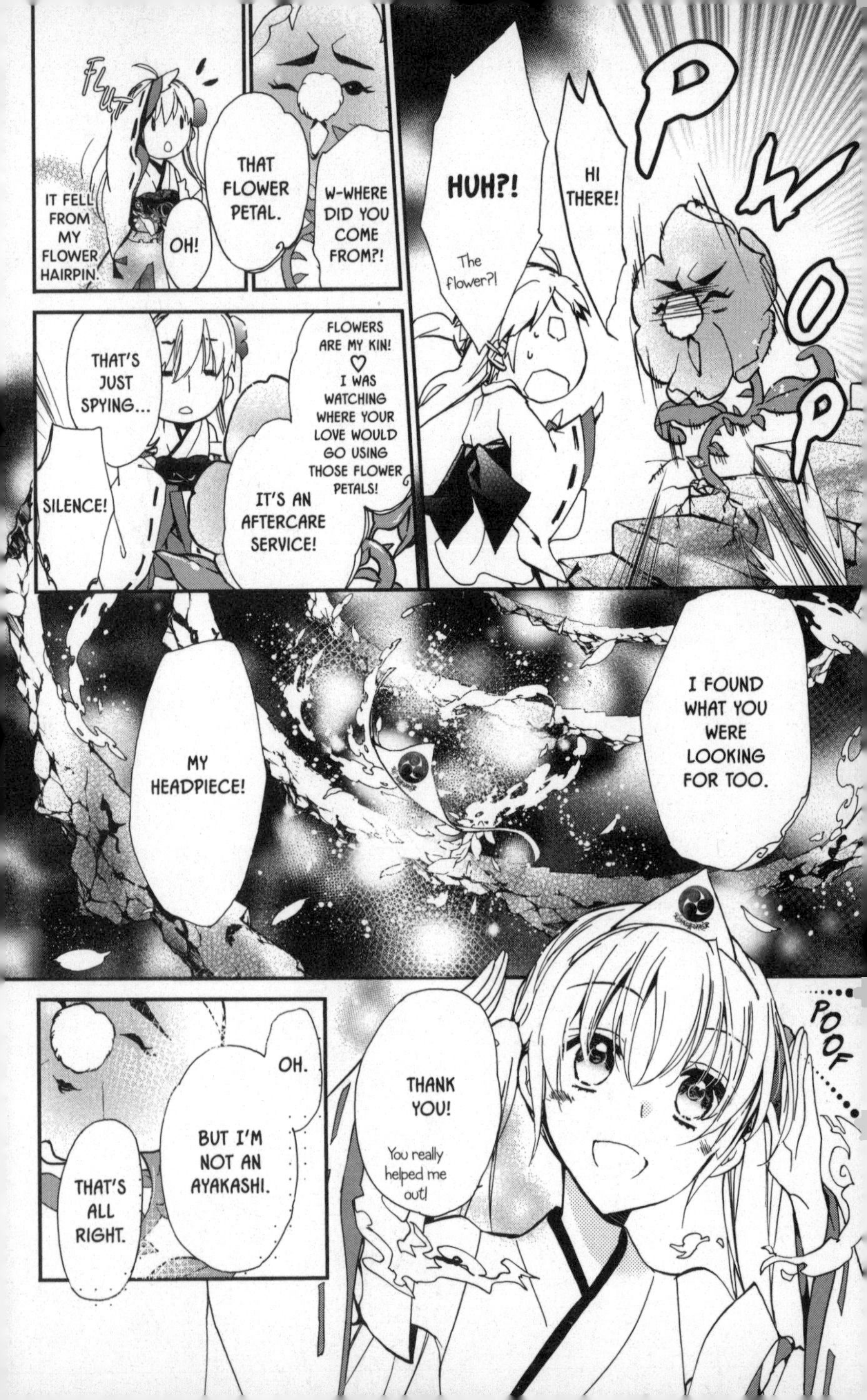
PWOP
HI THERE!
HUH?!
The flower?!
W-WHERE DID YOU COME FROM?!
THAT FLOWER PETAL.
FLUT
OH!
IT FELL FROM MY FLOWER HAIRPIN.
FLOWERS ARE MY KIN! ♡ I WAS WATCHING WHERE YOUR LOVE WOULD GO USING THOSE FLOWER PETALS!
THAT'S JUST SPYING...
IT'S AN AFTERCARE SERVICE!
SILENCE!
I FOUND WHAT YOU WERE LOOKING FOR TOO.
MY HEADPIECE!
POOF
THANK YOU!
You really helped me out!
OH.
BUT I'M NOT AN AYAKASHI.
THAT'S ALL RIGHT.

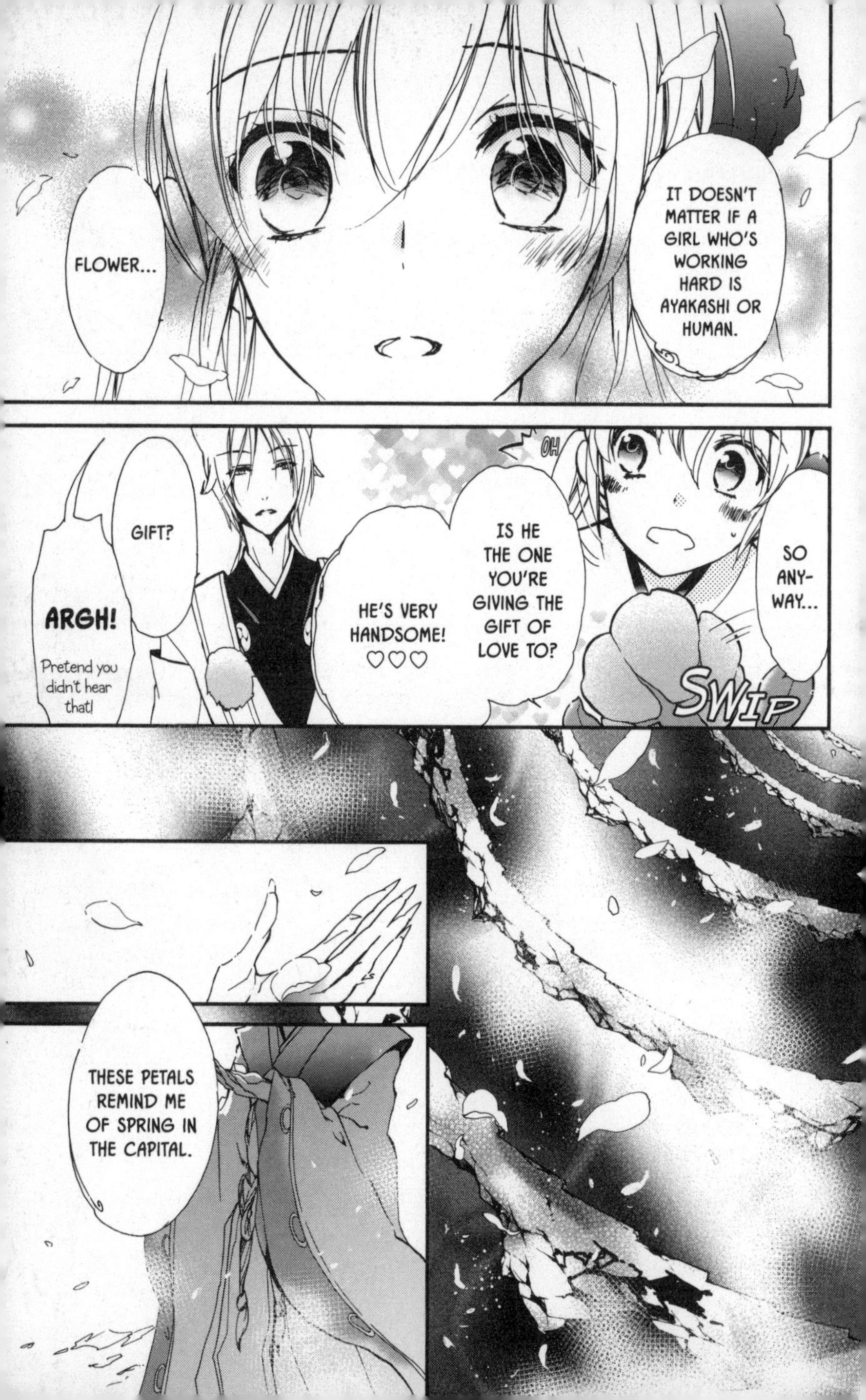
IT DOESN'T MATTER IF A GIRL WHO'S WORKING HARD IS AYAKASHI OR HUMAN.
FLOWER...
SO ANYWAY...
SWIP
OH
IS HE THE ONE YOU'RE GIVING THE GIFT OF LOVE TO?
HE'S VERY HANDSOME! ♡♡♡
GIFT?
ARGH!
Pretend you didn't hear that!
THESE PETALS REMIND ME OF SPRING IN THE CAPITAL.

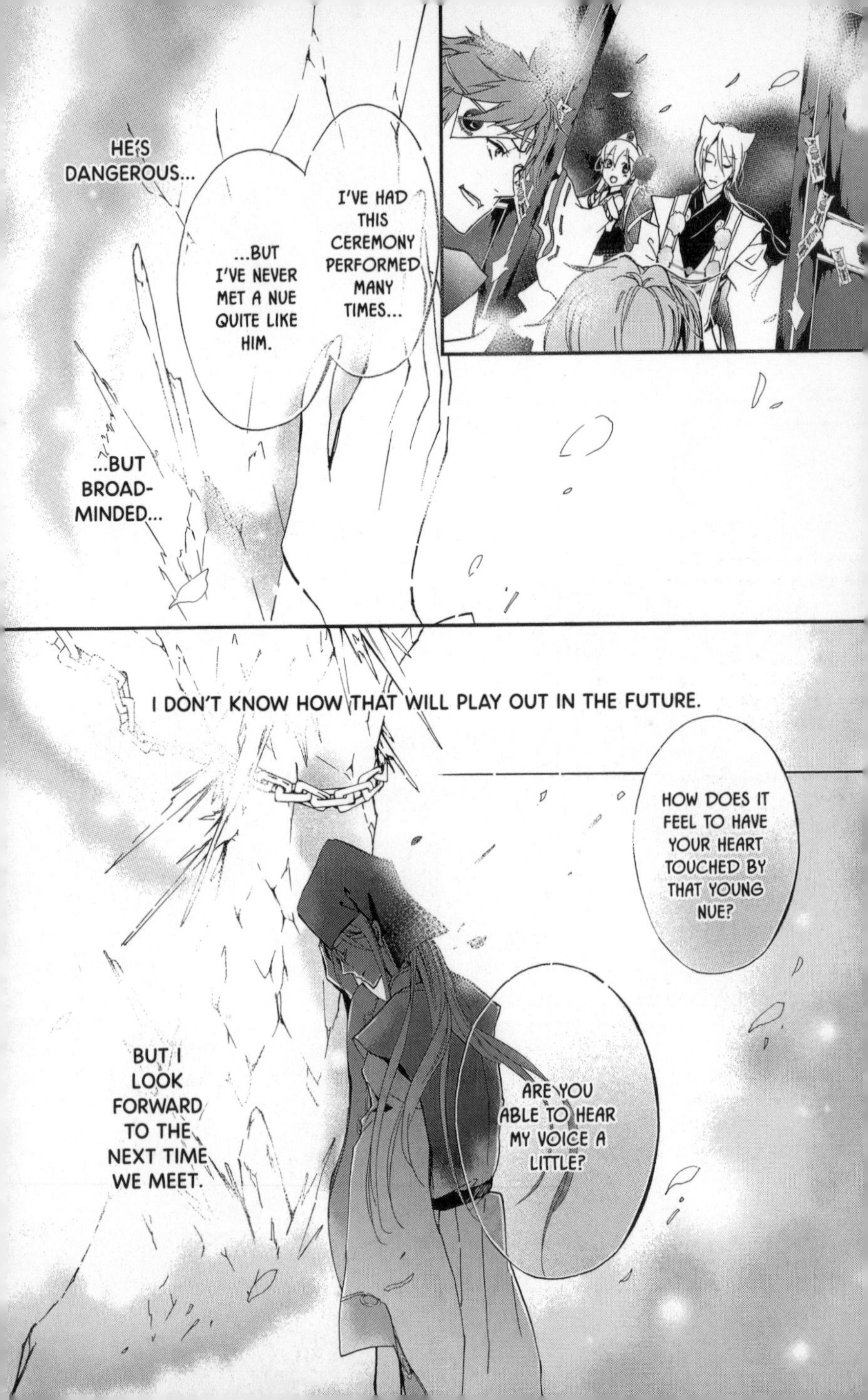
I'VE HAD THIS CEREMONY PERFORMED MANY TIMES...
...BUT I'VE NEVER MET A NUE QUITE LIKE HIM.
HE'S DANGEROUS...
...BUT BROAD-MINDED...
I DON'T KNOW HOW THAT WILL PLAY OUT IN THE FUTURE.
HOW DOES IT FEEL TO HAVE YOUR HEART TOUCHED BY THAT YOUNG NUE?
ARE YOU ABLE TO HEAR MY VOICE A LITTLE?
BUT I LOOK FORWARD TO THE NEXT TIME WE MEET.

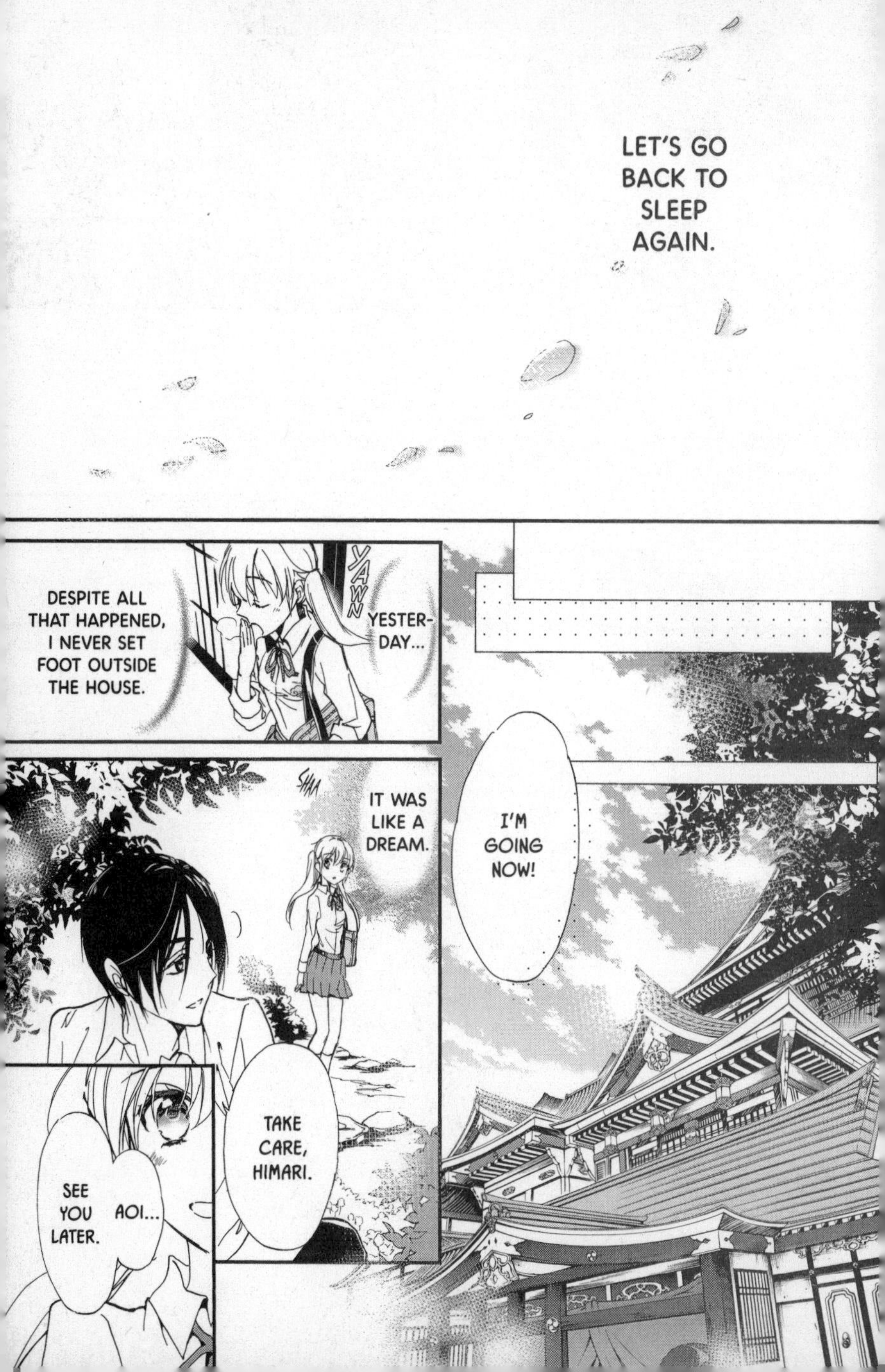
LET'S GO BACK TO SLEEP AGAIN.
I'M GOING NOW!
YESTER-DAY...
YAWN
DESPITE ALL THAT HAPPENED, I NEVER SET FOOT OUTSIDE THE HOUSE.
SHAA
IT WAS LIKE A DREAM.
TAKE CARE, HIMARI.
AOI...
SEE YOU LATER.

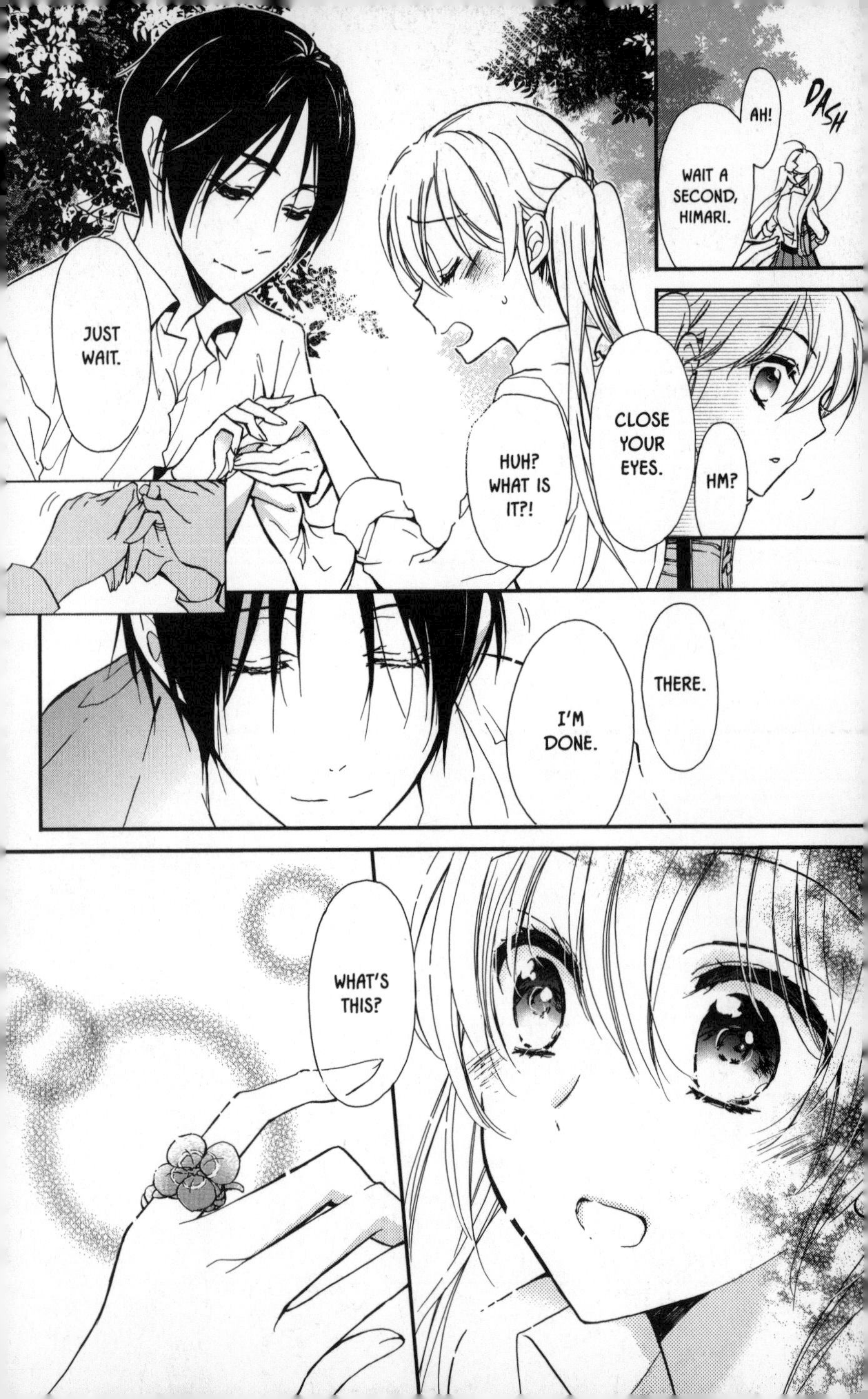
DASH
AH!
WAIT A SECOND, HIMARI.
HM?
CLOSE YOUR EYES.
HUH? WHAT IS IT?!
JUST WAIT.
THERE.
I'M DONE.
WHAT'S THIS?

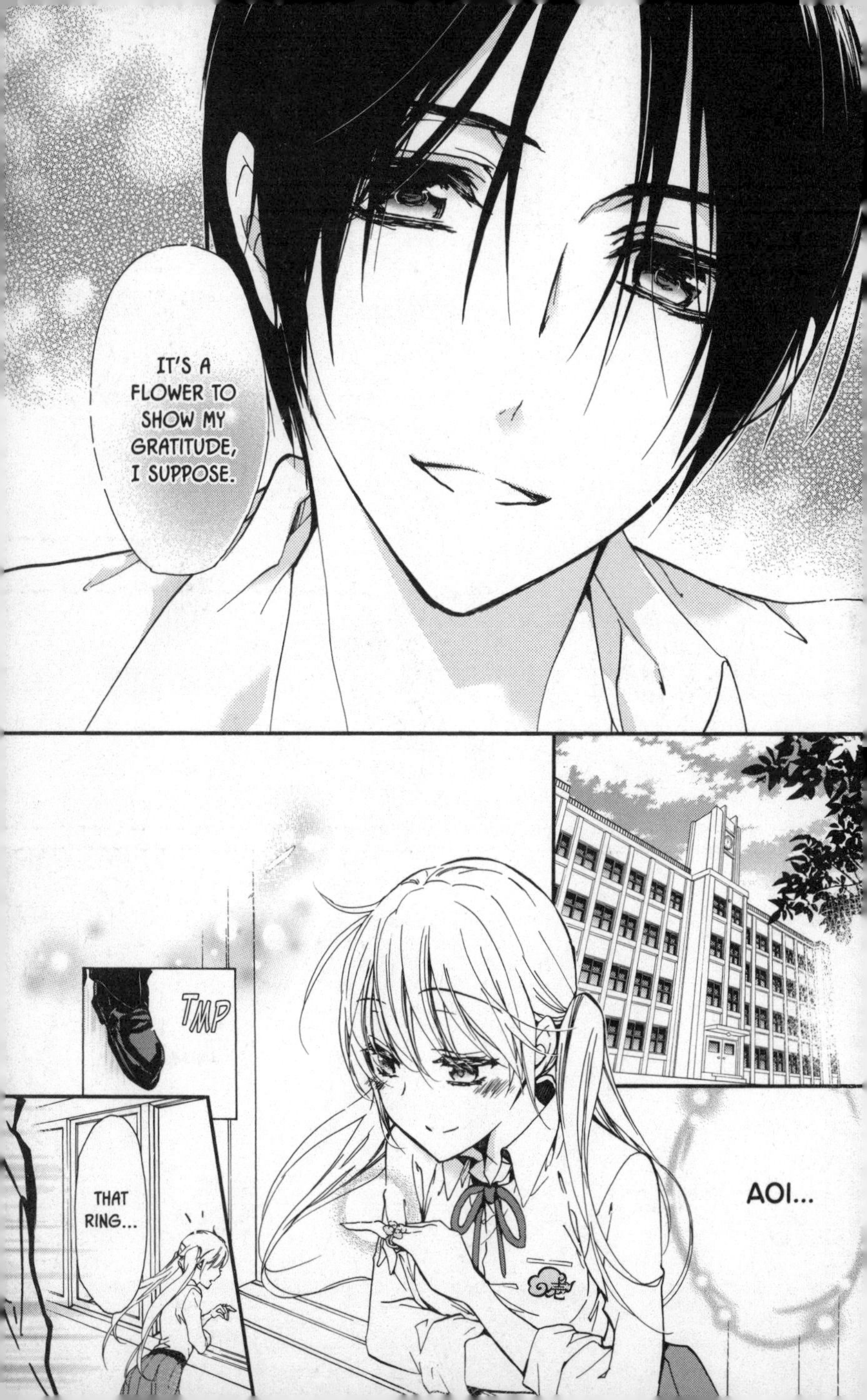
IT'S A FLOWER TO SHOW MY GRATITUDE, I SUPPOSE.
AOI...
TMP
THAT RING...

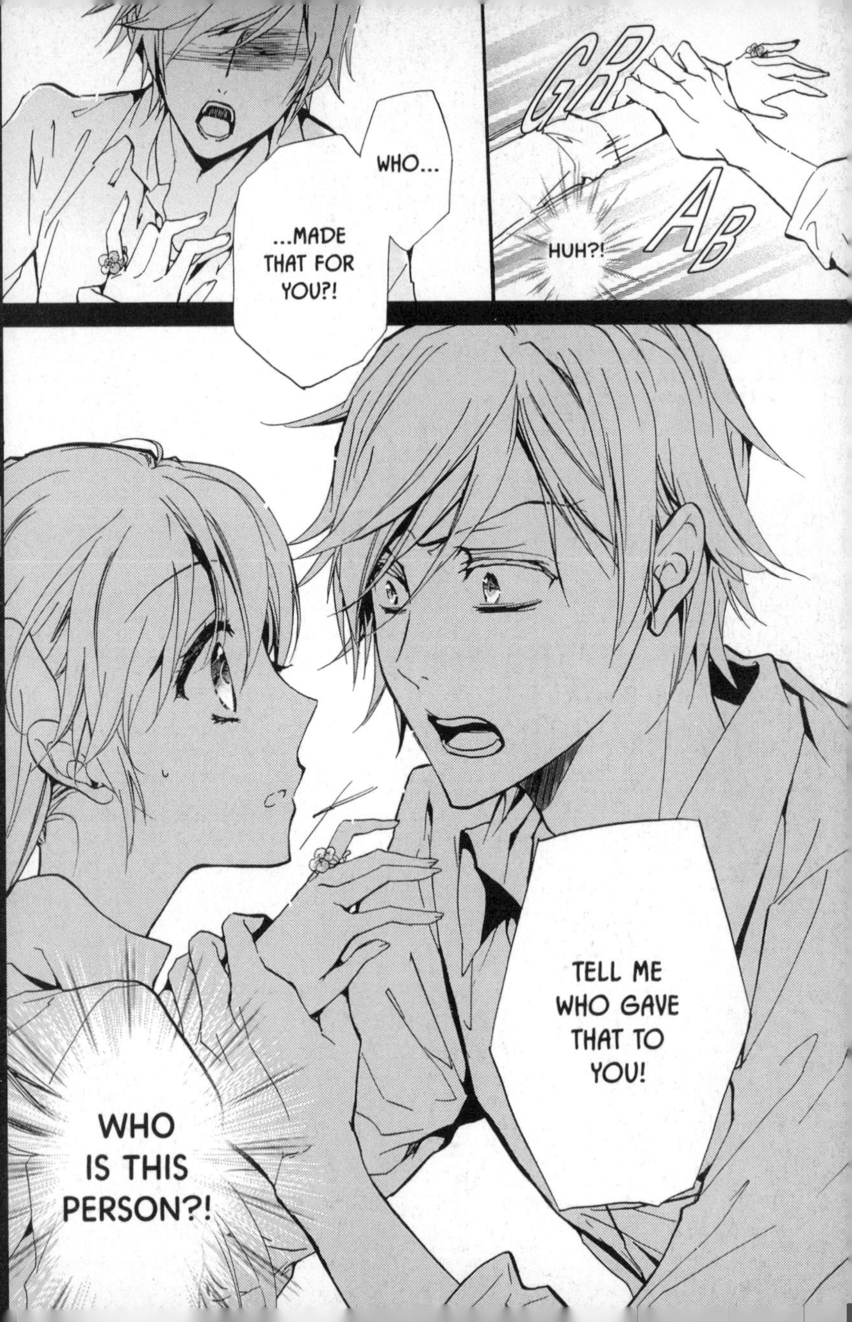
GRAB
HUH?!
WHO...
...MADE THAT FOR YOU?!
TELL ME WHO GAVE THAT TO YOU!
WHO IS THIS PERSON?!

The DEMON PRINCE of MOMOCHI HOUSE

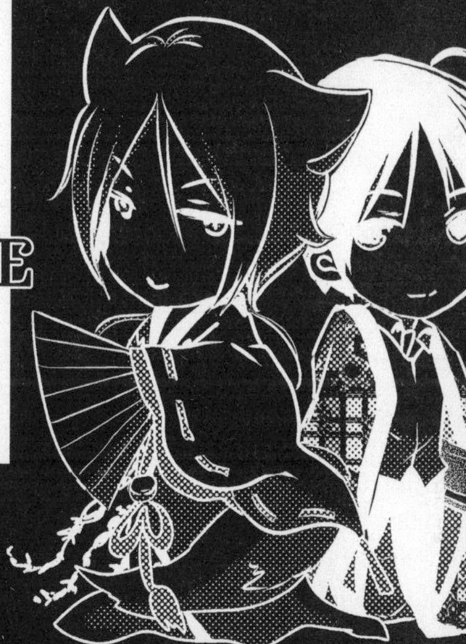

This is the third volume of *Momochi*. I'm surprised it's already this far along. The more I write, the more I need to write. And if I write one thing, I'm not able to write other things... It's agony, but I have a lot of fun. I'd like to build up this story, so I hope you continue to join me... There will be many more fun things to come!

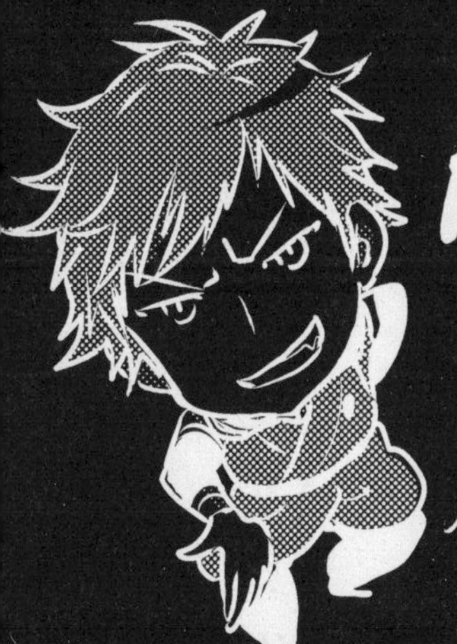

After-word

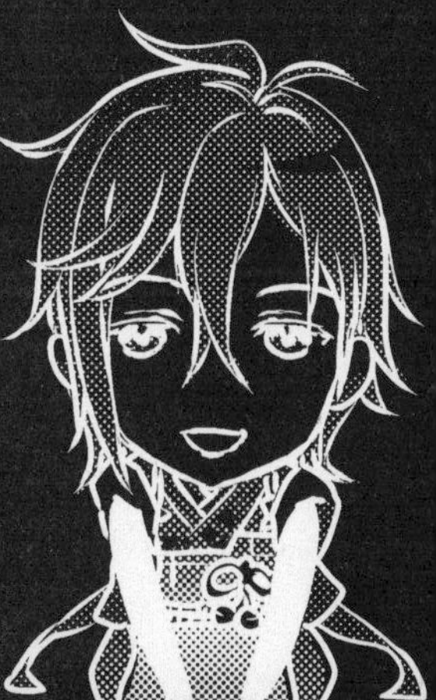

Special Thanx

Norico Ogawa Maico Yoshise
Aya Maeda
Juri Kodama Naoko Kimura
Kanae Saitoh Rica Kasahara
Sachico Hiyo

and MMCS Team ♥

I imagine this cover at twilight.
Come to think of it, whenever I draw
Himari's eyes in black and white,
I draw them like they're reflecting
the setting sun. Perhaps it's the
impression I get from the colors.

-Aya Shouoto

Aya Shouoto was born on December 25.
Her hobbies are traveling, staying at hotels,
sewing and daydreaming. She currently
lives in Tokyo and enjoys listening to J-pop
anime theme songs while she works.

The Demon Prince of Momochi House

Volume 3
Shojo Beat Edition

Story and Art by Aya Shouoto

Translation JN Productions
Touch-Up Art & Lettering Inori Fukuda Trant
Design Fawn Lau
Editor Nancy Thistlethwaite

MOMOCHISANCHI NO AYAKASHI OUJI Volume 3

Edited by KADOKAWA SHOTEN
First published in Japan in 2014 by KADOKAWA CORPORATION, Tokyo.
English translation rights arranged with KADOKAWA CORPORATION, Tokyo.

Printed in the U.S.A.

Published by VIZ Media, LLC
P.O. Box 77010
San Francisco, CA 94107

10 9 8 7 6 5 4 3 2 1
First printing, January 2016

www.viz.com

PARENTAL ADVISORY
THE DEMON PRINCE OF MOMOCHI HOUSE is rated T for Teen and is recommended for ages 13 and up.
ratings.viz.com

www.shojobeat.com

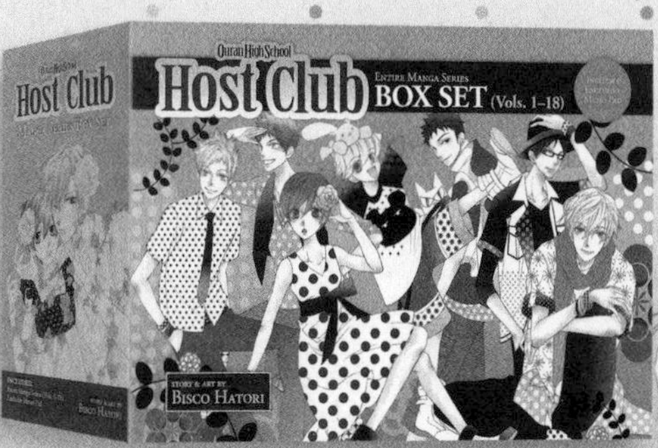
Ouran High School
Host Club
Entire Manga Series
BOX SET (Vols. 1–18)
Story & Art by
Bisco Hatori

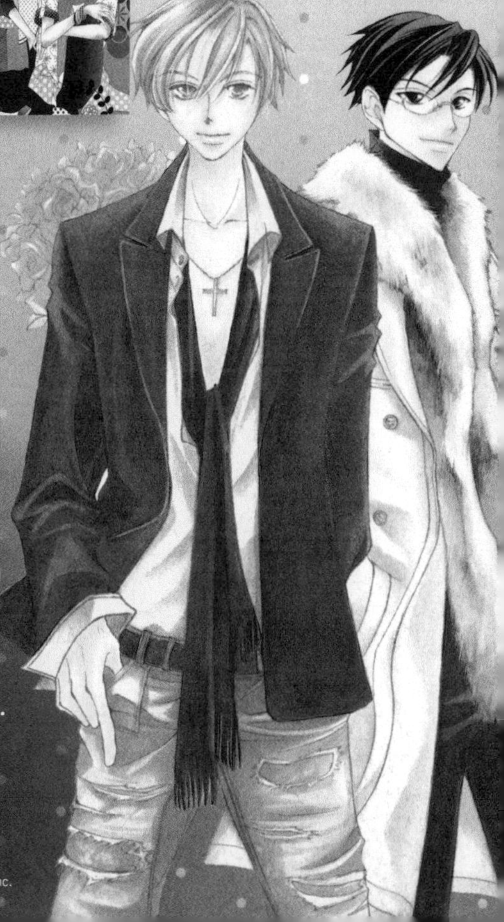

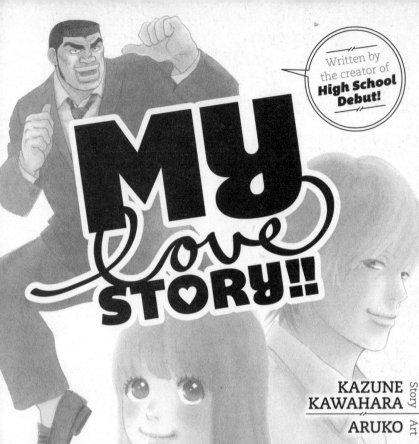

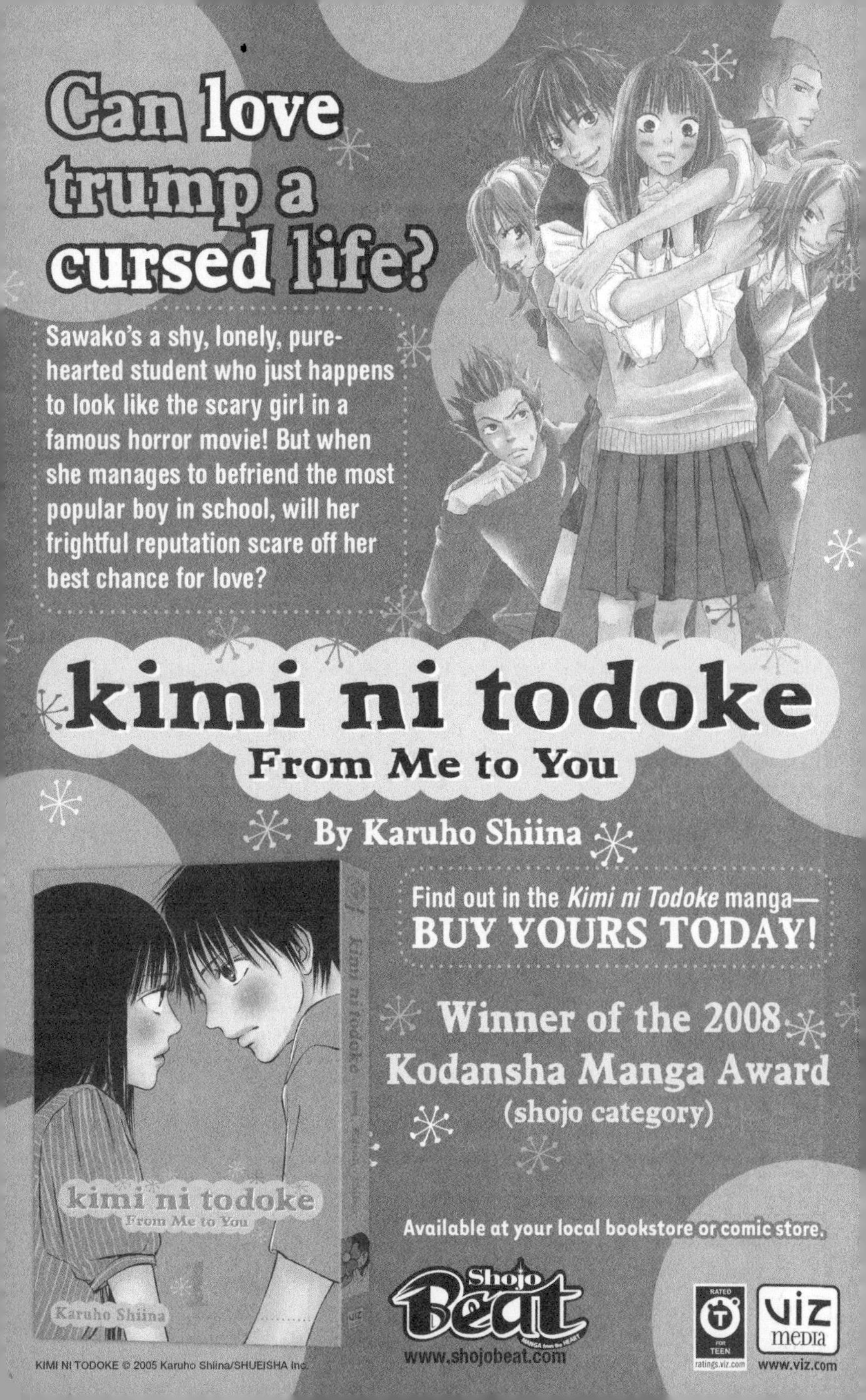
Can love trump a cursed life?
Sawako's a shy, lonely, pure-hearted student who just happens to look like the scary girl in a famous horror movie! But when she manages to befriend the most popular boy in school, will her frightful reputation scare off her best chance for love?
kimi ni todoke
From Me to You
By Karuho Shiina
kimi ni todoke
From Me to You
Karuho Shiina
Find out in the Kimi ni Todoke manga—
BUY YOURS TODAY!
Winner of the 2008
Kodansha Manga Award
(shojo category)
Available at your local bookstore or comic store.
Shojo Beat
www.shojobeat.com
RATED T FOR TEEN
ratings.viz.com
VIZ media
www.viz.com
KIMI NI TODOKE © 2005 Karuho Shiina/SHUEISHA Inc.

stop

You may be reading the
WRONG WAY!!

IT'S TRUE: In keeping with the original Japanese comic format, this book reads from right to left—so action, sound effects and word balloons are completely reversed. This preserves the orientation of the original artwork—plus, it's fun! Check out the diagram shown here to get the hang of things, and then turn to the other side of the book to get started!

'JAN -- 20171